RAPID GROWTH AND RELATIVE DECLINE

Rapid Growth and Relative Decline

Modelling Macroeconomic Dynamics with Hysteresis

Mark Setterfield
Assistant Professor of Economics
Trinity College
Hartford
Connecticut

First published in Great Britain 1997 by
MACMILLAN PRESS LTD
Houndmills, Basingstoke, Hampshire RG21 6XS and London
Companies and representatives throughout the world

A catalogue record for this book is available from the British Library.

ISBN 0–333–63736–4

First published in the United States of America 1997 by
ST. MARTIN'S PRESS, INC.,
Scholarly and Reference Division,
175 Fifth Avenue, New York, N.Y. 10010

ISBN 0–312–17268–0

Library of Congress Cataloging-in-Publication Data
Setterfield, Mark, 1967–
Rapid growth and relative decline : modelling macroeconomic
dynamics with hysteresis / Mark Setterfield.
    p. cm.
Includes bibliographical references and index.
ISBN 0–312–17268–0 (cloth)
1. Great Britain—Economic conditions—Econometric models.
2. Economic development—Mathematical models.   3. Macroeconomics–
–Mathematical models.   4. Hysteresis (Economics)   I. Title.
HC254.5.S42   1997
339.5'0941—dc21   96–46322
                                                            CIP

This book is printed on paper suitable for recycling and made from fully managed and
sustained forest sources.

10   9   8   7   6   5   4   3   2   1
06   05   04   03   02   01   00   99   98   97

Printed and bound in Great Britain by
Antony Rowe Ltd, Chippenham, Wiltshire

To the memory of my father

Contents

List of Tables

Acknowledgements

This book is based on research that I began as a doctoral student, and which contributed to my doctoral dissertation at Dalhousie University in Canada. Prior to my undertaking doctoral studies, I found myself drawn to Joan Robinson's distinction between logical and historical time, and the many questions regarding the analysis of economic dynamics that this distinction begs. That I was able to pursue this interest with any success is largely due to the efforts of two people. First, Geoff Harcourt at Cambridge University offered invaluable advice as to where I might find a dissertation supervisor sympathetic to my general interests. Second, John Cornwall at Dalhousie University proved to be that supervisor. John provided both the initial encouragement necessary for me to take the further development of my interests seriously, and then four years of meticulous supervision, during which he always found time for me despite the heavy demands of his own research schedule. I count myself among the most fortunate of people to have benefited not only from John's direction as an adviser, but also his friendship, and his enthusiasm for and attitude towards economics, both of which remain an inspiration.

At Dalhousie University, I also received many useful comments on my work from Wendy Cornwall of Mount Saint Vincent University, and Lars Osberg. Since the completion of my thesis, I have benefited greatly from the help of Tony Thirlwall of the University of Kent at Canterbury. Tony provided many of the suggestions that have enabled me to revise my dissertation and in the process, create this book. Numerous discussions with Basil Moore of Wesleyan University have also been productive, and have had a particular influence on parts of Chapter 2. While it is my hope that this book does some justice to those named above, it goes without saying that they bear no responsibility for any remaining errors.

Material in Chapter 5 is reprinted from the *Journal of Economic Issues* by special permission of the copyright holder, the Association for Evolutionary Economics.

Finally, I would like to thank Jennifer, for her love and support – and a great deal of patience – over the last few years.

Introduction

UNDERSTANDING THE GROWTH AND DEVELOPMENT OF
CAPITALISM: FACTS, THEORIES AND METHODOLOGICAL
APPROACHES

Of the many 'stylized facts' about growth, two are outstanding. First, growth rates differ between capitalist economies at any given point in time. Second, growth rates within individual capitalist economies differ over time. One consequence of these facts for the historical development of capitalism as a system has been that the relative growth rates of capitalist economies have varied over time. This point has recently found expression in the form of a 'new' stylized fact about growth, associated with the Regulation and Social Structure of Accumulation theories (see, for example, Boyer, 1990 and Bowles *et al.*, 1990 respectively). This states that the growth of capitalism can be periodized into distinct 'epochs', during which rapid growth and development is associated with markedly different technological and institutional structures. Furthermore, these epochs are characterized by the dominance of the world economy by different nation-states, the dominant economy in each epoch being the one with the currently most successful technological and institutional structures.

The view of capitalistic growth that this 'new' stylized fact inspires is that of a process intrinsically related to structural change. From the point of view of 'dominant' individual nation-states, it also suggests that a prolonged phase of relatively high growth may be superseded by a subsequent period of relative economic failure, as a new and more dynamic competitor gains international pre-eminence. The significance of this idea is already well known to scholars of the British economy, who have long lamented the relative economic decline of Britain since its nineteenth-century industrial heyday.[1] It is also an idea that has tremendous contemporary significance, as evidenced by the increasing concern of economists with the apparent relative decline of the US economy and the emerging Japanese/East Asian challenge since the late 1960s (see, for example, Baumol *et al.*, 1989; Lazonick, 1990).

Concern with the long-run competitive fate of nations – and, in particular, with the idea that a period of sustained and relatively high growth may be followed by one of relative economic decline – is by no means new. Indeed, discussion of the prospects of an established commercial society in an international trading environment is almost as old as the subject of economics itself. Such discussion can be traced back at least as far as the 'rich country–poor country' debate in eighteenth-century Scottish political economy.[2] Participants in this debate were concerned as to whether accumulation would indefinitely extend the wealth of a rich nation (subject to its securing sufficient markets for final output), or whether the acquisition of wealth was an inherently self-defeating process, by virtue of its adverse effects on the industry and ingenuity of a country's populace.

The issue of the long-run competitive fate of nations is therefore both timely and timeless. This book addresses the question as to whether the initial accumulation of wealth tends to favour or hinder its subsequent accumulation, with the aim of relating the answer to the growth 'epochs' described earlier. More specifically, it investigates the growth dynamics of capitalist economies, illustrating under what circumstances high growth may be self-perpetuating, and how high growth may ultimately bequeath the conditions for its own future deceleration, even giving rise to a period of relative economic decline.

An important feature of this exercise is its conception of capitalism as an endogenously evolving system. Following authors such as Cornwall (1977; 1990), Pasinetti (1981), Boyer (1990) and Bowles *et al.* (1990), growth is interpreted as a process of structural transformation, defined broadly to include both changes in the sectoral composition of final output, and changes in the technological and institutional structures of an economy. Moreover, structural transformation is not seen as being a smooth and continuous process. It is held that the transition between different technological, institutional and output structures or 'regimes' may not always be easy for an individual economy to undergo.

This conception of the dynamics of capitalism involves a rejection of steady-state approaches to modelling growth. In keeping with the 'stylized facts' already outlined, the historical growth and development of capitalism is interpreted as a history of *change*, involving variations in national growth rates over time, and more fundamental changes in international economic 'leadership'. Adopting a steady-state framework of analysis precludes discussion of changes in economic outcomes, unless the possibility of exogenous shocks is entertained. Since shocks constitute an unexplained and non-systematic element within a steady-state framework, however, they cannot, by definition, be construed as a systematic explanation of change. Yet even the most cursory reading of the history of capitalistic growth suggests that the systematic explanation of change is precisely what is required.

To this end, the steady-state approach is eschewed in favour of a framework of analysis which relies upon concepts of path dependency in order to explain macroeconomic evolution. The common methodological feature of these concepts is that they rest on the analysis of uni-directional, sequential patterns of economic activity; hence final economic outcomes are seen as being inherently dependent on the historical conditions that preceded them. This methodology contrasts markedly with that of standard equilibrium analysis (of which steady-state analysis forms a part), which conceives long-run economic outcomes as equilibria, defined and reached without reference to the path taken towards them. These equilibrium outcomes are ultimately 'explained' by exogenous data, imposed upon the economic system from without. As suggested earlier, this framework of analysis is not designed to explain the phenomenon of change. In contrast, concepts of path dependency may assist in this task. These mechanisms posit that economies are influenced not just by exogenous data, but also by the nature of endogenous adjustment processes which may, in and of themselves, affect final economic outcomes. By explicitly analysing the economy as an intertemporal sequence of events, concepts of path dependency provide an analytical framework for understanding the nature and significance of change.

OUTLINE OF THE BOOK

This book is divided into three parts, which pursue methodological, theoretical and empirical themes respectively.

In Part I, the traditional equilibrium approach to economic analysis, which conceives final economic outcomes as being defined and reached without reference to the path taken towards them, is contrasted with a methodology inspired by the concept of hysteresis, in which long-run outcomes are held to be path-dependent. Chapter 1 suggests that although there is no unique definition of the concept of 'economic equilibrium', equilibrium theories display a sufficient number of methodological similarities for us to identify a 'traditional equilibrium approach' to economic analysis. This approach is critiqued in terms of its lack of realism, frequent neglect of multiple equilibria, inattention to the problems of disequilibrium adjustment, and finally, in terms of the concept of hysteresis.

In Chapter 2, hysteresis is defined as existing when the long-run outcomes of an economic system depend on the (historical) adjustment path taken towards them. Recent attempts to characterize this process formally have relegated hysteresis to the status of a special case. It is shown, however, that these characterizations themselves constitute a special case. The concept of hysteresis is then 'reconstructed' and shown to be a potentially pervasive feature of dynamic economic systems. Following this, the compatibility of hysteresis with other concepts of path dependency such as cumulative causation and lock-in is discussed, with a view to using these various concepts as a means of analysing the long-run evolution of capitalist economies. Finally, Chapter 2 provides some reflections on the status of equilibrium as an organizing concept in light of the importance of path dependency.

The purpose of Part II is to construct a path-dependent theory of long-run growth, and illustrate its potential implications for the long-run competitive fate of an open economy in an interregional trading system. Chapter 3 takes the Kaldorian heritage of non-equilibrium growth modelling as a starting point. The nature of path dependency inherent in the idea of dynamic increasing returns to scale is discussed, and a model of cumulative causation is then constructed to illustrate the potential implications of dynamic increasing returns for growth.

Chapter 4 begins by identifying an important potential caveat in the process of cumulative causation – its apparent implication that given only initial conditions (and abstracting from the influence of exogenous shocks) the long-run competitive fate of a region is known with certainty. According to models of cumulative causation, success (that is, high growth) breeds success and failure (that is, low growth) begets failure indefinitely. It is then shown that this caveat can be overcome in a manner consistent with the concept of hysteresis by considering the technological and institutional context in which growth occurs. The technological evolution of a growing economy is treated as a function of the economy's prior growth and development, and it is illustrated that the process of technological evolution need not be efficient in the sense of being functional to the maintenance of high growth dynamics. In Chapter 5, the same is shown to be true of the evolution of an economy's institutions. Central to the demonstration of these results is the concept of lock-in (Arthur, 1988a, 1988b), which describes the propensity of dynamic economic systems to become stuck in 'grooves' from which they subsequently find it difficult to deviate. Taking the example of a high-growth 'virtuous circle' economy, the potential for an endogenously induced breakdown in the growth dynamics of cumulative causation is illustrated, with the possible future consequence that an initially fast-growing economy may enter a period of relative economic decline. In terms of the debate over the accumulation of wealth and its perpetuation, then, it is shown that there exist mechanisms in a capitalist economy which may act so as to sustain initially high growth (such as dynamic increasing returns), and mechanisms which may cause high-growth dynamics to break down (such as inefficient technological and/or institutional evolution).

Ultimately, it is the historical balance of these forces which determines the long-run competitive fate of a dominant (that is, relatively fast-growing and internationally pre-eminent) economy.

Part III serves to illustrate this point by means of reference to the historical development of the British economy since 1780. Britain is identified as having initially been a relatively fast-growing economy, which failed to undergo the type of structural transformation (primarily of a technological and institutional nature) necessary to maintain, in the face of emerging international competition, its position of relative economic dominance. Chapter 6 begins with a brief outline of the history of export, output and productivity growth in Britain since 1780, designed to illustrate that these variables have displayed the cumulative patterns of behaviour hypothesized in Part II. Chapters 7 and 8 then concentrate on explaining Britain's relative economic retardation after 1870, which followed its unprecedented growth as the world's 'first industrial nation'. In Chapter 7, the influence of lock-in on Britain's technological evolution is examined. The latter is found to have been inefficient, with negative consequences for the dynamics of key industries in the British economy. Chapter 8 then repeats this exercise, this time focusing on Britain's institutional evolution. This is again found to have been inefficient, and the adverse consequences for industries central to Britain's relative economic performance are again highlighted.

Finally, the conclusion offers a summary of the main findings of the book. It is suggested that capitalism is best interpreted as an endogenously evolving system, comprised of mechanisms whose very operation can influence the long-run configuration of the system as a whole.

PART I
Economic Modelling: Some Methodological Considerations

Introduction

The purpose of Part I is to assess two different approaches to modelling economic outcomes. The first, identified as the traditional equilibrium approach, conceives long-run economic outcomes as being determinate (Kaldor, 1934). This approach is common to the great majority of economic theorizing, regardless of whether it claims to be static or dynamic, or whether it is of a predominantly neoclassical or Keynesian nature.[1] Determinacy implies that economic outcomes evolve according to immutable 'natural laws'. Modelling the economy is thus reduced to the exercise of discovering what these 'laws' are, and deciding how much more or less knowledge about them can be imputed to the decision-making agents who make up the economy.

The second approach to modelling is identified with the concept of hysteresis. It is not unreasonable to think of hysteresis as having developed initially as a critique of traditional equilibrium economics. This is illustrated by the tendency of most authors who have thusfar appealed to the concept to concentrate on demonstrating its negative implications for traditional equilibrium constructs such as the natural rate of unemployment (see, for example, Jenkinson, 1987; Gordon, 1989; Layard et al., 1991). Furthermore, the methodology of these authors has not, as yet, progressed far beyond the confines of the traditional equilibrium approach.[2]

What arises from this seemingly narrow critique, however, is nothing less than a distinct approach to macroeconomic modelling – one which has logical antecedents in concepts such as cumulative causation and contemporary counterparts in ideas such as lock-in. Together, these concepts of path dependency provide a dynamic alternative to the traditional equilibrium approach that is broadly consistent with the notion of historical time. Allowing for historical time takes account of the fact that economic events occur in a uni-directional sequence. In historical time, any event occurring in the present exists in the context of a series of prior events corresponding to the periods which make up the past. In other words, what is current is so in the context of what has gone before.

As both Robinson (1980, p. 255) and Shackle (1958, p. 13) note, traditional equilibrium economics treats time, if at all, as a mathematical space rather than as the historical phenomenon described above. It is because of this that traditional equilibrium models may be criticized for being ahistorical. As a consequence, traditional equilibrium models tend to obscure precise (historical) sequences of events, and in so doing, deflect attention from the important possibility that such sequences might actually matter, in the sense that they may influence final economic outcomes. In contrast, hysteresis is complementary to the notion of historical time. Indeed, it is precisely the principle that sequences of events determine the nature of final outcomes on which the concept of hysteresis is based.

Part I is organized as follows. In Chapter 1, the traditional equilibrium approach is discussed, and a critique of this approach is seen to give rise to the concept of hysteresis. In Chapter 2, this concept is investigated and developed, and is shown to be suggestive of an alternative approach to macroeconomic modelling which is related to the later methodology of authors such as Kaldor (1972, 1985). Furthermore, an assessment of equilibrium as an organizing concept is used to illustrate the extent to which certain, apparently more conventional, tools may still be appropriate in the construction of hysteretic models of economic systems.

1 Economic Modelling and the Concept of Equilibrium

I THE TRADITIONAL EQUILIBRIUM APPROACH TO ECONOMIC MODELLING

There exist a number of definitions of the concept of economic equilibrium. One idea of equilibrium is that of a situation characterized by 'offsetting forces' – as, for example, when supply equals demand. A somewhat broader conception defines equilibrium as any state of rest which displays no endogenous tendencies to change over time.[1] There also exist a variety of model specific definitions of equilibrium. For example, in certain theories of the business cycle, equilibrium is characterized in terms of the way that individuals form conditional expectations.[2]

In spite of these differences in definition, however, it is possible to identify common methodological traits underlying what may be broadly construed as equilibrium analysis in economics. This 'traditional equilibrium approach' to economic modelling has two outstanding features. First, it involves identifying an array of structural equations, which define relationships determining the values of a set of endogenous variables, and (most importantly) which derive their structure from a set of *exogenous* variables and coefficients imposed upon the system from without. For example, in neoclassical partial equilibrium analysis of consumer and producer behaviour, individual consumption and production decisions (the endogenous variables) are related to exogenous variables such as relative prices, and coefficients representing preferences and technology.[3] These exogenous variables and coefficients are taken as given, forming what may be referred to as the 'data' of the system, determined independently of individual behaviour by the market, consumer psychology and the state of science respectively.

Second, traditional equilibrium models are typically constructed so as to yield stable equilibria – that is, points of rest to which the system will return following any arbitrary displacement.[4] This concern with stability follows naturally from concern with economic equilibria, since equilibrium configurations are not of general interest unless they are stable.

Stability is also important because it implies that an equilibrium configuration *defined* in terms of exogenous data may also be *reached* by the system to which it pertains from *any* arbitrary starting point. What the preceding considerations suggest, then, is a definition of the traditional equilibrium approach to economic analysis as one in which the long run or final outcomes of economic systems are seen as being determinate (Kaldor, 1934); they are both defined and reached without reference to the (historical) adjustment path taken towards them.

i) The Use of Traditional Equilibrium Methodology in Keynesian and Neoclassical Macroeconomics

The widespread use of the traditional equilibrium approach in macro-economics can be illustrated by considering two diverse examples of this methodology, both of which are characterized by stable equilibrium config-urations defined in terms of exogenous data. Equations [1.1] and [1.2] below comprise a highly simplified Keynesian income–expenditure model:

$$Y_t = C_t + \bar{I} \qquad [1.1]$$

$$C_t = \alpha Y_{t-1} \quad , \quad \alpha \in (0, 1) \qquad [1.2]$$

where Y_t represents national income, C_t represents realized aggregate consumption, α is the propensity to consume, $\bar{I}$ is the (exogenously given) desired level of investment, and t subscripts denote time periods.

In this system, there are two structural equations in two unknowns (Y_t and C_t), with Y_{t-1}, $\bar{I}$ and α taken as given. Substituting equation [1.2] into equation [1.1], we arrive at:

$$Y_t = \alpha Y_{t-1} + \bar{I} \qquad [1.3]$$

Setting $Y_t = Y_{t-1} = Y^E$, we arrive at:

$$Y^E = \frac{1}{1 - \alpha} \cdot \bar{I} \qquad [1.4]$$

Equation [1.4] describes an equilibrium income configuration, Y^E, defined in terms of the exogenous data $\bar{I}$ and α.

Suppose now that in some period t, a transitory shock gives rise to a once over increase in the value of income, so that $Y_t > Y_{t-1} = Y^E$. The effects of this are captured by the general solution of the difference equation [1.3], which can be written as:

$$Y_t = \alpha A b^{t-1} + \frac{\bar{I}}{1 - \alpha}$$

where $Y_t = Ab^t$, or:[5]

$$Y_t = A\alpha^t + \frac{\bar{I}}{1 - \alpha}$$ [1.5]

From equation [1.5] we can see that as $t \to \infty$, $A\alpha^t \to 0$ if $\alpha \in (-1, 1)$ – that is, that Y_t will converge to the steady state defined in equation [1.4] if $\alpha \in (-1, 1)$, which is clearly satisfied when $\alpha \in (0, 1)$ as initially hypothesized. Hence the specification of the model in equations [1.1] and [1.2] ensures that this model is stable around the equilibrium Y^E defined in equation [1.4] following any arbitrary disturbance; Y^E can be defined and reached without reference to the path taken towards it and is therefore determinate.

Now consider the following neoclassical model of the natural rate of unemployment:

$$(U_t - U_n) = \alpha(\dot{p}_t - \dot{p}_t^e) + \varepsilon_t \quad , \quad \alpha < 0, \, \varepsilon_t \sim (0, \sigma_e^2)$$ [1.6]

$$\dot{p}_t^e = \dot{p}_{t-1}^e + \beta(\dot{p}_{t-1} - \dot{p}_{t-1}^e) \quad , \quad \beta \in (0, 1)$$ [1.7]

$$\dot{p}_t = \dot{m}_t$$ [1.8]

where $\dot{p}_t$ is the rate of price inflation, $\dot{p}_t^e$ is the expected rate of price inflation, U_n is the (exogenously given) natural rate of unemployment, U_t is the actual rate of unemployment, $\dot{m}_t$ is the (exogenously given) rate of growth of the money supply, ε_t is a random error term with zero mean and constant variance, and t subscripts again denote time periods.

This time, there are three equations in three unknowns (U_t, $\dot{p}_t$ and $\dot{p}_t^e$) with α, β, $\dot{m}_t$, $\dot{p}_{t-1}^e$ and U_n taken as given. Setting $\dot{p}_t = \dot{p}_t^e = \dot{p}_{t-1}^e = \dot{p}^*$, equation [1.6] can be written as:

$$U_t = U_n + \varepsilon_t$$

Recalling that $E(\varepsilon_t) = 0$, we arrive at:

$$E(U_t) = U_n$$ [1.9]

Equation [1.9] defines an equilibrium unemployment rate defined in terms of the exogenous data U_n.

Suppose now that we introduce a once over increase in $\dot{m}$ in period t so that $\dot{p}^* = \dot{p}_t > \dot{p}_t^e$. This time, the effects of a disturbance to the model are captured by the general solution to the difference equation [1.7], which can be written as:

$$\dot{p}_t^e = (1 - \beta)Bd^{t-1} + \dot{p}^*$$

where $\dot{p}_t^e = Bd^t$, or:[6]

$$\dot{p}_t^e = B(1 - \beta)^t + \dot{p}^* \qquad [1.10]$$

From equation [1.10], we can see that as $t \to \infty$, $B(1 - \beta)^t \to 0$ if $(1 - \beta) \in (-1, 1)$ – that is, that $\dot{p}_t^e$ will converge to $\dot{p}^*$ as long as $(1 - \beta) \in (-1, 1)$, which is clearly satisfied when $\beta \in (0, 1)$ as originally hypothesized. The structure of the model in equations [1.6]–[1.8] again ensures that this model is stable in response to some initial disturbance, this time around the equilibrium configuration defined in equation [1.9]. Since the latter can, therefore, be defined and reached without reference to the path taken towards it, the equilibrium in equation [1.9] is once again determinate.

Both of the examples chosen appear dynamic, in so far as they impose a temporal ordering on variables in the form of time subscripts. This allows us to explicitly illustrate that both models are essentially *static*, in so far as the long-run outcomes deriving from them are both defined and reached without reference to the historical adjustment path taken towards them. It is *as if* their long-run outcomes were determined instantaneously. Many economic models are formally static, of course, their variables interacting simultaneously in a manner bereft of even the appearance of temporal ordering. In models of this nature, only the existence of equilibrium can be formally verified. In spite of this, explicitly static models usually assume or allege stability in an intuitive (albeit ultimately *ad hoc*) manner. For example, the assumption of stability is implicit in comparative static exercises, such as those commonly performed with the IS–LM system, and with the 'Marshallian cross' in the analysis of supply and demand. The simple Keynesian and neoclassical models discussed above may therefore be thought of as being representative of the dominant (traditional equilibrium) methodology in economic theory, whether of a formally static or allegedly 'dynamic' nature.

ii)   Towards a Critique of the Traditional Equilibrium Approach

The traditional equilibrium approach to economic modelling suggests both the existence and stability of a configuration which is independent of the past history of the system to which it pertains. In other words, it conceives long-run economic outcomes as being of a determinate nature, both defined and reached without reference to the path taken towards them. Furthermore, the diversity of the examples provided in the previous section illustrates the popularity of this approach in economic theory. However, the traditional equilibrium approach to economic modelling can be subject to a number of important criticisms. It is to these criticisms that we now turn our attention.

II THE 'REALISM' OF TRADITIONAL EQUILIBRIUM MODELS

Some authors (for example, Kaldor, 1972) have criticized particular variants of the traditional equilibrium approach on the basis that their assumptions lack realism.[7] These assumptions or axioms are a reflection of the general methodology of a model. For example, they influence not only the choice of data, (that is, what is taken as 'given'), but also the very questions a model asks (that is, what precisely it seeks to explain). Kaldor criticizes general equilibrium theory (and by extension, neoclassical theory as a whole) for making assumptions that are either impossible to falsify (for example, consumers 'maximize' utility) or which are at variance with what we observe in real world economies (for example, perfect competition and wholly impersonal market relationships).

The idea that it is legitimate to criticize a theory or group of theories for being 'unrealistic' has not met with unanimous approval. Friedman (1953) argues from a positivist perspective that a theory should be judged not by its descriptive realism, but on the basis of its predictive abilities. Hahn (1974), meanwhile, argues that by clearly specifying the restrictions necessary to obtain its results, even a patently unrealistic construct (such as the Arrow–Debreu model of general equilibrium) can be of great value in indicating what we likely *cannot* claim about the functioning of real world economies.

Coddington (1972, 1975) criticizes and rejects the methodological positions of both Friedman and Hahn. He argues that Friedman's positivism or 'instrumentalism' is ultimately unworkable, due to difficulties associated with unambiguously falsifying the predictions of economic hypotheses. These difficulties include data deficiencies, and the problem that economic hypotheses come in 'clusters', so that the apparent falsity of any particular hypothesis can always be blamed on the inadequacy of the supporting hypotheses necessary to generate the original testable proposition (see also McCloskey, 1983). Meanwhile, Coddington argues that Hahn's position is itself positivist; it rests on the idea that the mathematical precision of the Arrow–Debreu model is useful because precise statements permit the claims of a model to be subject to the test of falsification.

If economic theory cannot be evaluated solely on the basis of its predictions, then Kaldor's realist methodology – which essentially calls for the evaluation of theory at *all* levels, including its working hypotheses and assumptions – appears reasonable. However, in criticizing Friedman and Hahn, Coddington (1975) establishes a different basis for rejecting the criteria of realism. For Coddington, all theories are necessarily abstract, and hence are unrealistic by definition. Criticizing a theory for lacking realism involves the mistaken belief that theories should replicate their subject matter – something which they are not intended to do and, indeed, are incapable of doing. According to Coddington, the value of theory is that it 'can "impose coherence" and provide "insight" without being aimed primarily at description' (Coddington, 1975, p. 542).

Coddington is, of course, correct to point out that any abstraction and hence any theory is, by definition, unrealistic. However, since different models make different abstractions, a theory may be criticized as unrealistic not because it makes abstractions *per se*, but because it makes the *wrong* abstractions. Hence whilst the goal of theory is not to perfectly recreate the reality it seeks to model (such a task would be pointless since a perfect version of reality already exists in the form of reality itself) '. . . the necessity of abstraction . . . does not relieve one of the need to be somewhat descriptive' (Lavoie, 1992, p. 8) – in other words, to choose the most *appropriate* assumptions. For example, traditional equilibrium models will subsequently be criticized for treating as exogenous variables which should be thought of as being endogenous to economic activity. In this particular case, the 'wrong abstraction' compromises traditional equilibrium models by leading them to overlook the effects of intertemporal adjustment processes on final economic outcomes. Choosing the 'wrong abstractions' is significant not only because they may change the results of a theory, but also because they influence such things as the questions that it asks and its narrative content (that is, the nature of the 'story' that the theory is telling).

Essentially, what is at stake here is the way that we should seek to evaluate economic models, given the way we conceive the epistemic status of economic theory itself. Hence concern with avoiding the 'wrong abstractions' would not occur to a positivist, for whom any abstraction is, in principle, as good as the next, the only basis for evaluating a theory being its predictive ability. If, however, following Coddington (1975), Wilber and Harrison (1978) and McCloskey (1983), we reject the positivist conception of economics and its position of evaluating theory solely on the basis of predictions, and if we instead interpret economic theory as a collection of 'metaphors' and 'parables' designed to provide insight by telling convincing *stories* about the economy,[8] then it is legitimate to question *at all levels* how suitable any particular theory is as a story about reality. In other words, it is only reasonable to think of evaluating 'economic stories' at every stage of their argument, from the abstractions they make to the hypotheses they postulate through to their predictions. According to this storytelling view of economic discourse, predictions alone cannot bear sole responsibility for distinguishing between better and worse theories.[9] In the context of this storytelling conception of economic theory and its resulting conception of how economic theory should be evaluated, Kaldor's concern with the realism of abstractions makes good sense.

III   THE POSSIBILITY OF MULTIPLE EQUILIBRIA

Another objection to the traditional equilibrium approach involves the frequently overlooked possibility of multiple equilibria. This implies that even when we can adequately characterize an economic process in terms of a system of stable structural equations defined in terms of a given set of exogenous data, the solution of this system need not yield a *unique* equilibrium configuration. The importance of this possibility is twofold. First, multiple equilibria may be rankable – that is, different equilibrium configurations of the same system may have different welfare implications. In this case, the notion of equilibrium loses much of the normative significance that is usually attached to it;[10] a system can be 'in equilibrium' without this outcome being globally optimal.

Second, when there exist multiple equilibria, then by definition no one equilibrium configuration can be *globally* stable. This negates the usefulness of many comparative static exercises. It also raises the possibility that final outcomes in an economic system may depend on initial conditions, and hence which of the locally stable multiple equilibria the system converges towards.[11]

The possibility of multiple equilibria is given more explicit recognition in some variants of the traditional equilibrium approach than in others. For example, the neoclassical Second Fundamental Theorem of Welfare Economics recognizes that any Pareto optimal point is a market equilibrium for some initial distribution of resources.[12] Market equilibrium is not unique, therefore, in any circumstances where initial endowments are not fixed (for example, when there exists a government with redistributive functions.) Furthermore, even if initial endowments are fixed, it is well known that a general equilibrium may not be unique – the number of equilibria depends on the shape of preferences (see, for example, Varian, 1984, p. 241).

Similarly, explicit recognition of the possibility of multiple equilibria is made in game theory, especially when non-cooperative solutions to strategic interaction are considered. It is widely acknowledged that these solutions

Figure 1.1   Multiple Equilibria in a Strategic Form Game

Player 2

		A	B
Player 1	A	(5,1)	(3,1)
	B	(5,10)	(3,10)

may proliferate in any *n*-person non-cooperative game (Shubik, 1981, p. 307). This can be illustrated in the context of the two-player strategic form game in Fig. 1.1, in which all of the payoff vectors constitute non-cooperative (Nash) equilibria.

In this game, regardless of the behaviour of their opponent, neither player will express a preference between his/her available strategies. For example, if player 2 is known to have chosen strategy *A*, player 1 will be indifferent between strategies *A* and *B* (assuming that he/she is an individual welfare maximizer with no 'desire to punish') because they will each yield an identical payoff. Hence any of the outcomes of the game may be sustained as non-cooperative equilibria since, *ceteris paribus*, for any arbitrary strategy pair, no individual has any incentive to change his/her current behaviour.

However, in many variants of the traditional equilibrium approach, and particularly in macroeconomic analysis, the possibility of multiple equilibria is ignored. For example, the original formulation of the natural rate hypothesis postulates a natural rate of unemployment representing '. . . the level that would be ground out by the Walrasian system of general equilibrium equations' (Friedman, 1968, p. 8). Friedman simply assumes that this Walrasian equilibrium is unique, and indeed this assumption has continued to advise most subsequent theorizing on the natural rate hypothesis. A second example is provided by the theory of equilibrium business cycles in New Classical macroeconomics. Basic representations of this theory assume that the economy permanently gravitates around a unique Walrasian equilibrium, subject only to the perturbations caused by serially correlated random errors (see, for example, Lucas, 1975). Again, the possible implications of multiple equilibria are overlooked. These examples are particularly apt because, like most orthodox macroeconomics, they claim to be grounded in a Walrasian conception of the economy, whilst at the same time overlooking the Sonnenschein–Debreu–Mantel 'impossibility theorem' (see, for example, Kirman, 1989, 1992). This theorem suggests that, within the Walrasian approach, it is not, in fact, possible to find a set of restrictions on individuals that will generate 'well behaved' aggregate excess demand functions – that is, ones which generate unique (and stable) equilibria.[13] In fact, it appears that almost any continuous, homogeneous function satisfying Walras' Law may represent the aggregate excess demand function of an economy, making the global uniqueness (and stability) of equilibrium a special case. All this is in the nature of an aggregation problem; what holds at the individual level (in terms of the shape of agents' excess demand functions) does not hold at the level of the economy as a whole.[14] What is interesting, however, is the propensity – as illustrated by the examples given earlier – of much orthodox equilibrium theory which claims Walrasian foundations to ignore these results.

IV 'GETTING INTO' EQUILIBRIUM

A third criticism of the traditional equilibrium approach is related to the phenomenon of disequilibrium, or more precisely, the process of disequilibrium adjustment, by which a system is supposed to regain equilibrium following some initial disturbance.[15]

The informal characterization of an economic system 'getting into' equilibrium is one of the most frequently used and powerful allegories in the 'rhetoric of economics' (McCloskey, 1983). Robinson (1974a) argues that the most curious feature of equilibrium in this allegory is that it is conventionally conceived as representing the end of an economic process – a state that attains after a discrete interval of time during which the economy has been in disequilibrium. For Robinson, it seems almost counter-intuitive that a situation where economic agents are forming the 'wrong' present expectations on the basis of the 'wrong' current prices, levels of output, capital stock and so on (as is the case under conditions of disequilibrium) should lead to the state of order that is equilibrium. Concerns of this nature can be summarized by the following question: once an economic system is *out* of equilibrium, can it be supposed that forces will operate so as to get it *back into* equilibrium?

Considerable scepticism has been expressed on this issue, not least by some eminent theorists from within the equilibrium tradition. Hahn (1970) notes that while:

- [e]quilibrium economics,[16] because of its well known welfare economics implications, is easily convertible into an apologia for existing economic arrangements . . . (there is) no support for the view that any of the traditional methods of response of various agents to changes in their economic environment makes the '[invisible] hand' perform as it is often taken to perform.[17]

(Hahn, 1970, p. 1)

One conventional approach to the problem of disequilibrium adjustment is to postulate the existence of an auctioneer-type figure, whose task is to reconcile all economic activity by means of adjusting all relevant variables to their equilibrium values before any production, consumption or exchange activity actually takes place. In effect, this 'solves' the problem of disequilibrium adjustment by removing the phenomenon from the sphere of economic activity. The auctioneer is implicit in the notion of instantaneous disequilibrium adjustment,[18] and is therefore more widely appealed to than is commonly recognized. However, the assumption of what amounts to a central planner is clearly unrealistic in the context of an economy in which decision making is decentralized. Acknowledging this forces us to conceive disequilibrium adjustment as a process of sequential recontracting endemic to the economy, and occurring in historical time. But this in turn means that we must contend with the reservations of authors such as Robinson and Hahn, regarding the capacity of such a process to guide an economic system into equilibrium.

Unfortunately, economic theory has not gone out of its way to address these reservations. Indeed, the majority of investigations into the disequilibrium behaviour of economic systems do not extend far beyond pure allegory, usually based on the statement of heuristic adjustment rules such as 'excess demand leads to a change in price'. Such adjustment rules possess no innate features that guarantee the type of adjustments necessary to lead a system back into equilibrium. The mere fact that economic agents in a state of disequilibrium will seek to change their behaviour does not in and of itself imply that these changes will subsequently result in the attainment of equilibrium.

As illustrated earlier, it is possible to specify the mathematical conditions necessary for stability in formal dynamic models. However, even then, attention is seldom paid to the necessary *economic* conditions that these mathematical conditions imply.[19] In spite of the contribution made by mathematical formulations of stability conditions, the following problems remain regarding the process of disequilibrium adjustment and the prospects for 'getting into' equilibrium.

i) The Problem of Control over Economic Variables

Models which make the assumption of perfect competition suffer the conceptual weakness of failing to specify precisely who is supposed to signal disequilibrium by changing prices (Arrow, 1959). Recall that in a perfectly competitive economy, no one individual has any direct control over prices. If perfect competition is interpreted literally, then, models which make this assumption require an auctioneer to make disequilibrium price adjustments. But the assumption of what amounts to central planning in a decentralized economy is, as we have already seen, untenable. This problem is, of course, easily overcome by relaxing the assumption of perfect competition. However, this cannot be done without forfeiting the accompanying neoclassical welfare propositions which, as Hahn notes, motivate a good deal of the attention which is paid to models within the traditional equilibrium approach.

ii) Stocks and Flows, and Their Impact on Disequilibrium Adjustment

Further problems arise if we allow for the fact that some goods may accumulate in the form of stocks, so that in the process of disequilibrium production and trading, 'mistakes' can carry over from period to period.[20] Unless all goods are flows, in which case they can only exist within a specific period, we cannot postulate that all agents necessarily begin each period of activity with the same initial 'endowments' (which now include variable stocks of capital, debt, information and so forth). In the absence of an auctioneer to prevent production, consumption and trade from occurring until equilibrium is reached, the process of tatonnement, by which the system is supposed to 'get into' equilibrium, will therefore break down (Varian, 1984 p. 247).[21] What this means is that tatonnement can only really be interpreted as an instantaneous process occurring in logical time, because it is self-evidently true that stocks (of debt, capital, information and so forth) of varying sizes can and in all probability will carry over from period to period as a result of disequilibrium activity in historical time. In other words, as soon as we insist on considering adjustment processes in historical time (rather than as *de facto* instantaneous processes occurring in logical time), then conventional stability analysis begins to break down. Under these circumstances, the conventional notion of 'getting into' equilibrium associated with the mechanical stability properties of determinate equilibria, becomes ambiguous.[22]

iii) The Speed of Disequilibrium Adjustment

A third problem concerns the speed with which disequilibrium adjustment is supposed to take place. Although assumed 'given', the data of a traditional equilibrium model may change over time. For example, we would not expect consumer preferences to remain fixed indefinitely. It is quite common in the context of the traditional equilibrium approach to postulate exogenous changes in the data of a model in order to motivate comparative static/dynamic analysis. An important and neglected point, therefore, is how fast the process of disequilibrium adjustment takes place relative to the speed with which the 'data' of a model is changing over time. As Cornwall (1991) notes:

> ... if ... real world change[s] in tastes, technologies and other institutional features are very rapid relative to the rate at which the economy can adjust, the convergence properties of the model take on much less interest and importance than the institutional changes themselves.
>
> (Cornwall, 1991, p. 107)

iv) Connections between Markets, or, Income versus Substitution Effects

Each problem with the process of disequilibrium adjustment that has been discussed so far applies equally to individual market (that is, 'partial equilibrium') and economy wide (that is, 'general equilibrium') analyses. There exists a further problem, however, which relates specifically to general equilibrium analysis, and concerns the existence of connections between markets. This problem is central in Keynesian macroeconomic analysis. Hence for Keynes (1936), wages play an important dual role, as both a cost of production, and as a source of aggregate demand in the circular flow of income. Part of Keynes' contribution was to argue that this neglected interrelatedness between the labour market and the demand side of the product market denies the possibility of automatic adjustment towards a full employment equilibrium, since strategies designed to reduce labour costs (that is, wages) will simultaneously reduce aggregate demand, and hence the derived demand for labour.[23] The notion, developed by Keynes, that income effects dominate substitution effects is not lost on a number of critical neo-Walrasians, who acknowledge within the context of Walrasian General Equilibrium models the deleterious effects this has on the stability of Walrasian equilibrium.[24]

v) Signalling and Coordination Problems in Disequilibrium

A final problem associated with the process of disequilibrium adjustment concerns the issues of signalling and coordination. Some proponents of the traditional equilibrium approach insist that equilibrium must be reached, since otherwise unexploited gains from trade will persist. This is held to be inconsistent with the postulate of individual (substantive) rationality that is central to most variants of mainstream equilibrium economics. However, there is an important caveat in this argument. Unexploited gains from trade cannot be regarded as a sufficient condition to entice rational individuals to change their current behaviour in an equilibrating manner. Even rationally chosen changes in behaviour depend not only on preferences but also on constraints, and clearly there may exist circumstances where the constraints on choice are such that self-equilibrating change may not occur. Even if we overlook phenomena such as power, which are seldom acknowledged, much less addressed, within the traditional equilibrium approach, simple problems with information may thwart the process of 'getting into' equilibrium. As Hahn (1982) points out, if mutually beneficent trades are to take place, the opportunities for these trades must be both *recognized* and *successfully signalled*. But the extent to which such opportunities will be recognized and successfully signalled depends vitally on the ways in which potential parties to a trade are able to communicate, and hence what signals can be sent and how they are interpreted.

In a decentralized economy with incomplete information in which individuals communicate impersonally, the problems associated with signalling are enormous. Indeed, the interpretation of even the most elementary signal, such as a fall in price, is open to doubt. For example, if price is taken as an indication of quality, lowering the selling price of a good may be interpreted as a signal of its inferiority. Rather than increasing the number of prospective buyers as in conventional exchange theory, a fall in price may therefore reduce the demand for a product (Stiglitz, 1987). If the interpretation of market signals under conditions of imperfect information is uncertain, then, it is not clear whether the communication that takes place between agents in a state of disequilibrium will be of a nature that will lead these agents into a state of equilibrium.

As complicated as they are, the difficulties associated with recognizing and signalling opportunities for trade arguably *understate* the nature of the problem at hand. In order to exploit gains from trade, these opportunities must not only be recognized and successfully signalled, there must also exist a coordinating mechanism which enables interested parties to interact to their mutual benefit. Frequently, it is assumed that such a mechanism always exists in the form of a market. In this view, markets are (at least implicitly) treated as part of a pre-existing 'state of nature' in which agents find themselves acting. However, an alternative view is that markets (along with other economic, social and political coordination mechanisms) are humanly devised institutions. The problem here is with the creation of appropriate coordination mechanisms in the first place, something which may be neither easy nor costless, whilst the foresight necessary to create an appropriate set of coordination mechanisms *a priori* may not be available to agents under conditions of fundamental uncertainty.[25] As a result, we will likely observe missing coordination mechanisms which can only conflate the problems associated with realizing gains from trade and 'getting into' equilibrium.

V HYSTERESIS

The arguments of the preceding section question the stability of equilibrium configurations in the traditional equilibrium approach by asking whether it is conceivable for an economic system to 'get into' a pre-specified equilibrium as the result of a prior period of disequilibrium adjustment. However, the stability issue can be pursued further. In particular, it is important to ask whether it is at all legitimate to model economic processes in terms of determinate equilibria – that is, as having long-run outcomes which can be defined, much less reached, without reference to the prior adjustment path taken towards them.

Recall that the orthodox notion of equilibrium constitutes a stable configuration derived from a series of structural equations defined in terms of exogenously given data.[26] What is especially interesting about this notion is that the equilibrium configuration (or set of configurations in the case of multiple equilibria) is conceived as being completely independent of the process of disequilibrium adjustment – that is, it is independent of the path the system takes towards equilibrium. Traditional equilibrium models postulate equilibrium configurations that depend only on alleged exogenous 'data', the precise nature of which is, of course, left unexplained by the models themselves. The equilibria of such models are therefore entirely independent of the past history of the systems from which they derive.

As was noted earlier, the intertemporal adjustment behaviour of economic systems is seldom explicitly considered by traditional equilibrium models. Yet as Kaldor (1934) notes:

It is not possible . . . to determine the position of equilibrium from a given system of data, since every successive step taken in order to reach equilibrium will alter the conditions of equilibrium . . . and thus change the final position – unless the conditions are such that either (1) an equilibrium . . . [is] established immediately, or (2) the [situation] . . . actually established leaves the conditions of equilibrium unaffected (in which case the final position will be independent of the route followed.)

(Kaldor, 1934, p. 124)

It is precisely these limiting assumptions which are implicit in most variants of the traditional equilibrium approach. Clearly, the first assumption must be rejected if we are to take serious account of the genuinely intertemporal nature of economic processes. What remains to be seen is whether the second assumption should also be rejected. Is it appropriate to conceive long-run economic outcomes as being independent of the prior adjustment paths taken by the systems from which they derive? This issue brings us to the concept of path dependency and, more specifically, to the concept of hysteresis.

2 An Alternative Approach – Modelling with Hysteresis

I   INTRODUCTION

If we assume that an economic system is permanently in a state of long-run equilibrium (that is, that it will adjust instantaneously to this state from any arbitrary starting point), then questions posed by the nature of the inter-temporal behaviour of the economy are of little importance.[1] As long as economic activity is governed by conditions of long-run equilibrium, a configuration which is itself determined at any point in time by a set of exogenously given data, the economy will simply replicate itself through time in the form of a determinate equilibrium time path.[2] There will be no endogenous tendencies for the existing configuration of the economy to change, whilst the disturbing effects of random shocks will be instant-aneously corrected.

However, in Chapter 1, it was suggested that equilibrium is tradi-tionally conceptualized as being the end of an economic process. Even within the traditional equilibrium approach to economic modelling, then, there is tacit recognition of the fact that economic outcomes arise from sequential patterns of economic activity (in this case, a sequence of dis-equilibrium adjustments) – that is, that economic outcomes arise from economic processes which occur in historical time. Furthermore, it was seen that consideration of the genuinely intertemporal nature of economic activity poses important problems for traditional equilibrium analysis. The prospects of an economic system 'getting into' equilibrium become less favourable. There is also the possibility, indicated towards the end of Chapter 1, that by neglecting to consider the precise adjustment path taken by an economic system in a state of disequilibrium, traditional equilibrium analysis overlooks an important potential influence on the determination of final economic outcomes. It is to the discussion of the far reaching implications of this latter possibility that the present chapter is devoted.

II THE IMPORTANCE OF ADJUSTMENT PATHS IN DETERMINING ECONOMIC OUTCOMES: THE PROCESS OF HYSTERESIS

The term hysteresis originates in the natural sciences where, for example, it is used to describe the electromagnetic properties of ferric metals in the process of their magnetization and subsequent demagnetization.[3] Hysteresis exists when the long-run or final value of a variable depends on the value of the variable in the past, by virtue of the influence of this past value on the current alleged exogenous variables, coefficients and structural equations which characterize the system that determines the variable.[4] The central characteristic of hysteresis is, therefore, that it causes the *long-run* or *final* outcome of a system to depend on its previous outcomes – that is, the long run or final outcome depends on the path taken towards it. Notice that this distinguishes hysteretic systems from other dynamic systems whose short-run outcomes are path specific, but which ultimately converge to configurations defined independently of the path taken towards them.[5]

Recent attempts to characterize mathematically the process of hysteresis (for example, Wyplosz, 1987; Franz, 1990) have tended to proceed in terms of systems of equations similar to the following:

$$X_t = \Omega W_t \qquad [2.1]$$

$$W_t = f(X_{t-1}, Z_t) \qquad [2.2]$$

In this 'mainstream' characterization, hysteresis may occur as a result of the influence of past values of the endogenous variable X on the current values of the alleged exogenous variable W; both the coefficient Ω and the variable Z are treated as genuinely exogenous data. Consider the case where equation [2.2] can be given the linear functional form:

$$W_t = \alpha + \beta X_{t-1} + \gamma Z_t \qquad [2.3]$$

Substituting [2.3] into [2.1] yields:

$$X_t = \nu + \mu X_{t-1} + \phi Z_t \qquad [2.4]$$

where $\nu = \Omega\alpha$, $\mu = \Omega\beta$ and $\phi = \Omega\gamma$. By setting $X_t = X_{t-1} = X^*$, equation [2.4] may be solved to obtain:

$$X^* = \frac{\nu + \phi Z^*}{1 - \mu} \qquad [2.5]$$

where an asterisk (*) represents the steady state value of a variable. However, if $\mu = 1$, that is if the difference equation [2.4] possesses a unit root, equation [2.5] cannot be solved for X^*. Instead, given the existence condition $Z^* = -\dfrac{v}{\phi}$,[6] we can only define from [2.4] the system of equations:

$$X_t = v + \mu X_{t-1} + \phi Z_t$$

$$X_{t-1} = v + \mu X_{t-2} + \phi Z_{t-1}$$

$$\cdot$$
$$\cdot$$
$$\cdot$$

$$X_1 = v + \mu X_0 + \phi Z_1$$

which can be solved to yield:

$$X_t = X_0 + tv + \phi \cdot \sum_{i=1}^{t} Z_i \qquad [2.6]$$

where Z_i represents the time dependent values of Z.[7] This suggests that at any point t in time, all that can be derived is some 'contemporaneous' value of the variable X which depends on its own past history. Note that this is true even in the long run, where the 'long-run outcome' given by equation [2.6] is defined as such by virtue of its temporal distance, measured in calendar time, from the initial period 0. When $\mu = 1$, then, the system in equations [2.1] and [2.3] is hysteretic.

The model summarized in [2.6] is useful for illustrating an important feature of hysteretic systems. Note that in equation [2.6], X_t depends on the entire timepath of Z.[8] This implies that the system has a 'long memory', the importance of which is that it will never 'forget' any feature of its timepath – even what appear to be transitory shocks. Hence in complete contrast to, for example, New Classical macroeconomics, hysteresis suggests that even random disturbances may have long-lasting effects which permanently influence the future behaviour of an economic system, and hence its long run configuration.

i)   Hysteresis and Persistence

Hysteresis occurs in equation [2.6] only as a result of the assumption that $\mu = 1$, which was neither explained nor justified. This leads authors such as Wyplosz (1987) and Franz (1990) to conclude that hysteresis is a special case, which occurs only when a dynamic system comprising a set of difference equations possesses a unit root,[9] and which is encompassed by the more general traditional equilibrium approach. Nowhere is acceptance of this more evident than in the literature that claims to investigate the incidence of hysteresis in the natural rate of unemployment. Following Gordon (1989), this may be illustrated in the context of the following version of the natural rate hypothesis:

$$\dot{p}_t = \alpha \dot{p}_{t-1} + \beta(U_t - U^*) \qquad [2.7]$$

where $\dot{p}_t$ and $\dot{p}_{t-1}$ are the rates of inflation in periods t and $t-1$ respectively, and $U_t - U^*$ represents the difference between the actual and the natural rates of unemployment in period t. Given [2.7], it is usually argued that hysteresis exists if U^* depends on the past history of unemployment, as well as other (alleged exogenous) microeconomic variables captured by the vector Z_t. Hence we can write:

$$U^* = \eta U_{t-1} + \gamma Z_t \qquad [2.8]$$

Substituting [2.8] into [2.7], we arrive at:

$$\dot{p}_t = \alpha \dot{p}_{t-1} + \beta(1 - \eta)U_t + \beta\eta \cdot \Delta U_t - \beta\gamma Z_t \qquad [2.9]$$

Under the assumptions of the natural rate hypothesis, we may set $\alpha = 1$. In the steady state, $\dot{p}_t = \dot{p}_{t-1} = \dot{p}^*$, and $U_t = U_{t-1} = U^*$, which would conventionally allow us to solve for the natural rate as follows:

$$U^* = \frac{\gamma Z^*}{1 - \eta} \qquad [2.10]$$

However, if $\eta = 1$, equation [2.10] cannot be solved for U^*. Indeed, there exists no determinate natural rate in this case, so once again hysteresis, or what is sometimes referred to as 'full hysteresis' exists. The latter term is clearly intended as a contrast with what some authors (for example, Layard *et al.*, 1991) interpret as 'partial hysteresis' which arises in the case of 'persistence'. Hence suppose that $0 < \eta < 1$.[10] Then equation [2.10] will admit a determinate solution for U^*. However, there may exist situations in the short run where, with $\dot{p}_t = \dot{p}_{t-1} = \dot{p}^*$, we can derive from equation [2.9] the expression:

$$U_t^* = \gamma Z_t + \eta U_{t-1} \qquad [2.11]$$

Here, U_t^*, the 'contemporaneous' natural rate, represents '. . . that level of unemployment which is consistent with stable inflation *during the current period* . . .' (Layard *et al.*, 1991, p. 382). This case is referred to as persistence. U_t^* is intended to represent a temporary equilibrium sensitive to past rates of unemployment (Cross, 1991, p. 10), as distinct from the determinate long-run or steady-state equilibrium defined in [2.10]. Thus whilst full hysteresis is regarded as a special case, 'hysteresis', it is argued, may nevertheless occur in the short run in the form of unemployment persistence, as indicated by equation [2.11]. However, in the case of persistence, there continues to exist a determinate long-run or steady-state value of the natural rate defined solely in terms of exogenous data, and uninfluenced by the timepath of previous unemployment (equation [2.10]). Hence the system ultimately gravitates towards a configuration which is independent of the path taken towards it; it is ahysteretic, and belongs in the domain of traditional equilibrium analysis.

ii) A Familiar Example

The idea of persistence is not, in fact, new. In order to understand it more fully, it is constructive to consider a special case of a familiar macroeconomic model which displays 'persistence'. The system of equations which follows will immediately be recognized as Samuelson's multiplier–accelerator model, where Y is the level of national income, C represents aggregate consumption, I and $\overline{G}$ are the levels of investment and (exogenously given) government expenditure respectively, and the subscripts denote time periods:

$$Y_t = C_t + I_t + \overline{G} \tag{2.12}$$

$$C_t = \alpha Y_{t-1} \tag{2.13}$$

$$I_t = \beta(C_t - C_{t-1})$$

$$= \alpha\beta(Y_{t-1} - Y_{t-2}) \tag{2.14}$$

Substituting [2.13] and [2.14] into [2.12] yields:

$$Y_t = \alpha(1 + \beta)Y_{t-1} - \alpha\beta Y_{t-2} + \overline{G} \tag{2.15}$$

and if we assume that $\alpha\beta < 1$ and $\alpha < \dfrac{4\beta}{1 + \beta^2}$, it can be shown that the general solution of this model will yield an income time path which displays damped cycles.[11]

It appears from the nature of these equations that the model is hysteretic, since it is apparent from equation [2.15] that the variable Y depends, in any period t, on its own past values. However, the specific values of the parameters chosen above ensure that following any arbitrary disturbance, the system will converge to the determinate equilibrium:

$$Y^* = \frac{\overline{G}}{1 - \alpha}$$

What the model in fact describes is a process of oscillatory disequilibrium adjustment, in which the current or 'contemporaneous' value of income in equation [2.15] depends on its values in the past, but in which the level of income ultimately converges to an equilibrium which is independent of its prior adjustment path. The simple multiplier–accelerator model is therefore ahysteretic, although it does display what has been described earlier as persistence. In spite of its sometimes elaborate interpretation in the context of the unit root characterization of hysteresis, the notion of persistence is simply a rediscovery of the idea of sequential disequilibrium adjustment.[12]

III CRITICISMS OF THE HYSTERESIS/PERSISTENCE DICHOTOMY: RECONSTRUCTING HYSTERESIS AS A GENERAL CASE

Whilst the characterizations outlined earlier suggest that hysteresis is a special case, closer inspection suggests the contrary – that the importance of unit roots and the distinction between hysteresis and persistence are more apparent than real, and that hysteresis is a potentially pervasive phenomenon.

i) Hysteresis and the Process of Disequilibrium Adjustment

If $\mu \neq 1$ the system of equations [2.1] and [2.3] yields the steady state solution:

$$X^* = \frac{v + \phi Z^*}{1 - \mu} \qquad [2.5]$$

However, for this to be a relevant description of the system at any point in time, we must be able to show that the configuration in [2.5] can be reached. As was pointed out in Chapter 1, regardless of the existence of a steady state, we cannot conclude that a system will 'get into' equilibrium without specifying the appropriate dynamic convergence process. Fortunately, the system that is currently being contemplated is of a simple nature. The only form of hysteresis that is being admitted is the influence of past values of the endogenous variable X on the alleged exogenous variable W. Other channels of hysteresis (such as the possible influence of past values of X on the parameters and the form of the structural equations of the system) are being ignored.

As we have already seen, this enables us to characterize equations [2.1] and [2.3] as a simple difference equation of the form:

$$X_t = \nu + \mu X_{t-1} + \phi Z_t \qquad [2.4]$$

Studying the general solution of equation [2.4] enables us to be quite specific about the behaviour of the timepath of the variable X. This general solution can be written:

$$X_t = \mu A b^{t-1} + \frac{\nu + \phi Z^*}{1 - \alpha}$$

where A and b are constants, and $X_t = Ab^t$. This equation can in turn be rewritten as:[13]

$$X_t = A\mu^t + \frac{\nu + \phi Z^*}{1 - \alpha}$$

which implies that X_t will converge to the equilibrium value indicated by equation [2.5] for all values of μ such that $-1 < \mu < 1$.

From a mathematical point of view, this suggests that under conditions more general than those previously invoked to generate hysteresis, the equilibrium in equation [2.5] is determinate. However, it is important to consider what assumptions are necessary for this result to be relevant for an *economic* system. Perhaps the most important, as noted in section IV(iii) of Chapter 1, is that the speed of adjustment of X towards the equilibrium in [2.5] must be fast relative to the speed at which the data underlying this equilibrium are themselves changing. But suppose that the convergence of X is a long-run phenomenon, or at least of sufficient longevity to allow the equilibrium in [2.5] to alter its configuration before it is ever reached.[14] Essentially, we are assuming that 'persistence' occurs over a sufficiently long period of time to allow the data which determine long-run equilibrium to change. Then this long-run equilibrium will not provide an appropriate description of the configuration of the system at any point in time. In this case, the 'contemporaneous' value of X in equation [2.4] is all that is of interest. The behaviour of X will be described by the equations:

$$X_t = \nu + \mu X_{t-1} + \phi Z_t$$

$$X_{t-1} = \nu + \mu X_{t-2} + \phi Z_{t-1}$$

$$\vdots$$

$$X_1 = \nu + \mu X_0 + \phi Z_1$$

which upon substitution yields:

$$X_t = \mu' X_0 + \nu \cdot \sum_{i=1}^{t} \mu^{i-1} + \phi \cdot \sum_{i=1}^{t} \mu^{t-i} Z_i$$

which in turn implies that the value of X in any period t is specific to its prior adjustment path – that is, that it is hysteretic.

What this illustrates is that an important implicit assumption in the literature that distinguishes between hysteresis and persistence is that the speed of adjustment towards long-run equilibrium is relatively fast. If, however, persistence occurs over a sufficient period of time to allow the data underlying this long-run equilibrium to change – that is, if the speed of disequilibrium adjustment is relatively slow – long-run equilibrium may never be reached. Instead, as already illustrated, the distinction between hysteresis and persistence breaks down; the current value of X *always* depends on its prior adjustment path. This is true even in the long run, where the 'long run' is now conceived purely in terms of its temporal distance, measured in calendar time, from the initial period 0. Our analysis therefore suggests that hysteresis can exist even in systems with unique equilibria defined independently of the path taken towards them, if these equilibria fail to govern the long-run behaviour of such systems, which instead remain in a constant state of disequilibrium.[15]

ii) The Importance of Functional Forms

The second problem with mainstream characterizations of hysteresis is that the results to which they give rise are contingent on linear functional forms. Suppose that instead of equations [2.1] and [2.3] we have:

$$X_t = \Omega W_t \qquad [2.1]$$

$$W_t = \delta X_{t-1} \cdot Z_t \qquad [2.3a]$$

where the coefficient δ is again taken as given. Substituting [2.3a] into [2.1] now yields:

$$X_t = \lambda X_{t-1} \cdot Z_t \qquad [2.16]$$

where $\lambda = \Omega\delta$. Imposing steady state conditions on [2.16] admits no solution for X^*. Instead given the existence condition $Z^* = \dfrac{1}{\lambda},$[16] we can only define the system of equations:

$$X_t = \lambda X_{t-1} \cdot Z_t$$

$$X_{t-1} = \lambda X_{t-2} \cdot Z_{t-1}$$

.

.

.

$$X_1 = \lambda X_0 \cdot Z_1$$

which can be summarized as:

$$X_t = \lambda^t X_0 \cdot \prod_{i=1}^{t} Z_i \qquad\qquad [2.17]$$

This indicates that the value of X depends on its prior timepath for any value of $\lambda \neq 0$ – that is, that the system is hysteretic for any non-trivial value of λ.[17]

The specific example illustrated above does not take us far beyond the unit root methodology. Equation [2.16] can be written in a log-linear form which gives us a difference equation in $\ln X$ with a unit root.[18] However, more general discussions of the pervasiveness of hysteresis in the presence of non-linearities can be found in Cross (1991, 1993). One important feature of the systems considered by Cross is that their current outcomes are influenced only by the *dominant extrema* of past 'inputs' to the system, rather than by all past inputs.[19] Hence models of this nature have 'selective memories', in the sense that only *some* of their history is relevant in the determination of current outcomes arising from them (see Cross, 1991, pp. 32–34).

iii) Hysteresis and the Concept of 'Deep Endogeneity'[20]

It is evident from the definition given at the beginning of Section II that the concept of hysteresis poses fundamental questions about the nature of adjustment processes in economic models. This is obvious even in the unit root characterization of hysteresis, where once over shocks ($Z_i \neq 0$ for some i) have a permanent effect on subsequent outcomes in equation [2.6], *contra* the conventional (orthodox equilibrium) wisdom which suggests that, due to subsequent offsetting adjustments, shocks have no impact on long-run (steady-state) outcomes. However, if hysteresis is primarily a critique of the conventional treatment of adjustment processes, it is clear that the unit root characterization of hysteresis does not barely begin to rethink these processes. Embarking more fully on this exercise suggests that our theoretical treatment of both the extent and (in particular) the nature of endogeneity in economic models – not the existence or otherwise of unit roots – may be the critical factor determining the pervasiveness of hysteresis.

In order to begin examining these ideas, consider once again the steady state solution to the system described by equations [2.1] and [2.3]:

$$X^* = \frac{v + \phi Z^*}{1 - \mu} \qquad [2.5]$$

Notice that this outcome is defined in terms of the 'data' of equations [2.1] and [2.3] – that is, the coefficients and variables which are alleged to be exogenous to the structural model from which the expression in [2.5] is derived.

However, a central point of the hysteresis critique of traditional equilibrium analysis is to question whether conventional 'data' can in fact be regarded as exogenous in this manner. Might it not be preferable to interpret such traditional 'data' as tastes, technology and institutions as being endogenous to the economic outcomes they are held to explain?[21] Suppose, then, that in addition to equations [2.1] and [2.3] we have:

$$v_t = f_1(X_{t-1}) = \delta_1 X_{t-1} \qquad [2.18]$$

$$Z_t = f_2(X_{t-1}) = \delta_2 X_{t-1} \qquad [2.19]$$

that is, v and Z are dependent on the time path of X, or are what may be described as 'deeply endogenous'.[22] Given the conditions postulated in [2.18] and [2.19], equation [2.4] now becomes:

$$X_t = (\delta_1 + \mu + \delta_2\phi) \cdot X_{t-1} \qquad [2.4a]$$

$$\Rightarrow \quad (1 - (\delta_1 + \mu + \delta_2\phi)) \cdot X^* = 0 \qquad [2.5a]$$

where $X^* = X_t = X_{t-1}$ represents the steady state value of X. This expression yields the unique steady state solution $X^* = 0$, given the existence condition $\delta_1 + \mu + \delta_2 \neq 1$.[23] However, this solution is unlikely to be of general economic interest, suggesting that because of the (hitherto overlooked) deep endogeneity of the 'data' in equations [2.1] and [2.3], our model admits only trivial steady state solutions for X. We can, however, derive more general long-run outcomes from the system of equations:

$$X_t = (\delta_1 + \mu + \delta_2\phi) \cdot X_{t-1}$$

$$X_{t-1} = (\delta_1 + \mu + \delta_2\phi) \cdot X_{t-2}$$

$$\cdot$$
$$\cdot$$
$$\cdot$$

$$X_1 = (\delta_1 + \mu + \delta_2\phi) \cdot X_0$$

$$\Rightarrow \quad X_t = (\delta_1 + \mu + \delta_2\phi)^t \cdot X_0 \qquad [2.20]$$

but in equation [2.20], the long-run value of X clearly depends on the value of X established in the past, and is consequently hysteretic. It appears, then, that the deep endogeneity of what is conventionally regarded as 'data' may be sufficient to generate hysteresis as a general case outcome.

iv) Is Deep Endogeneity Enough? The Extent versus the Nature of Deep Endogeneity and the Importance of Adjustment Asymmetries

One possible objection to the result of the previous section is that it depends vitally on the precise *extent* to which deep endogeneity affects the data of equations [2.1] and [2.3]. Suppose, for example, that only [2.9] is valid – that is to say, Z is deeply endogenous, but v is genuinely exogenous. Then equation [2.4] now becomes:

$$X_t = v + (\mu + \delta_2\phi) \cdot X_{t-1} \qquad [2.4b]$$

$$\Rightarrow \quad X^* = \frac{v}{1 - \mu - \delta_2\phi} \qquad [2.5b]$$

where $X^* = X_t = X_{t-1}$ denotes the steady state value of X.[24] This suggests that as long as there are *some* genuinely exogenous data in our structural model, the system it describes will yield a traditional steady-state outcome. Hysteresis is again reduced to the status of a special case, contingent on the existence of a unit root. It would appear that unless we treat all separable elements of our structural model as deeply endogenous – in other words, unless we make a special case assumption about the *extent* of deep endogeneity – the latter is not sufficient to generate a hysteresis result.

Further consideration suggests, however, that the *extent* of deep endogeneity may not be the key issue. Rather, it is the *nature* of endogeneity – specifically, the way that the adjustment of deeply endogenous variables is modelled – that is of primary importance. In equation [2.19], the behaviour of Z is modelled in such a way that changes in Z brought about by the disequilibrium adjustment of X 'cancel out' over the course of the disequilibrium time path, leaving the long-run value of X unaffected. In other words, the *cumulative* change in Z induced by the disequilibrium adjustment of X sums to zero in the long run, so that the long-run value of X is, despite the deep endogeneity of Z, unaffected by its own prior disequilibrium values. Hence the long-run value of X can be appropriately characterized in terms of a traditional (determinate) steady state equilibrium as in [2.5b].

In order to see this explicitly, it is useful to re-write equation [2.19] as:

$$Z_t = f_t(X_{t-1}) \qquad [2.20]$$

and consider the impact of this expression on equation [2.5].[25] Under what circumstances, then, can Z^*, the long-run value of Z, be treated as independent of the prior disequilibrium time path of X, making the original equilibrium in [2.5] determinate?

We begin by considering a disturbance which causes X to depart from the equilibrium value X^* in equation [2.5]. Denote the sequence of changes in X as it moves along its disequilibrium adjustment path between periods 1 and t as $dX_i = X_i - X_{i-1}$ for all $i = 1, \ldots, t$. Define $DX = \sum_{i=1}^{t} dX_i$ as the cumulative change in X along the hypothesized disequilibrium adjustment path between periods 1 and t. Now suppose that $DX = 0$. This implies that the hypothesized changes in X between periods 0 and t are 'cumulatively neutral', so that $X_t = X^*$. In other words, we are hypothesizing that following the initial disturbance, X has followed a disequilibrium adjustment path along which it has returned to its original value by period t. Whether X is now back in equilibrium, however, or whether $X_t = X^*$ is merely a disequilibrium point through which X is passing *en route* to a new long-run value, remains to be seen. It transpires that whichever of these two scenarios is the more accurate depends very much on the behaviour of Z in equation [2.20]. Suppose, then, that [2.20] is subject to the conditions:

(a) $\qquad\qquad f_i' \neq 0 \quad \text{for some} \quad i = 2, \ldots, t{+}1$

(b) $\qquad\qquad DZ = \sum_{i=1}^{t} f_{i+1}' \cdot dX_i = 0$

What this means is that changes in X along its disequilibrium adjustment path (dX_i) have a short-run effect on Z ($f_i' \neq 0$ for some i in assumption (a), so that $f_{i+1}' \cdot dX_i \neq 0$ for some i) but that these variations in Z 'cancel out' over the course of the adjustment path ($\sum_{i=1}^{t} f_{i+1}' \cdot dX_i = 0$ in assumption (b)). Ultimately, then, the long-run value of Z, Z^*, is unaffected by the disequilibrium behaviour of X, and so the long-run value of X, X^*, will also be unaffected by its own prior time path. Instead, X^* will be given by the determinate equilibrium in equation [2.5].

It is disequilibrium dynamics of this nature that are implicitly postulated in equation [2.19], and which prevent this equation from being sufficient to generate hysteresis in the system described by equation [2.1] and [2.3]. Precisely the same reasoning is implicit in the hysteresis/persistence dichotomy discussed in Section II(i). This dichotomy admits the possibility of some heretofore overlooked endogeneity in economic relationships (assumption (*a*)), but assumes that endogenously induced changes in economic 'data' have no lasting significance – that they effectively 'cancel out' over time (assumption (*b*)). The result of this assumption is that whilst short-run outcomes display persistence, long-run outcomes are nevertheless determinate.

Clearly, the preceding results are dependent on the particular treatment of the nature of endogeneity in adjustment processes captured in assumption (*b*). Suppose, then, that we retain assumption (*a*), but forgo assumption (*b*) in favour of:

(*c*)
$$DZ = \sum_{i=1}^{t} f'_{i+1} \cdot dX_i \neq 0$$

This time, the variations in Z_t with respect to X_t do not 'cancel out' over time. Although $DX = 0$ for $i = 1, \ldots, t$, these cumulatively neutral changes in X are *not* cumulatively neutral with respect to Z. Consequently, although $X_t = X^*$, X^* is no longer the equilibrium value of X. To see this, let Z^{**} denote the new long-run value of Z that emerges from the process described in assumption (*c*), where $Z^{**} \neq Z^*$ since $DZ \neq 0$. Assume for simplicity that any subsequent adjustments in the value of X during the periods $i = t+1, \ldots, n$ are cumulatively neutral with respect to Z – that is, that $DZ = \sum_{i=t+1}^{n} f'_{i+1} \cdot dX_i = 0$. Then the new long-run value of X, denoted X^{**}, towards which X will now converge during the periods $i = t+1, \ldots, n$ is given by:[26]

$$X^{**} = \frac{v + \phi Z^{**}}{1 - \mu} \neq \frac{v + \phi Z^*}{1 - \mu} = X^* \qquad [2.21]$$

When the long-run value of Z depends on the prior disequilibrium adjustment path of X as in assumption (*c*), then the long-run value of X will depend on the values of X established in the past. This is clearly illustrated by the final result in [2.21]. Under the conditions postulated in assumption (*c*), we will, therefore, observe hysteresis, so that this assumption can be identified as expressing the sufficient condition for hysteresis to occur. Note, moreover, that hysteresis does not depend on the special case existence of unit roots. Indeed, it occurs under more general formal conditions (assumption (*c*)) than those necessary to generate a determinate long-run equilibrium outcome (assumption (*b*)).

It is instructive at this stage to pause to reflect on the intuitive basis of assumption (*c*). In general, the outcome in assumption (*c*) will be observed whenever there exist 'adjustment asymmetries' in economic variables displaying deep endogeneity. In our example, the deeply endogenous variable Z can be said to display adjustment asymmetries if a change in this variable induced by a change in the variable X cannot be reversed simply by restoring the original value of X. Suppose, for example, that an increase in X along its disequilibrium adjustment path induces an increase in Z. Then if Z is subject to adjustment asymmetries, a series of offsetting reductions in X in subsequent periods will not induce Z to return to its original value. As a result, the adjustment path followed by X will induce changes in the long-run value of Z, which will in turn induce changes in the long-run value of X itself – that is, the long-run value of X will depend on the values of X established in the past, and will therefore display hysteresis.

There are already well known examples of how such adjustment asymmetries can occur, and how they can give rise to hysteresis. For example, there may exist adjustment asymmetries in behavioural norms due to 'revenge motives'. Cornwall (1991) argues that labour may feel that it has been 'made to pay' the costs of an anti-inflationary policy which relies on high unemployment to reduce wage demands. Hence even if unemployment subsequently falls, there may exist a strong desire to 'get even' for the perceived inequities of previous periods, which will change workers' attitudes towards the wage bargaining process. This can give rise to hysteresis in the long-run Phillips curve (Cornwall, 1991). Adjustment asymmetries may also arise in firms' costs of production, due to sunk costs which are incurred as a result of entry into a market. Sunk costs are, by definition, expenditures which cannot be recovered if the action that led to them being incurred is subsequently reversed. This can give rise to hysteresis in investment decisions (Dixit, 1989).[27]

v) Adjustment along a Given Time Path versus Changes in the Time Path Itself

On the basis of equation [2.20], we can define some g such that:

$$Z_t = g(X_1, \ldots, X_{t-1}) \qquad [2.22]$$

Equation [2.22] is an analog of equation [2.20], expressing Z as a function of the entire disequilibrium adjustment path $(X_1, \ldots, X_{t-1})$ prior to period t. Suppose that we now define $\Delta X = \sum_{i=1}^{t-1} dX_i$, where $dX_i = X_i' - X_i$ for all $i = 1, \ldots, t-1$ represents the difference at each point in time between values of X along a new disequilibrium time path (denoted by X_i') and values of X along the 'base' disequilibrium time path (denoted by X_i) which comprises the arguments of the function g in equation [2.22]. We make no initial assumption here as to whether $\Delta X \gtreqless 0$. Suppose, however, that the following conditions apply:

(d) $\qquad\qquad\qquad g_i' \neq 0 \quad for\ some \quad i = 1, \ldots, t-1$

(e) $\qquad\qquad\qquad \Delta Z = \sum_{i=1}^{t-1} g_i' \cdot dX_i \neq 0$

In light of assumption (d), ΔZ in assumption (e) represents the cumulative change in Z arising from a small change in X's disequilibrium time path. (Note the contrast to DZ in assumptions (b) and (c), which captures the cumulative change in Z arising from the movement of X *along* a *given* disequilibrium time path.) The notion that $\Delta Z \neq 0$ implies that Z is not only sensitive to the process of disequilibrium adjustment *per se* (as is the case when $DZ \neq 0$), but to the *precise* disequilibrium time path taken. In this case, 'history matters' in the fullest sense; we need to know the *exact* past history of the system we are considering in order to understand the evolution of the deeply endogenous variable Z and hence the long-run value of X. The outcome in assumption (e) and its implications will be of substantial use to us when we confront the issue of modelling the impact of prior growth trajectories on the subsequent relative growth prospects of competing regions in Part II.

IV   AN ALTERNATIVE APPROACH TO MACROECONOMIC MODELLING

The preceding arguments illustrate the limits of the unit root characterization of hysteresis, and suggest that the distinction between hysteresis and persistence to which it gives rise is not useful. In so doing, they show that hysteresis is not a special case, but must be treated as a potentially pervasive feature of macroeconomic systems.

Incorporating a generalized notion of hysteresis into macroeconomic models can therefore be identified as an important research agenda for macroeconomics. Such a research agenda would avoid the ahistoricism of the traditional equilibrium approach, the results of which are ultimately determined by unexplained external data. It would also avoid the pitfall, inherent in current theorizing, of permitting an illusory escape from hysteresis back into the traditional equilibrium approach via the notion of persistence. What remains to be seen, however, is precisely what the treatment of hysteresis as a general phenomenon implies for macroeconomic modelling. The first implication is clearly negative. If hysteresis is a prevalent feature of economic activity, then the traditional equilibrium approach to macroeconomic modelling is guilty of overlooking an important aspect of macroeconomic dynamics. More specifically, hysteresis suggests that it is misleading to conceive the behaviour of an economic system as being governed by a determinate equilibrium. The orthodox notion of equilibrium posits a long-run outcome that *governs* the path taken towards it, since all disequilibrium adjustment paths ultimately lead to the same final outcome. With hysteresis, however, any long-run or final configuration that is reached by a system will *depend on* the path taken towards it. The evolution of a system – even in the long run – will, therefore, be best described by 'contemporaneous' values of variables expressed in terms of their own past history.

However, the second implication is positive – namely, that within the hysteresis critique of traditional equilibrium analysis lie the foundations of an alternative methodology for macroeconomic modelling. The key element of this alternative methodology is the notion that economies function in historical time – economic events occur in a uni-directional sequence rather than instantaneously, and these sequential patterns of activity matter in the sense that they affect final outcomes. The challenge with which we are presented, then, is to identify practical 'organizing concepts' suited to the pursuit of this methodology in macroeconomic modelling. The generalized notion of hysteresis developed previously is one such organizing concept. However, the notion that economic events unfold in a uni-directional sequence also calls forth other 'new' organizing concepts into the macro-economic debate – concepts which have hitherto been widely overlooked because they have no place in traditional equilibrium analysis. Of particular importance in this regard are the concepts of cumulative causation and lock-in.

i) Cumulative Causation

The insight that macroeconomic dynamics occur sequentially in historical time is an inherent feature of the Keynesian tradition in macroeconomics.[28] Recognition of the importance of sequential patterns of economic activity can be found in the General Theory, where Keynes' analysis of the general equilibrium effects of falling real wages is based explicitly on the fact that '[t]he hiring of workers and the marketing of the output produced by those workers are separated in time' (Skott, 1983, p. 23). That is, that the hiring of workers, the implementation of a specific production plan, and the sale of final output comprises a distinct sequence of activities and that this sequence matters when we come to analyse the levels of output and employment in an economy. Emphasis on the importance of history as a determinant of current and future outcomes is also explicit in the work of authors such as Robinson (1974a, 1980) and Kaldor (1972, 1985). Of particular importance is Kaldor's promotion of the concept of cumulative causation.[29] Cumulative causation involves a circular interaction between economic variables, in such a way that an initial change in a variable x induces supporting changes in the vector of variables Z which reinforce the initial change in x. Hence, with cumulative causation, 'the actual state of the economy during any one "period" cannot be predicted except as a result of the sequence of events in previous periods that led up to it' (Kaldor, 1972, p. 1244).

Comparing the definition and consequences of cumulative causation with the definition and consequences of hysteresis discussed earlier, it is immediately apparent that a close correspondence exists between these concepts. This correspondence is not exact (that is, the concepts are not formally equivalent) because cumulative causation dictates that successive changes in a variable be positively correlated. For example, an initial increase in x will induce subsequent increases in x. This is not necessarily true of hysteretic systems, in which an increase in the value of x in the present period might give rise to changes in the structure of the system determining x which cause its subsequent value to *decline*.[30] However, cumulative causation is based on the same basic methodological conception of the economy that we have already identified with hysteresis – that of the economy as a historical entity, which instead of adjusting inevitably towards some determinate equilibrium, comprises sequential patterns of activity which can, in and of themselves, affect the nature of final economic outcomes. In this way, Kaldor's treatment of the principle of cumulative causation can be interpreted as a preliminary attempt to understand the workings of a macroeconomy in hysteretic terms.[31] It offers a concrete indication of how we might at least begin to conceive the process of modelling macroeconomic systems with hysteresis – a point to which we will subsequently return in Chapter 3.

ii) Lock-In

Lock-in is a property of dynamic systems that arises when sequential patterns of activity form a 'groove' from which it subsequently becomes difficult for a system to deviate. Lock-in occurs when current behaviour is conditional on either past events, or the behaviour of other agents in the system. These 'frequency dependency effects' may give rise to situations where to deviate from the pursuit of a particular activity requires non-marginal adjustments, which it does not pay any one individual to undertake within a given period, or which are beyond the control of the individual decision making unit. Hence the system becomes 'locked in' to this activity. Results of this nature can be observed even within the rubric of the conventional (neoclassical) theory of rational choice. The key premise of lock-in is that decisions are made sequentially (rather than simultaneously within some initial period) *not* that individual decision makers are in some way 'irrational'.

Lock-in can occur in a variety of ways. Suppose, for example, that we are faced with a set of economic activities, each of which is designed to fulfil the same objective. Suppose further that the returns to these activities are directly proportional to the extent that they have been practised in the past – for example, they may involve learning by doing. Then it may be that at each point in time, the rational choice of activity will be the one first chosen – even if, in some long-run sense, it is inferior to one or all of the alternative activities (Arthur, 1988a, p. 13). Hence the system becomes locked in to this initial activity.

A simple example serves to illustrate this point. Consider a person faced with a career choice – say law or medicine – where the rewards to each activity increase with experience.[32] Suppose that the initial rewards to law are highest, but are relatively quickly surpassed by those of medicine. Then a rational agent with a high discount rate may choose law as his/her career. However, after a brief period of time in law, the person may come to realize that an equivalent time spent in medicine would have ensured higher earnings at all future dates, and therefore decide that medicine was in fact the career with the greater long-term potential. Despite this realization, it may be that the returns over the remainder of the individual's working life to *continuing* in law, in which experience has already been accumulated, exceed the returns to *beginning* a new career in medicine.[33] At no point in time will it pay the individual to switch careers from law to medicine; he/she is effectively locked in to a career in law by virtue of his/her initial choice.

A second, and particularly important, phenomenon which may generate lock-in is interrelatedness (Frankel, 1955). Interrelatedness can be defined as interconnections between components of the production process (technologies, institutions, individual decision-making units) which are usually thought of as being divisible and separable. There are two dimensions to interrelatedness, both of which can give rise to lock-in. First, interrelatedness can occur *within* the individual decision-making unit, when current behaviour is conditional on the individual's own past behaviour. Suppose, for example, that the components of the production process under the control of an individual decision maker are interrelated. Then changing any one of these components may require complementary changes in other components with which it is interrelated. This possibility is vividly illustrated by David's (1985) documentation of the difficulties firms face in switching from QWERTY to the more efficient DSK typewriter keyboards. These difficulties arise due to the accompanying expenditures on the human capital of firms' employees, whose current skills are complementary to QWERTY, that such a switch would require. In this scenario, the problem which interrelatedness poses is that change may become prohibitively costly. As a result, the current choices of the individual decision maker are constrained in such a way that he/she becomes locked in to his/her own past practices.

Second, interrelatedness can occur *between* individual decision-making units, in which case the current behaviour of any one individual is conditional on the behaviour of others in the system. Suppose now that the components of the production process under the control of *different* individual decision-making units are interrelated. Then a change in any one of these components by a particular individual decision maker may require accompanying changes in other components which are beyond the range of his/her control. For example, no individual firm can adopt broad gauge rolling stock if railway companies remain committed to narrow gauge tracks. The problem which interrelatedness now poses is that the decision-making unit is small relative to the size of the unit of change required. This results in the system (that is, all individual units) becoming locked in to current practices.[34]

It should be clear from the nature of lock-in as described above that this phenomenon may constitute an important source of the adjustment asymmetries discussed in Section III(iv). If it is possible for certain features of the economy – such as its technological or institutional structures, for example – to become locked in to certain forms from which it is subsequently difficult for them to deviate, then simply restoring the external conditions that existed prior to the creation of these technological and institutional forms may not be sufficient to eliminate them. Lock-in to technological and institutional structures may, therefore, play an important role in generating hysteretic macroeconomic outcomes. In Chapters 4 and 5, we will further explore this possibility, with the aim of demonstrating its potential implications for the evolution of an economy. For the time being, however, note that what lock-in illustrates is that even when agents are making rational choices, they may yet experience 'regret', arising from the awareness that the type of activities that they are undertaking are demonstrably inferior to an available alternative (Arthur, 1988a).

V   WHAT REMAINS OF EQUILIBRIUM?

It is important to realize that hysteresis, cumulative causation, and lock-in are not equivalent concepts. Nor, indeed, does the existence of, say, hysteresis necessarily imply the existence of phenomena such as lock-in. Rather, it is simply the case that all three of these concepts are mutually compatible, and this is so because of a methodological feature common to each of them; emphasis on the notion that economic activity occurs in historically sequential patterns which 'matter' in the determination of long-run outcomes. What hysteresis, cumulative causation and lock-in provide is a set of organizing concepts suitable for use in modelling macroeconomic dynamics in a manner which is broadly consistent with the notion of historical time. The challenge that is presented to us, then, is to construct a path-dependent model of macroeconomic activity which conceives the long run as an evolutionary sequence of short runs, and which allows us to discuss the implications for long-run macroeconomic outcomes of sequential short-run patterns of economic activity.

Before addressing this challenge, however, we might stop to consider whether the usefulness of hysteresis, cumulative causation and lock-in as organizing concepts in economic theory implies that the concept of equilibrium is redundant? Of course, the orthodox notion of equilibrium defined in Chapter 1 as a determinate long-run outcome is clearly antithetical to the principle of path dependence. However, the general idea of a 'state of rest' or a 'balance of forces' may not, in and of itself, contradict the idea of path dependence. What is crucial is the way in which any such equilibrium is conceived in light of preceding periods of disequilibrium.

In order to explore these ideas further, it is useful to refer back to the work of Kaldor (1934). As we have already seen in Chapter 1, Kaldor defined a determinate outcome as one which depends only on exogenous data and which can therefore be defined and reached independently of the path taken towards it. He defined indeterminate outcomes as those possessing the opposite characteristics – that is, as depending on the past outcomes of the systems from which they derive by virtue of the influence of these past outcomes on the 'data' defining the final outcome.[35] What is important for our purposes is that Kaldor made a further distinction between definite and indefinite indeterminate outcomes. An indeterminate outcome is also indefinite if it shows no tendency to ever approximate a position of equilibrium.[36] An indeterminate outcome may be definite, however, if it *does* eventually approximate a position of equilibrium. An important point to note, though, is that because the outcome is indeterminate as well as definite, the equilibrium must depend on the prior (disequilibrium) adjustment path taken towards it. In sum, an indeterminate outcome '. . . may still be one which is tending towards an equilibrium (that is, it may be definite) . . . ; but the point at which [the system] ultimately come[s] to rest can no longer be deduced from the data of the initial situation' (Kaldor, 1934, p. 132). On the contrary, the definite or equilibrium outcome will depend also on the precise sequence of adjustments which take place subsequent to the 'initial situation'. It appears, then, that the idea of equilibrium is not altogether incompatible with the principle of path dependence. Clearly, however, the notion of equilibrium we are appealing to here is radically different from the orthodox notion of equilibrium as previously defined. If an outcome is indeterminate but definite, equilibrium is nothing more than a position reached *ex post*. It is *not* an *ex ante* 'centre of gravity' towards which all adjustment paths inexorably tend, as is the orthodox notion of equilibrium.

There may, however, be another, qualitatively different objection to the use of equilibrium as an organizing concept. This objection is concerned less with the problems associated with 'getting into' equilibrium (in which we have, up until now, been chiefly interested) than it is with what happens once equilibrium is achieved – or, more precisely, with what being 'in equilibrium' implies about the nature of the economic future. One characteristic property of an equilibrium time path is that once it has been reached, a system will display no endogenous tendency to deviate from it. Deviations may occur, of course, by virtue of exogenous shocks, but these are, by definition, unexplained within the confines of any system itself. Once reached, then, equilibrium implies a state of extreme stasis – an 'end to history', as it were, since, in the absence of shocks, any subsequent evolution of a system is pre-determined by the equilibrium time path that has been achieved. Along this time path, the precise sequence of events of which economic activity over time is comprised does not 'matter', since it will have no effect on the subsequent outcomes of the system. It appears, therefore, that the invocation of equilibrium as a solution concept – even qualified by the caveat that any equilibrium achieved is path dependent – entails an intolerable departure from the strictures of historical time, according to which sequential patterns of activity *do*, in principle, matter.

There are, however, two possible responses to this concern. The first involves an admission of the problem identified earlier, but seeks to argue that, nevertheless, equilibrium remains a useful organizing concept. This argument relies on the idea that 'not all equilibrium concepts were created equally'. As was noted at the beginning of Chapter 1, the term 'equilibrium' can mean many different things in economics. Most importantly, however, its treatment as an organizing concept differs crucially between schools of thought. Hence according to Kregel (1976), Keynes used the idea of equilibrium as a pedagogic device in an otherwise essentially historical model of the economy. In the General Theory, Keynes eschewed the notion of long-run equilibrium, but assumed a constant state of long-run expectations. This was designed to ' "lock up" [the] effect of general expectations and uncertainty without assuming that they did not exist' (Kregel, 1976, p. 212) and hence to facilitate demonstration of the principle of effective demand via the use of a new equilibrium concept – the short-run under employment equilibrium. However, Kregel goes on to argue that Keynes' lectures of 1937 reveal his consideration of a model in which long-run expectations are subject to revision in light of the prior disappointment of short-run expectations, implying that the underlying determinants of aggregate demand (the propensity to consume, liquidity preference, and the marginal efficiency of capital) are endogenous to the past history of the economy. The important feature of this model is that:[37]

if . . . realization of error alters the state of expectations and shifts the independent behavioural functions, Keynes' model of shifting equilibrium will describe an actual path of an economy over time chasing an ever changing equilibrium . . .

(Kregel, 1976, p. 217)

that is, the model displays what we have defined earlier as hysteresis – its final or long-run configuration depends on the prior adjustment path of the economy. Furthermore, this long-run outcome may be, in Kaldor's terminology, indefinite. However, Kregel goes on to argue that:

the extreme complexity of such a situation explains why Keynes was willing to 'tame' this system, first making assumptions that allowed the definition of functions that he knew did not exist through their entire range, expressly in order to give force to the theory of effective demand.

(Kregel, 1976, p. 216)

In other words, Keynes invoked the notion of the short-run under employment equilibrium as a pedagogic device to illustrate the workings of his short-run theory. It is for similarly strategic reasons that equilibrium may, in some circumstances, be usefully retained as an organizing concept in economic theory, even if path dependency is pervasive.

The second response is to advocate a rethinking of the concept of equilibrium itself, designed to overcome the appearance that equilibrium implies an 'end to history'. This requires a re-examination of the 'no endogenous tendency to change' property of an equilibrium time path. Essentially, what is involved is challenging the idea that there can ever be, at least in the long run, a state of the world where there is 'no endogenous tendency to change'. Critical here is the belief that human action is motivated not just by well defined expected future consequences (as in conventional neoclassical behavioural theory) but also by reference to past and/or present states of mind (Witt, 1991, p. 88). For example, if expectations are *not* well defined because agents exist in an environment of fundamental uncertainty, then the repetition associated with a state of equilibrium may arouse suspicion – a feeling that 'things are too quiet'. This may alter agents' animal spirits and hence their actions, perturbing the economic system from within.[38] Alternatively, suppose that repetition in equilibrium results in boredom which inspires some individuals to seek novelty (Witt, 1991, pp. 88–9). This will likely result in innovative actions being undertaken by these individuals, which will again perturb the system from within. Finally, suppose that agents are, in part, motivated by previously defined aspirations and that repeated (equilibrium) outcomes fall short of these aspirations (Witt, 1991, p. 89). We may again observe innovative actions by disappointed individuals which will endogenously perturb the economic system.

In any of the instances discussed, the state of tranquillity associated with conditions of equilibrium may simply be a precursor to some subsequent, endogenously generated, change. If so, then conditions of equilibrium need not imply an indefinite state of rest from which there is 'no endogenous tendency to change'. As such, there is no 'end to history' once equilibrium is achieved, because subsequent endogenous change may arise even at a position of equilibrium.

What the preceding arguments suggest is that in some models, equilibrium is deliberately used as a pedagogic device to 'lock up without ignoring' the effects of historical time whilst in others, we may conceive of situations where being in equilibrium is simply a precursor to a process of 'innovating out' of equilibrium. It might be argued that what the latter implies is really a *de facto* abolition of equilibrium as an organizing concept. Alternatively, *both* of the points made can be interpreted as suggesting that all equilibria should really be treated as 'conditional' equilibria – positions which are either entirely artificial (as when history has been 'locked up') or which have been established by some prior, path-dependent process and await subsequent redefinition by forces endogenous to the sequential progression of the economy through historical time.[39] In either case, a conditional equilibrium represents a state of rest brought about by some real or imagined temporary suspension of the forces of change endogenous to a system. And in either case, the notion of a conditional equilibrium might prove to be a useful organizing concept without implying that there has been some 'end to history'.

The notion of equilibrium plays a much diminished role in the modelling exercise in Part II. However, in principle the use of conditional equilibria as organizing concepts would not appear to be antithetical to the project of modelling macroeconomic systems with hysteresis. Indeed, the modelling exercise in Sections III(iii)–(v) may be thought of as ample illustration of this point. As long as any equilibrium is treated as dependent on the prior adjustment path taken towards it and is shown to be the long-run outcome emergent from some precise prior sequence of short-run adjustments,[40] or as long as the idea of equilibrium is invoked when such evolutionary properties of a system are to be artificially 'locked up without being ignored', then the notion of equilibrium may, at times, be useful as an organizing concept in economic theory. Since it does not appear necessary to insist that the very idea of equilibrium is redundant in order to move concepts such as hysteresis, cumulative causation and lock-in to the fore, it is not, therefore, the recommendation of this analysis that we should insist on the complete redundancy of equilibrium as an organizing concept.

PART II
Modelling Macroeconomic Systems with Hysteresis: Growth and Structural Change in Capitalist Economies

Introduction

In Part I, it was argued that hysteresis, along with cumulative causation and lock-in, may provide suitable organizing concepts for the construction of a model of long-run macroeconomic performance which is broadly affine with the notion of historical time.[1] This involves placing emphasis on the role of past outcomes in determining the current and future configuration of a system. Although by some interpretations the concept of equilibrium is not entirely antithetical to this project, the modelling exercise that follows will, by necessity, involve a rejection of the orthodox notion of equilibria as determinate 'centres of gravity' governing the long-run outcomes of macroeconomic systems.

Chapter 3 begins by identifying an important potential source of path dependency – the existence of increasing returns to scale. This recalls Kaldor's contributions to non-equilibrium growth theory. Much of the chapter is devoted to the construction of a Kaldorian model of cumulative causation, which is interpreted as a first step towards understanding path dependent macroeconomic dynamics. Chapters 4 and 5 extend these beginnings by considering the impact of technological and institutional structures on growth. Particular emphasis is placed on the possibility of an economy experiencing lock-in to specific technological and institutional 'regimes' in the context of which cumulative causation is occurring. This is shown to extend the model of cumulative causation developed in Chapter 3 into a more generally hysteretic long-run form. In so doing, the model illustrates the possibility that self-reinforcing growth dynamics in a capitalist economy will break down in the course of growth and development.

3 A Model of Cumulative Causation

In Chapter 2, it was suggested that there exists a close correspondence between hysteresis and the principle of cumulative causation associated with authors such as Kaldor. This correspondence suggests that the work of Kaldor may represent a useful point of departure for our attempt to construct a hysteretic model of long-run macroeconomic dynamics. The aim of this chapter is to explore this possibility in detail.

I INCREASING RETURNS AND THE KALDORIAN HERITAGE

i) Sources of Increasing Returns

Central to Kaldor's models of cumulative causation (see, for example, Kaldor, 1970, 1972 and 1985) is the concept of increasing returns to scale. Increasing returns may be of either a static or dynamic nature. Static economies of scale result directly from increases in the physical size of production units, as increases in the surface area of a production unit give rise to more than proportional increases in its volume and hence productive capacity. For example, constructing a $4 \times 4 \times 4$ storage facility requires four times the building materials needed to construct a $2 \times 2 \times 2$ storage facility, due to the fourfold increase in the surface area of the facility that is being contemplated. However, this quadrupling of inputs will increase storage capacity, which varies with the volume of the facility, eight fold. Assuming that building materials are priced at a uniform rate per square unit, this will halve storage costs per cubic unit.

For authors such as Kaldor, however, the most important types of economies of scale are dynamic in nature. Dynamic increasing returns result from induced technological progress in the course of the expansion of output, and accrue through a variety of channels. Several of these channels are motivated, either explicitly or implicitly, by the significance which attaches to increases in current output by virtue of their effects on firms' expectations of future product demand in an environment where productive activity is demand constrained and subject to fundamental uncertainty. Hence, as first emphasized by Adam Smith and subsequently by Young (1928), increases in the division of labour (that is, increased specialization) occur in response to increases in the size of the market. According to this view, demand led increases in output will promote increases in the degree of specialization of work tasks within the firm, which will in turn raise average productivity.

Technical progress may also be associated with the accumulation of new and specific types of fixed capital, within which technological advances are embodied. However, firms may hesitate to accumulate these assets if they must win market share from competitors in order to achieve the level of output that will fully utilize such newly acquired fixed capital.[1] However, if the market as a whole is expanding, then even if market shares remain constant, individual firms may achieve a level of output that will fully utilize a more capital intensive technique of production (Scitovsky, 1956; Lamfalussy, 1961, 1963). Dynamic returns to scale therefore accrue as increases in output in response to growing demand facilitate the accumulation of new fixed capital embodying technological progress which raises firms' productivity.

Finally, according to authors such as Schmookler (1966), innovative activity is demand led. As a result, dynamic economies of scale may occur as increases in current output stimulate productivity enhancing innovations within the economy.

The economy may also experience dynamic increasing returns which are external to the individual firm. The growth of output and the concomitant expansion of industry within a concentrated geographical area typically encourages the emergence of specialized firms at intermediate stages of production, the development of a local infrastructure of physical and human capital and so forth – all of which are productivity enhancing. Externalities may also arise by virtue of the technical nature of knowledge as a commodity.[2] Two important attributes of knowledge are that it is a non-rival commodity, and that it is, at least partly, non-excludable. Hence the larger the output and so the greater the number of firms in an industry, the greater the flow of non-rival, non-excludable knowledge into a general 'pool' of information from which all producers are simultaneously able to draw (see, for example, Grossman and Helpman, 1991).

Dynamic returns to scale may also arise from the process of 'learning by doing'. This source of increasing returns derives from the notion that the more production occurs during a given period, the more is learnt about the production process through its repeated use, and so the more this production process is likely to be improved and refined. Arrow (1962) argues that learning is a product of experience – that it takes place as a consequence of engaging in production activities which are imperfectly understood. Arrow argues that learning gives rise to both improved knowledge of existing processes, and improvement in processes themselves, that is, technological progress. Note that in Arrow's account, learning by doing occurs over time, but arises simply through repetition. It is conceivable, then, that even if output is stationary, productivity will grow over time due to learning by doing, as long as useful experience can always be gained from the repeated act of production. Hence, as noted by Boyer and Petit (1991, p. 494), the principle of learning by doing is not analytically identical to the proposition that productivity growth is a function of output growth, which is characteristic of the other channels, surveyed earlier, through which dynamic increasing returns accrue. However, learning by doing is at least confluent with this output growth–productivity growth nexus. As output expands over time, then, this will increase the amount of production per period, increasing the degree of repetition in production and so the amount of learning by doing. It only remains to point out that this increase in learning over time will further enhance productivity over time – that is, output growth will stimulate productivity growth by increasing the amount of learning by doing per period.

ii) The Existence of Large-Scale Increasing Returns

An important implicit assumption underlying Kaldor's discussion of increasing returns is that they are 'large relative to the size of the economy', by which we mean that increasing returns cannot be exhausted by the scale of production in any period.[3] Two important dynamic properties of modern capitalist economies suggest the existence, at any point in time, of 'large-scale' increasing returns as defined earlier. The first of these, emphasized by Kaldor (1970) and Cornwall (1977), stems from the conception of capitalism as a 'dual economy' in which a basic dichotomy exists between 'land based' and 'processing' activities. The distinguishing feature of the latter is their reliance on 'produced means of production' (that is, capital goods), which are intimately related to increasing returns. For example, capital goods embody technological progress, and this in turn is affected by the process of learning by doing. The use of produced means of production implies that the 'scarcity of resources' in processing activities cannot be thought of as being independent of the level of activity in the economy. What is chiefly important in processing activities is the dynamic propensity of the economy to *create* resources (that is, to deepen and/or widen its stock of capital) rather than the static problem of resource *allocation*. The endogeneity of this resource creation process gives rise to the potential for continuous dynamic economies of scale related to increases in the quantity and quality of the capital stock – that is, the potential for increasing returns which, at any given point in time, are large relative to the size of the economy.[4]

However, it is not only the ability of capitalism to manufacture an important source of increasing returns that accounts for the large-scale nature of the latter. As Cornwall (1972) illustrates, this is also due to the inherently unbalanced nature of the growth of capitalist economies, or more precisely, the nature of growth as a process of structural transformation. According to Cornwall, growth can be characterized as a movement through a hierarchy of commodities with different goods becoming 'necessities' (that is, having high income elasticities of demand) and 'luxuries' (low income elasticities of demand) at different levels of per capita income (see also Pasinetti, 1981, pp. 71–5). In this way,

> [a]ll that really needs to be argued to support the economies of scale position is that the growth of productivity in some firm or industry is more responsive to demand conditions when the rate of growth of demand is high and rising. When the market for the good becomes relatively saturated and demand shifts to other industries, a slowing down in the rate of productivity and the exhaustion of scale economies can be expected. [But this] comes at a time when it is less consequential for the overall growth of productivity.
>
> (Cornwall, 1972, p. 64)

In other words, as demand transfers through the commodity hierarchy towards new products, the new industries producing them are able to reap dynamic economies of scale. Hence the growth of productivity in these industries will be rising just as demand and resources are being transferred towards them, that is, as their weight in the economy is becoming larger. Thus the process of growth as transformation – the continuous and overlapping rise and decline of industries, and the local (that is, intra-industry) exploitation and then exhaustion of increasing returns – implies that in aggregate, economies of scale are always present and hence may be considered large relative to the size of the economy. Whilst economies of scale may not always be present in a given industry, they may yet continuously exist in the economy as a whole because movement through the commodity hierarchy will enable the continual exploitation of new sources of economies of scale.[5]

iii) Dynamic Increasing Returns as a Source of Path Dependency

The importance of dynamic increasing returns is their implication that the technical possibilities for economic activity in any period depend crucially on the nature and extent of economic activity in the past, and that the ways in which these opportunities are currently being exploited will, in turn, create opportunities for the future which previously did not exist. Hence as the economy expands and in so doing accumulates capital, experiences learning by doing, and moves through the commodity hierarchy, it will realize dynamic increasing returns which may subsequently facilitate the further expansion of its output. Under these conditions, some part of the 'state of technology' in an economy is deeply endogenous to the process of growth and development itself. More importantly, the potential for growth in any period will be influenced by the extent to which growth has been realized in the past – that is, growth will become a path dependent process. In light of this, we can identify dynamic increasing returns as an important potential source of path dependency.

II   MODELLING CUMULATIVE CAUSATION

The question remains, however, as to precisely how the dynamics of an economy with large scale increasing returns will operate, and how they may be modelled.

An early attempt to address this issue was Young's (1928) combination of Adam Smith's insights into the division of labour with Say's Law. Young argues that, at a very aggregate level, economic activity can essentially be seen as a process which involves the exchange of goods for goods. Hence every increase in the supply of a commodity enlarges, at least potentially (a vital qualification in the context of a monetary production economy), the market for other commodities. This leads Young to conclude that whilst Smith was correct to point out that the division of labour depends on the extent of the market, the extent of the market also depends on the division of labour, in the sense that rising output accruing from an increase in the latter will potentially increase the former. Hence Young argues that the division of labour depends on the division of labour – not just in a simple, tautological sense, but because the division of labour and the extent of the market are involved in a 'joint interaction' over time, or what may be defined as a process of cumulative causation.

However, this combination of Say's law and Smith's theorem does not in itself provide a complete dynamic theory of progressive cumulative change. As Young himself realized, something more needs to be said about the demand side.[6] From a Keynesian perspective, what is missing is a link between the effects of a change in the level of production and the level of aggregate demand, in order to ensure that any given increase in production is accompanied by an increase in aggregate demand sufficient to support this new, higher level of economic activity. One of the central contributions of Kaldor (1970, 1972, 1985) was to realize this, and show that the gap may be filled by Keynes' theory of effective demand. In his 1985 model, Kaldor emphasizes the importance of external trade as the leading source of aggregate demand.[7] For Kaldor, the process of economic development and the accompanying division of labour imply a continuous subdivision of industries, and the growth of specialist firms at intermediate stages of production.[8] He argues that there is an obvious tendency for this process to become concentrated in and around geographical centres, since its success depends in part on such factors as the local presence of skilled manpower and the frequent transfer of unfinished goods between specialized firms. Hence if success in industrial development is at all uneven between different centres, then there will exist scope for mutually advantageous exchanges to take place – that is, we would expect interregional trade to occur. From a Keynesian perspective, then, the 'geography of development' suggests that external trade is a potentially important source of aggregate demand.

i) A Formal Model

Following Dixon and Thirlwall (1975), Thirlwall (1980) and McCombie and Thirlwall (1994), the relationship between interregional trade, aggregate demand, dynamic increasing returns and growth in a Kaldorian model of cumulative causation can be illustrated by the interaction of the following equations:

$$\dot{q}_{jt} = r_t + \alpha_j \dot{Y}_{jt-1} \quad , \quad \alpha_j > 0 \qquad [3.1]$$

$$\dot{p}_{jt} = \dot{w}_{jt} - \dot{q}_{jt} \qquad [3.2]$$

$$\dot{X}_{jt} = \beta_j(\dot{p}_{wt} - \dot{p}_{jt}) + \gamma_j \dot{Y}_{wt} \quad , \quad \beta_j, \gamma_j > 0 \qquad [3.3]$$

$$\dot{Y}_{jt} = \lambda_j \dot{X}_{jt} \quad , \quad \lambda_j > 0 \qquad [3.4]$$

where for any region j, $\dot{q}_j$ is the rate of growth of productivity, r represents exogenous influences on the rate of productivity growth, $\dot{Y}_j$ is the rate of growth of output (which is assumed to be positive in the long run),[9] $\dot{p}_j$ and $\dot{w}_j$ are domestic price and wage inflation respectively, $\dot{X}_j$ is the rate of growth of exports, $\dot{p}_w$ and $\dot{Y}_w$ represent price inflation and output growth in the 'rest of the world' respectively, and subscripts denote time periods.[10] The model is intended to be couched in terms of traded goods which are subject to dynamic increasing returns.

Rapid Growth and Relative Decline

Equation [3.1] expresses productivity growth as a function of exogenous influences (r) and the 'Verdoorn component', $\alpha_j \dot{Y}_{jt-1}$.[11] The coefficient α_j essentially reflects the extent to which output growth facilitates the realization of dynamic increasing returns, and hence productivity growth in region j. Equation [3.2], meanwhile, follows from the mark up price equation:

$$p_{jt} = \left(\frac{w_{jt}}{q_{jt}} \right) \cdot \tau$$

where p_j is the price level, w_j is the nominal wage, q_j is the level of labour productivity and $\tau = 1 + \theta$ where θ is the (fixed) percentage mark up of prices over labour costs in region j.

Equation [3.3] is derived from Thirlwall's (1980) export function:

$$X_{jt} = \left(\frac{p_{jt}}{e \cdot p_{wt}} \right)^{\phi} \cdot Y_{wt}^{\gamma}$$

where $-\phi = \beta_j$ is the absolute value of the own and cross price elasticities of region j's exports, γ_j denotes the income elasticity of demand of region j's exports and e represents the (fixed) exchange rate. Finally, equation [3.4] relates export growth to the subsequent growth of income. In keeping with Kaldor's emphasis on the demand side, it makes the Hicksian assumption that the growth of autonomous demand determines the long-run rate of output growth (Thirlwall, 1980). In this case, exports are assumed, for simplicity, to be the only source of autonomous demand that is non-constant, in order to highlight Kaldor's particular emphasis on the importance of export led growth.

ii) Interpreting the Structural Model

The structural model outlined above is of a simple form, and is by no means intended to be a complete structural specification of a capitalist economy. Notice, for example, that the model does not involve a balance of payments equilibrium condition. It assumes that trade surpluses and deficits can be accumulated indefinitely, overlooking the fact that this would require deficit regions to be able to attract a permanent net inflow of capital (Thirlwall, 1980).[12]

Despite its obvious limitations, the structural model developed supports a variety of equilibrium and non-equilibrium interpretations which offer useful, if stylized, characterizations of the process of cumulative causation. To see this, note that by substituting equations [3.3], [3.2] and then [3.1] into equation [3.4], we arrive at the expression:

$$\dot{Y}_{jt} = \lambda_j \alpha_j \beta_j \dot{Y}_{jt-1} + \lambda_j \beta_j (\dot{p}_{wt} - \dot{w}_{jt} + \dot{r}_t) + \lambda_j \gamma_j \dot{Y}_{wt} \qquad [3.5]$$

From the analogous conditions to [3.1] and [3.2] for region w, we have:

$$\dot{q}_{wt} = \dot{r}_t + \alpha_w \dot{Y}_{wt-1} \qquad [3.1a]$$

$$\dot{p}_{wt} = \dot{w}_{wt} - \dot{q}_{wt} \qquad [3.2a]$$

$$\Rightarrow \quad \dot{p}_{wt} = \dot{w}_{wt} - \dot{r}_t - \alpha_w \dot{Y}_{wt-1} \qquad [3.6]$$

In order to proceed, we now make two simplifying assumptions. First, following Kaldor, we assume that $\dot{w}_{jt} = \dot{w}_{wt}$.[13] Second, following Dixon and Thirlwall, 1975), we assume that $\dot{Y}_{wt} = \dot{Y}_{wt-1} = \dot{Y}_w$ is an exogenously given positive constant.[14] Utilizing these assumptions, substituting equation [3.6] into equation [3.5] yields:

$$\dot{Y}_{jt} = \lambda_j \alpha_j \beta_j \dot{Y}_{jt-1} + \lambda_j (\gamma_j - \alpha_w \beta_j) \dot{Y}_w \qquad [3.7]$$

Suppose that we now impose steady state conditions, such that $\dot{Y}_{jt} = \dot{Y}_{jt-1} = \dot{Y}_j^*$. Assuming that $\lambda_j \alpha_j \beta_j \neq 1$, this allows us to rewrite [3.7] as:

$$\frac{\dot{Y}_j^*}{\dot{Y}_w} = \frac{\lambda_j (\gamma_j - \alpha_w \beta_j)}{1 - \lambda_j \alpha_j \beta_j} \qquad [3.8]$$

Furthermore, it is straightforward to verify that if $0 < \lambda_j \alpha_j \beta_j < 1$, then the steady-state equilibrium in [3.8] is stable. This implies that the model in equations [3.1]–[3.4] yields a traditional equilibrium interpretation, in which the long-run relative growth rate of region j is determinate, being both defined (as in equation [3.8]) and reached ($0 < \lambda_j \alpha_j \beta_j < 1$ is a sufficient condition for the stability of [3.8]) independently of the path taken towards it. Whilst this traditional equilibrium interpretation is mathematically admissible, it seems quite unlike the result intended by Kaldor, whose verbal models of cumulative causation envisage initial relative growth rates having a permanent effect on long-run growth outcomes in a system without a determinate equilibrium (see, for example, Kaldor, 1985, pp. 61–3).

However, alternative, non-equilibrium interpretations of the model are possible, which restore the Kaldorian influence of initial conditions on long-run relative growth outcomes.[15] Hence recall from Section III(i) of Chapter 2 that even in a system where a unique, determinate equilibrium exists, long-run outcomes may nevertheless be path dependent if the speed of adjustment towards this equilibrium is slow relative to the speed at which the data underlying it are changing. Even if $0 < \lambda_j \alpha_j \beta_j < 1$, then, the equilibrium in [3.8] may not be relevant as a description of the configuration of the system in equations [3.1]–[3.4] at any point in time. This possibility would seem especially likely in the current context, not least because the 'data' in equation [3.8] may themselves vary with the growth paths $\dot{Y}_{jt}$ and $\dot{Y}_w$. We will pursue this likelihood in extensive detail in Chapters 4 and 5. At present, however, simply note that the coefficient γ_j, the income elasticity of demand of region j's exports, will depend on j's progress through the commodity hierarchy, which is itself a function of j's stage of development and hence prior growth path (Cornwall, 1977).

Making the 'slow relative adjustment' assumption allows us to use the model in equations [3.1]–[3.4] to illustrate the dynamics of cumulative causation without, at present, making assumptions about the effects of growth on the 'data' in equation [3.8], but with the Kaldorian emphasis on the influence of initial conditions fully restored. Under the assumption of 'slow relative adjustment', equations [3.1]–[3.4] can be treated as a recurring sequence in order to demonstrate their interaction in a process of cumulative causation, in which initial relative growth rates influence long-run relative growth outcomes.

iii)   The Process of Cumulative Causation – an Illustration

According to Kaldor, an important feature of the process of economic development is that differences in productivity growth are likely to emerge between regions. This claim may appear curious given the conventional notion that rational entrepreneurs, regardless of their location, will always adopt the least-cost (that is, most efficient) method of production currently available. However, in Kaldorian models, efficiency gains result from dynamic increasing returns, and may therefore accrue to regions unevenly simply as a result of the fact that economic development does not occur simultaneously in all regions. It is clear from equation [3.1] that an economy which experiences an initially high rate of output growth will also experience a high rate of productivity growth.

The consequences of this are demonstrated by equations [3.2]–[3.4]. From equations [3.2] and [3.3], we can see that, other things being equal, a region with a high rate of productivity growth will experience a high rate of growth of exports. With $\dot{w}_{jt}$ given in equation [3.2], efficiency wages (the ratio of money wages to productivity) and hence unit costs of production will fall in an economy with a high rate of productivity growth. Kaldor argues that this will occur because whilst productivity growth varies with output growth due to increasing returns, wage relativities tend to remain constant between regions over time. Hence differences between regions in the rate of productivity growth will not be offset by equivalent differences in the rate of growth of money wages.

In this way, a region with a high rate of productivity growth should be able to exploit its low efficiency wages by realizing a relatively low domestic rate of inflation. The region will thus gain a competitive advantage over other regions which, as indicated by equation [3.3], will enable it to win market share from them and so improve its rate of growth of exports. Note, however, that price competition is not the only determinant of export success in equation [3.3]. Non-price competition, to the extent that it can be thought of as influencing the size of the income elasticity of demand, γ_j, is also important. Indeed, as will become clear, the size of γ_j (and hence the influence of non-price competition on exports) plays a critical role in influencing the evolution of the model and hence the determination of long-run relative growth outcomes.[16]

The model is completed by equation [3.4], according to which a higher rate of growth of exports will raise the level of economic growth. However, in the presence of dynamic increasing returns, the process will not end here. Returning to equation [3.1], we can see that the growth of income in [3.4] will lead, once more, to the subsequent realization of dynamic increasing returns. This will act so as to reinforce the initial productivity growth advantage of region j, further enhancing its trade position and hence the growth of its income and so on. In this way, the recursive interaction of equations [3.1]–[3.4] describes a process of cumulative causation, which can be summarized by the causal chain:

$$\dot{X}_{jt} \rightarrow \dot{Y}_{jt} \rightarrow \dot{q}_{jt+1} \rightarrow \dot{X}_{jt+1} \rightarrow \text{and so on}$$

More formally, referring back to the reduced form of equations [3.1]–[3.4] in equation [3.7], we can summarize the recursion of our structural model and hence the process of cumulative causation in the form of the expression:

$$\dot{Y}_{jt} = (\lambda_j \alpha_j \beta_j)^t \dot{Y}_{j0} + \lambda_j(\gamma_j - \alpha_w\beta_j)\dot{Y}_w \cdot \sum_{i=0}^{t-1}(\lambda_j \alpha_j \beta_j)^i \qquad [3.9]$$

where $\dot{Y}_{j0}$ represents the rate of growth of region j in some initial period 0. Dividing through by $\dot{Y}_w$, equation [3.9] yields the following expression for relative growth rates:

$$\frac{\dot{Y}_{jt}}{\dot{Y}_w} = (\lambda_j \alpha_j \beta_j)^t \frac{\dot{Y}_{j0}}{\dot{Y}_w} + \lambda_j(\gamma_j - \alpha_w\beta_j) \cdot \sum_{i=0}^{t-1}(\lambda_j \alpha_j \beta_j)^i \qquad [3.10]$$

We can clearly see that the determinate equilibrium outcome in equation [3.8] is a limit result of the more general expression for relative growth rates in equation [3.10].[17] However, given the assumption of 'slow relative adjustment', this limit result will not provide a relevant description of the precise configuration of the system in equations [3.1]–[3.4] at any point in time. Instead, for any period during which the data defining equation [3.8] are unchanging, equation [3.10] affords the relevant description of long-run relative growth rates, which can only be construed as such by virtue of their temporal distance (in calendar time) from the initial conditions $\frac{\dot{Y}_{j0}}{\dot{Y}_w}$ established in period 0. Equation [3.10] clearly illustrates that in our recursive interpretation of equations [3.1]–[3.4], long-run growth outcomes depend on initial relative growth rates. Furthermore, there will, by construction, be no tendency for equation [3.10] to converge to a determinate relative growth equilibrium, due to its assumed slow speed of adjustment. These features confirm the correspondence between our disequilibrium interpretation of the Dixon-Thirlwall model and the principles of cumulative causation originally enunciated by Kaldor, according to whom long-run relative growth outcomes are path dependent, being sensitive to initial conditions in a system without determinate equilibria.

iv) The Consequences of Cumulative Causation

An important feature of cumulative causation is that the growth of one region is not altogether neutral with respect to its effects on the other regions with which it competes. This can be illustrated by studying the distributional consequences of cumulative causation in the context of the formal model already developed.

First, note that in equation [3.10]:

$$\frac{\partial\left(\dfrac{\dot{Y}_{jt}}{\dot{Y}_w}\right)}{\partial\left(\dfrac{\dot{Y}_{j0}}{\dot{Y}_w}\right)} = (\lambda_j\,\alpha_j\,\beta_j)^t > 0$$

for all t – in other words, $\dfrac{\dot{Y}_{jt}}{\dot{Y}_w}$ varies directly with $\dfrac{\dot{Y}_{j0}}{\dot{Y}_w}$. What this means is that following some initial enhancement of region j's relative growth rate in period 0, relative growth in this region remains permanently higher than it otherwise would have been. This gives rise to the notion of virtuous and vicious circles of cumulative causation, that is, self perpetuating high/low relative growth rates arising from an initially high/low relative growth rate.

Suppose now that, following an initial enhancement of its relative growth rate due to an early start to development, region j experiences a virtuous circle such that $\dfrac{\dot{Y}_{jt}}{\dot{Y}_w} > 1$ for all t. Then it follows that region j's share of world income will rise over time in a cumulative fashion.[18] More importantly, assume that $\dot{P}_{jt} \leq \dot{P}_{wt}$ for all t, where $\dot{P}_i$ denotes the rate of growth of population in region $i = j, w$. With $\dot{Y}_{jt} > \dot{Y}_w$, this means that region j's rate of growth of per capita income will be higher than region w's, and that region j's share of world per capita income will also increase cumulatively over time.[19] If region j was relatively rich initially (that is, if $\dfrac{Y_{j0}}{P_{j0}} > \dfrac{Y_{w0}}{P_{w0}}$) – an assumption which is quite reasonable given the early start to development which we have hypothesized to be the cause of region j's initial relative growth advantage – these conditions will imply divergence in the level of per capita income between region j and the rest of the world. In a model of cumulative causation, then, we might expect increasing inequalities to emerge over time between initially prosperous and initially poor regions as a result of self-reinforcing growth and interregional trade outcomes.

III A NOTE ON WAGE AND PRICE ASSUMPTIONS IN THE MODEL OF CUMULATIVE CAUSATION

i) Flexible Wages and Competitiveness

In discussing the process of cumulative causation in Section II, the assumption was made that wage relativities between regions tend to remain constant over time. It may therefore appear that cumulative causation as described above depends on a 'special case' sticky wage (or sticky *relative* wage) assumption, and that its quantity dynamics will be offset if wages are flexible, and a vicious circle region experiences declining relative money wages.

Note, however, that the adjustment of relative wages necessary to restore the price competitiveness of a vicious circle region would have to be instantaneous in order to completely mitigate the quantity effects of cumulative causation. Such instantaneous adjustment could occur if, for example, the economy was regulated by an auctioneer, or if economic agents were forming strong form rational expectations on the basis of complete information in the context of a perfectly competitive labour market. As illustrated in Part I, however, no form of instantaneous adjustment endears itself to models based on the notion that adjustment is an intertemporal process. What the following analysis suggests is that without instantaneous relative wage (and, in Section III(ii), exchange rate) adjustment, wage (exchange rate) flexibility *per se* is not sufficient to offset the quantity dynamics of cumulative causation.

To see this, we need only examine equations [3.2], [3.2a] and [3.3], which can be restated as follows:

$$\dot{p}_{jt} = \dot{w}_{jt} - \dot{q}_{jt} \qquad\qquad [3.2]$$

$$\dot{p}_{wt} = \dot{w}_{wt} - \dot{q}_{wt} \qquad\qquad [3.2a]$$

$$\dot{X}_{jt} = \beta_j (\dot{p}_{wt} - \dot{p}_{jt}) + \gamma_j \dot{Y}_{wt} \qquad\qquad [3.3]$$

It follows from [3.2] and [3.2a] that $\dot{p}_{wt} - \dot{p}_{jt} = (\dot{w}_{wt} - \dot{w}_{jt}) + (\dot{q}_{jt} - \dot{q}_{wt})$. Suppose now that $\dot{w}_{jt} \neq \dot{w}_{wt}$. If, in any 'round' of the process of cumulative causation, we have $\dot{w}_{wt} - \dot{w}_{jt} = -(\dot{q}_{jt} - \dot{q}_{wt})$, then $\dot{p}_{wt} - \dot{p}_{jt} = 0$. Hence, as inspection of equation [3.3] reveals, there will be no enhancement of export growth in region j as a result of its faster productivity growth. Instantaneous (that is, within period) adjustment in relative wages can, therefore, negate the inflation differential effect through which cumulative causation works in equations [3.1]–[3.4]. Under these circumstances, the process of cumulative causation will break down. However, if relative wage adjustment is incomplete in any period t, this result does not follow. Even if we have $\dot{w}_{jt} \neq \dot{w}_{wt}$ in any period t, as long as $|\dot{w}_{wt} - \dot{w}_{jt}| < \dot{q}_{jt} - \dot{q}_{wt}$, we will also observe $\dot{p}_{wt} - \dot{p}_{jt} > 0$, so that the quantity dynamics described by the recursion of equations [3.1]–[3.4] will proceed as previously described. If $\dot{w}_{jt} \neq \dot{w}_{wt}$, the quantity dynamics of cumulative causation will certainly be modified by the wage dynamics that accompany our relaxation of the constant wage relativities assumption. Specifically, if $\dot{q}_{jt} > \dot{q}_{wt}$ but $\dot{w}_{wt} < \dot{w}_{jt}$, then region j's relative rate of growth of exports and output will be diminished compared to the case where $\dot{w}_{wt} = \dot{w}_{jt}$. However, as long as instantaneous relative wage adjustment does not occur, then although the competitive advantage realized in any round of cumulative causation by a region experiencing relatively high productivity growth may be *reduced* by changes in relative money wages, it will not be *entirely offset*. The quantity dynamics of cumulative causation will therefore continue to operate in the manner described in Section II.

Ironically, regardless of the speed of wage adjustments, it is not altogether obvious that we would expect a vicious circle region to experience declining relative money wages. Since $\dot{Y}_w$ is positive by assumption, employment may be increasing in this region in spite of its *relative* economic decline.

If adjustments to wage bargaining procedures do not occur unless the level of employment is falling, and hence a region is experiencing *absolute* decline, region *w* will not experience a downward pressure on its relative money wages, and wage relativities may therefore remain unchanged (Skott, 1985).

ii) The Exchange Rate and Competitiveness

A second assumption made in the development of the model discussed in Section II was that of a fixed exchange rate, *e*. If this assumption is relaxed, equation [3.3] can be rewritten as:

$$\dot{X}_{jt} = \beta_j(\dot{p}_{wt} + \dot{e}_t - \dot{p}_{jt}) + \gamma_j \dot{Y}_{wt} \qquad [3.11]$$

Is it the case, then, that changes in *e* may prevent a region from gaining and maintaining the type of competitive advantage necessary to generate cumulative causation?

In order to completely mitigate the quantity effects of cumulative causation, it would again be necessary for the exchange rate to adjust instantaneously in order to completely negate the changes in relative competitiveness that occur within any given round of the process of cumulative causation. To see this, we need only consider the workings of equation [3.11]. Suppose, then, that $\dot{p}_{wt} > \dot{p}_{jt}$ in equation [3.11]. Suppose further that $\dot{e}_t < 0$ – that is, that the exchange rate depreciates in favour of region *w*.[20] If, in spite of this, it is nevertheless the case that $\dot{p}_{wt} + \dot{e}_t > \dot{p}_{jt}$, there will still be a positive net effect on $\dot{X}_{jt}$ in equation [3.11]. If the exchange rate does not adjust instantaneously within any given period in such a way as to completely offset regional inflation differentials, then as in the case of sluggish wage adjustment, quantity effects will be realized and cumulative causation will continue as previously described.

The effects of a flexible exchange rate on the quantity dynamics of cumulative causation may also be impaired if the exchange rate has only a limited impact on relative price competitiveness, fails to adjust appropriately in response to changes in interregional trade flows, or simply fails to affect interregional trade flows. For example, note that in the model developed in Section II, whilst the *producer* real wage in region *j* within any period *t* is given by $\omega_{jt} = \dfrac{w_{jt}}{p_{jt}}$, the *consumer* real wage in the same period can be written as:

$$\omega_{jt}^c = \frac{w_{jt}}{p_{jt}^\delta \cdot (e_t \cdot p_{wt})^\varepsilon} \qquad [3.12]$$

where δ and ε are weights such that $\delta, \varepsilon \in (0, 1)$ and $\delta + \varepsilon = 1$. It follows from equation [3.12] that the rate of growth of the consumer real wage is given by:

$$\dot{\omega}^c_{jt} = \dot{w}_{jt} - \delta\dot{p}_{jt} - \varepsilon(\dot{e}_t + \dot{p}_{wt}) \qquad [3.13]$$

Equation [3.13] suggests that consumer real wage growth varies inversely with fluctuations in the exchange rate, e_t. Suppose, then, that during some period we have $\dot{e}_t > 0$ – that is, that the exchange rate depreciates in favour of region j. Other things being equal, this will reduce the rate of growth of the consumer real wage during this period. However, if region j now experiences real wage resistance – that is, if workers bid up money wages in an attempt to offset the decline in $\dot{\omega}^c_{jt}$ – then this will reduce the effects on competitiveness of the original devaluation (Skott, 1985). To see this, note that with real wage resistance, money wage inflation in region j must be remodelled as:

$$\dot{w}'_{jt} = \dot{w}_{jt} + \varepsilon\dot{e}_t$$

where total money wage inflation $\dot{w}'_{jt}$ now comprises a domestic component ($\dot{w}_{jt}$) as before, and a real wage resistance component $\varepsilon\dot{e}_t$, which represents the change in money wages necessary to offset the effects of exchange devaluation on the consumer real wage. This implies that price inflation in region j must now be remodelled as:

$$\dot{p}'_{jt} = \dot{w}'_{jt} - \dot{q}_{jt}$$

$$= \dot{w}_{jt} + \varepsilon\dot{e}_t - \dot{q}_{jt}$$

$$\Rightarrow \quad \dot{p}'_{jt} = \dot{p}_{jt} + \varepsilon\dot{e}_t \qquad [3.14]$$

given the definition of $\dot{p}_j$ in equation [3.2]. In light of [3.14], equation [3.11] now becomes:

$$\dot{X}_{jt} = \beta_j(\dot{p}_{wt} + \dot{e}_t - \dot{p}'_{jt}) + \gamma_j\dot{Y}_{wt}$$

$$= \beta_j(\dot{p}_{wt} + \dot{e}_t - \dot{p}_{jt} - \varepsilon\dot{e}_t) + \gamma_j\dot{Y}_{wt}$$

$$= \beta_j(\dot{p}_{wt} - \dot{p}_{jt} + \dot{e}_t(1 - \varepsilon)) + \gamma_j\dot{Y}_{wt} \qquad [3.15]$$

Since $1 - \varepsilon > 0$ by assumption, comparing equation [3.15] with equation [3.11] clearly illustrates that any level of real wage resistance will reduce the effects of a given exchange depreciation $\dot{e}_t > 0$ on relative competitiveness and hence export growth in region j. It is also clear from equation [3.15] that the greater the value of ε (that is, the more sensitive wage earners are to prices in the 'rest of the world' and so the greater their degree of real wage resistance), the smaller will be the impact of apparently favourable exchange rate devaluations on a region's export and hence output growth.

Aside from real wage resistance, the exchange rate may be deliberately manipulated in response to political economy considerations, or its movements may be dominated by speculative capital flows rather than trade in goods and services (Dornbusch, 1987). If the exchange rate therefore fails to adjust appropriately in response to changes in interregional trade flows, then once again, exchange rate devaluations will not systematically offset the quantity dynamics of cumulative causation.

Finally, changes in the exchange rate simply may not have large effects on trade flows between regions, at least in the short run. If entry into foreign markets involves sunk costs, there will exist a range over which the exchange rate may fluctuate without encouraging exit from a particular regional market (Dixit, 1989; Krugman, 1989). Current incumbents may practise a policy of 'pricing to the market' by varying their mark ups, in order to offset currency fluctuations and so avoid the loss of hard won (through expenditure on sunk costs) market share. If trade flows are thus invariant to exchange rate movements, changes in currency values will have little or no short run effect on the quantity dynamics of cumulative causation.

iii) Summary

Without formally specifying an appropriate theory of wage and exchange rate dynamics, the preceding comments illustrate the possibility that relaxing the wage and price assumptions implicit in the model developed in Section II need not systematically negate the implications of this model. This suggests that the assumptions of a fixed exchange rate and constant wage relativities can be retained as simplifying abstractions throughout the remainder of our analysis in Part II.

IV CONCLUSION

The model developed in this chapter and summarized in equations [3.1]–[3.4] serves as a useful tool to illustrate the dynamics of cumulative causation. As intimated earlier, it by no means represents a complete specification of the dynamics of a capitalist economy. However, as illustrated in Section III, the model is not unduly compromised by its simplicity and consequent 'neglect' of factors such as wage and exchange rate flexibility. Furthermore, a disequilibrium interpretation of the model affords some basic insights into the dynamics of a path dependent economy. In view of the correspondence between cumulative causation and hysteresis discussed in Chapter 2, the modelling exercise in this chapter enables us to begin to grasp some of the potential consequences of hysteresis for macroeconomic evolution. Indeed, it seems possible to interpret Kaldor's analysis of cumulative causation as nothing less than a preliminary attempt to understand the workings of the economy under generalized conditions of hysteresis.

4 The Supply Side and Macroeconomic Performance I: Technological Evolution

In Chapter 3, it was suggested that Kaldor's model of cumulative causation can be interpreted as a first step towards understanding macroeconomic dynamics under conditions of hysteresis. Recall that our characterization of this model in equations [3.1]–[3.4] can be summarized as:

$$\frac{\dot{Y}_{jt}}{\dot{Y}_w} = (\lambda_j \alpha_j \beta_j)^t \frac{\dot{Y}_{j0}}{\dot{Y}_w} + \lambda_j(\gamma_j - \alpha_w \beta_j)\sum_{i=0}^{t-1}(\lambda_j \alpha_j \beta_j)^i \qquad [3.10]$$

where $0 < \lambda_j \alpha_j \beta_j < 1$. The limit result of this expression was shown to be a determinate equilibrium (equation [3.8]). However, in Chapter 3, it was suggested that this determinate long-run outcome will be of no practical consequence if we assume that adjustment towards it is slow relative to the speed at which the data defining it are themselves changing over time. This assumption was, in part, justified by the suggestion that these data may themselves ultimately be sensitive to the prior growth path of a region. In this and the following Chapter, we will explicitly study mechanisms which may give rise to changes in the coefficients α_j and γ_j, which play a key role in defining the long-run growth outcome in equation [3.10] (and its limit, equation [3.8]). This will be shown to transform the model of cumulative causation developed in Chapter 3 into a more generally hysteretic model of long-run growth and development.

I PROBLEMS WITH THE KALDORIAN MODEL OF CUMULATIVE CAUSATION

i) Initial Conditions and Cumulative Success/Failure

There exists an important caveat in Kaldor's concept of cumulative causation as discussed in Chapter 3. In this model, success breeds success and failure begets failure indefinitely. This is because initial conditions are the only feature of a region's prior growth trajectory which enter into the determination of its long-run relative growth outcomes, as can be seen by inspection of equation [3.10]. It appears, therefore, that an initially faster growing economy will permanently experience faster growth, whilst its less successful trading partners will endure slower growth in perpetuity. In sum, once the initial relative success or failure of a region is known, so too, it seems, is the rest of its history.

The extent of this problem should not, however, be overstated. Consider the case of a virtuous circle, which can be summarized by the causal chain:

$$\text{high } \dot{X}_t \rightarrow \text{high } \dot{Y}_t \rightarrow \text{high } \dot{q}_{t+1} \rightarrow \text{high } \dot{X}_{t+1} \rightarrow \text{and so on}$$

a

In any 'round' of the process of cumulative causation, the dynamics of a virtuous circle depend on sufficient demand (that is, export growth) being forthcoming in response to the realization of scale economies both to support the new full employment level of output and to propagate the next 'round' of cumulative causation. In other words:

> [w]hether the process keeps its momentum . . . or gets stopped (and probably reversed) depends on the 'next round' of demand, on the response of demand to the inducement to further growth provided by the rise in efficiency.
>
> (Ricoy, 1987, p. 733)

Hence there exists a potential 'weak link' in the causal chain of a virtuous circle, if the rate of growth of exports is subject to exogenous shocks over time. This 'weak link' is marked at point *a* in the causal chain illustrated above. In any 'round' of this causal chain, if insufficient export demand is forthcoming to foster continued rapid growth, the cumulative process on which a virtuous circle is based will break down.

In order to explicitly demonstrate this possibility, we begin by considering an augmented export function of the form:

$$X_{jt} = \left(\frac{p_{jt}}{e \cdot p_{wt}} \right)^{\phi} \cdot Y_{wt}^{\gamma} \cdot \psi^{\eta} \qquad [4.1]$$

where $\eta \sim (0, \sigma_{\eta}^2)$ and ψ is some constant such that $\psi > 1$. The term ψ^{η} therefore captures random demand shocks influencing the value of X_j in any period t.

Because $\dot{Y}_w$ is an exogenous constant by assumption, it is possible to define a variable ε such that:

$$\varepsilon = \eta \cdot \frac{1}{\dot{Y}_w} \qquad [4.2]$$

where $\varepsilon \sim \left(0, \frac{1}{\dot{Y}_w^2} \cdot \sigma_\eta^2\right)$. Using the information in equation [4.2], the dynamic analog of our export function [4.1] can be written as:

$$\dot{X}_{jt} = \beta_j(\dot{p}_{wt} - \dot{p}_{jt}) + \gamma_j \dot{Y}_w + \dot{Y}_w \cdot (\ln\psi) \cdot v_{jt} \qquad [4.3]$$

where $v_{jt} = \varepsilon_{jt} - \varepsilon_{jt-1}$. Finally, this enables us to rewrite the reduced form of the model developed in Chapter 3 as:

$$\dot{Y}_{jt} = \lambda_j \alpha_j \beta_j \dot{Y}_{jt-1} + \lambda_j (\gamma_j - \alpha_w\beta_j)\dot{Y}_w + \lambda_j \dot{Y}_w(\ln\psi) \cdot v_{jt} \qquad [4.4]$$

so that our expression for the long run relative growth rate in region j becomes:

$$\frac{\dot{Y}_{jt}}{\dot{Y}_w} = (\lambda_j \alpha_j \beta_j)^t \frac{\dot{Y}_{j0}}{\dot{Y}_w} +$$

$$\lambda_j \left[(\gamma_j - \alpha_w\beta_j)\sum_{i=0}^{t-1}(\lambda_j \alpha_j \beta_j)^i + (\ln\psi)\sum_{i=1}^{t}(\lambda_j \alpha_j \beta_j)^{t-i} \cdot v_{ji} \right] \qquad [4.5]$$

Note that equation [4.5] nests equation [3.10] as a special case when $v_{ji} = 0$ for all $i = 1, \ldots, t$. However, consider the case of a once over demand shock in period n such that $\varepsilon_{jn-1} = 0$, $\varepsilon_{jn} > 0$ and $\varepsilon_{jn+1} = 0$. In this case, $v_{jn} = -v_{jn+1} = \varepsilon_{jn} \neq 0$.[1] However, inspection of equation [4.5] reveals that $\frac{\dot{Y}_{jt}}{\dot{Y}_w}$ varies with $\sum_{i=1}^{t}(\lambda_j \alpha_j \beta_j)^{t-i} \cdot v_{ji}$. This is significant, because clearly $(\lambda_j\alpha_j\beta_j)^{t-n} \cdot v_{jn} \neq -(\lambda_j\alpha_j\beta_j)^{t-n-1} \cdot v_{jn+1}$ despite the fact that $v_{jn} = -v_{jn+1} = \varepsilon_{jn}$. In other words, the introduction and removal of the positive demand shock ε_{jn} has a permanent rather than a temporary effect – it leaves behind a 'trace' which influences the long-run relative growth outcome $\frac{\dot{Y}_{jt}}{\dot{Y}_w}$. The precise magnitude of this trace, denoted as θ_j, can be written as:

$$\theta_j = (\ln\psi) \left((\lambda_j \alpha_j \beta_j)^{t-n} \cdot v_{jn} - [-(\lambda_j \alpha_j \beta_j)^{t-n-1} \cdot v_{jn+1}] \right)$$

$$= (\ln\psi) \left((\lambda_j \alpha_j \beta_j)^{t-n} \cdot \varepsilon_{jn} - (\lambda_j \alpha_j \beta_j)^{t-n-1} \cdot \varepsilon_{jn} \right)$$

$$\Rightarrow \quad \theta_j = (\ln\psi) \cdot (\lambda_j\alpha_j\beta_j)^{t-n-1} \cdot \varepsilon_{jn}(\lambda_j\alpha_j\beta_j - 1) \qquad [4.6]$$

and hence $\theta_j < 0$ since $\ln\psi > 0$, and $\varepsilon_{jn} > 0$ and $0 < \lambda_j\alpha_j\beta_j < 1$ by assumption. This suggests that a once-over positive demand shock ($\varepsilon_{jn} > 0$) has a negative impact on long-run growth outcomes in equation [4.5]. This apparently perverse result is explained by the fact that the initially positive impact of the shock (v_{jn}) carries less weight in equation [4.5] than the negative impact of its subsequent removal (v_{jn+1}).[2] More generally, what the result illustrates is that demand shocks can play a crucial role in the interrupting the apparently smooth progress of cumulative causation as modelled in equations [3.1]–[3.4].

ii) Demand-Led Growth and Endogenously Induced Supply Side Changes: The Notion of Technological and Institutional 'Regimes'

One possible objection to the preceding argument is that it relies on *unexplained* changes in export demand to generate the breakdown of a virtuous circle. This is analogous to the reliance of traditional equilibrium models on exogenous 'shocks' to explain changes in macroeconomic performance. The changes in export demand already postulated have not been shown to arise endogenously in the course of growth and development. Hence the 'weak link' we have identified on the demand side of the model does not arise from *within* the process of cumulative causation itself. In the absence of shocks, then, the model continues to predict that only initial conditions affect long-run growth outcomes, and that initially fast/slow growth is indefinitely self perpetuating. This is a rather awkward prediction for two reasons. First, it suggests that whilst cumulative causation does not suffer the extreme ahistoricism of traditional equilibrium models, since it explicitly conceives long-run outcomes as being path dependent, it does not greatly attenuate the determinism inherent in the traditional equilibrium approach. Abstracting from exogenous shocks, only one feature of history – initial conditions – matters in a model of cumulative causation. All other features of history unfold in a mechanical fashion from these initial conditions and therefore exert no independent influence on the nature of long-run outcomes. Second, the stylized facts of long-run growth suggest that some initially fast growing regions (such as Britain and now arguably the US) have, in the course of their long-run growth and development, transformed into relatively slow growing economies.

How, then, might we rethink the process of cumulative causation in order to capture the influence on long-run growth outcomes of not just initial conditions, but also the subsequent features of a region's relative growth trajectory? One approach is to begin by considering that cumulative causation does not occur within a vacuum, but in a precise technological and institutional context. These technological and institutional 'regimes' characterize the technical and social structure of the supply side of the economy. They may be influenced by the process of growth, and may in turn help determine long-run growth outcomes by influencing the structural stability of the process of cumulative causation as modelled in Chapter 3. Consider, for example, the case of a relatively fast growing economy. Intuitively, what we are suggesting is that if, as a result of its relatively fast growth, this region suffers inefficient technological and/or institutional evolution – specifically, if its technological or institutional structures cease to be functional to the maintenance of high growth dynamics – then its virtuous circle of cumulative causation will endogenously break down. More formally, it may be that growth induced changes in the technological and/or institutional regimes that exist on the supply side of the economy can be interpreted as permanently influencing the size of key coefficients such as α_j or γ_j in the model of cumulative causation developed in Chapter 3. In other words, α_j and γ_j may be thought of as being deeply endogenous to the prior growth path of a region and subject to adjustment asymmetries. If this is the case, even the most cursory inspection of equation [3.10] reveals that long-run relative growth outcomes will be affected.

The question remains, however, as to how technological and institutional regimes and their evolution can be conceived, and how their impact on coefficients such as α_j and γ_j can be modelled. In what remains of the current chapter, we will analyse the nature of technological regimes, returning to the topic of institutions in Chapter 5. In analysing both technological and institutional evolution, we will make use of similar concepts which indicate potential asymmetries in the adjustment of technology and institutions over time. Particular use will be made of the concept of lock in discussed in Chapter 2. In each case, the treatment of α_j and γ_j as deeply endogenous variables subject to adjustment asymmetries will be shown to extend the Kaldorian model of cumulative causation into a more generally hysteretic representation of the growth process.

II TECHNOLOGICAL INTERRELATEDNESS AND THE PROBLEM OF LOCK-IN

In Chapter 2, it was suggested that the concept of lock-in is methodologically compatible with hysteresis, and that it may provide important insights into the workings of a hysteretic economy. One way in which this is so is if lock-in affects the technological evolution of an economy. In what follows, we will show that technological lock-in may have an adverse effect on the rate of productivity growth in an economy, by limiting its capacity to undergo technological change and hence to realize dynamic increasing returns associated with technological change. Furthermore, technological lock-in may impair the ability of an economy to realize transformational growth – that is, movement through the commodity hierarchy that Cornwall (1977) and Pasinetti (1981) associate with different levels of per capita income. This may have adverse consequences for the elasticity of demand of a region's tradeable output. In either case, the technological evolution of an economy may be inefficient. The current technological regime will cease to be functional to the maintenance of high growth dynamics, with potentially adverse consequences for a region's virtuous circle and hence its relative rate of growth.

i)   Technological Interrelatedness and Lock-In

A 'technological regime' can be defined as the matrix of technologies embodied in physical and human capital that can be found at the point of production in an economy at any point in time. In principle, because of the process of technological change, we would not expect the technological regime in an economy to remain constant over time. In practice, however, switching regimes may be a difficult feat to achieve.

This argument, developed originally by Frankel (1955), is based on the central idea that as an economy industrializes and develops, interconnections arise amongst the components of its production processes – machines, plant, raw material supplies, transport network, human capital and so forth.[3] For example, plant specifications, such as the size or the strength of flooring, may be deliberately contrived to accommodate machinery of an existing vintage. Alternatively, haulage facilities may be designed to complement existing features of a region's infrastructure, such as the weight capacity or the height of bridges, the width of roads, or the gauge of railway tracks. This growing *interrelatedness* in the process of production may limit the ability of more developed economies to undergo technological change, locking them in to practices inherited as a legacy of the past. As previously intimated in Chapter 2, there are two dimensions to interrelatedness that can give rise to lock-in – interrelatedness *within* and interrelatedness *between* individual decision-making units.

ii)   Technological Interrelatedness within Decision-Making Units

Technological interrelatedness within individual decision-making units – or what may be referred to as intra-firm technological interrelatedness – occurs when interconnections arise between the components of an individual firm's production process. Under these circumstances, replacing an individual component of the production process may require complementary changes in other components with which it is interrelated, and this may hinder technological change by making it prohibitively costly. Referring back to the example used in Chapter 2, any firm wishing to change from QWERTY to the more efficient DSK typewriter keyboard must contend with not only the purchase of new keyboards, but also additional expenditures associated with re-training QWERTY-schooled typing staff in their use (David, 1985).

This problem can be illustrated by means of a formal example involving two firms, one of which is a new entrant to the market, and the other of which is an established, incumbent firm. Assume that these firms have identical time horizons, and identical rates of time preference. Consider now a technological innovation – say, the development of a new piece of machinery – which, when combined with complementary components, gives rise to a technological regime which is more efficient than that currently employed by the incumbent firm. How will the two firms respond to this technological advance? For the new entrant with no previous production history, the choice between technologies is unambiguous, due to the assumed greater efficiency of the new machine and its associated technological regime. Hence by hypothesis:

$$\int_0^T (R_{nt} - C_{nt}) \cdot e^{-rt} dt = \pi_n > \pi_o = \int_0^T (R_{ot} - C_{ot}) \cdot e^{-rt} dt \qquad [4.7]$$

where R represents revenue, C fixed and variable costs, π denotes profits, T is the time horizon of the firm and r its rate of time preference, and n and o denote, respectively, the new piece of machinery and the old one that it is designed to replace. However, for the incumbent firm, the relative profitability of the two technologies is less definite, since:

$$\int_0^T (R_{nt} - C_{nt}) \cdot e^{-rt} dt - S = \pi_n \lessgtr \pi_o = \int_0^T (R_{ot} - C_{ot}) \cdot e^{-rt} dt \qquad [4.8]$$

In equation [4.8], the new variable S represents costs associated solely with the act of *changing between* technological regimes, and hence abandoning components of a *previously existing* regime. Because they correspond to past production decisions, these costs are unique to incumbents in the market – they do not influence the choice between techniques of new entrants. Costs of this nature fall into three main categories. First, there exist direct costs of abandonment. These include severance payments to redundant employees, and expenditures associated with the scrapping of plant and equipment. Essentially, these are costs which negate the standard assumption of the 'free disposal' of inputs into the production process.

Second, a firm may encounter indirect costs associated with switching regimes, in the form of forgone revenues which would have accrued to the old regime during the time it takes to change between technological regimes. Indirect costs of this nature will be important whenever implementing technological change is not an instantaneous process, and when changing interrelated technologies interrupts the production process to the point where throughput is impeded – conditions which appear, intuitively, to be generally applicable.

Finally, there exist sunk costs of production. As defined in Chapter 2, a sunk cost is any expenditure that cannot be recovered if the action that led to its being incurred is subsequently reversed. Sunk costs of production are past outlays that can only be recovered from future revenues. An example of a sunk cost is the depreciation of capital values that may occur due to asymmetric information in the market for used plant and equipment (Akerlof, 1970). This accrues as a sunk cost since it ensures that the original purchase value of plant and equipment (net of an appropriate discount for its physical depreciation) cannot be recovered through its subsequent resale.[4] If a firm abandons its existing technological regime, the sunk costs associated with this regime will 'carry over', and will have to be recovered from future revenues accruing to the new technological regime.

The important thing to note is that the greater the degree of technological interrelatedness, the more changes to its existing production process the incumbent firm will have to make in order to adopt the new technology. Hence the higher will be the costs, S, associated with the act of changing the production process, and so the lower will be π_n in equation [4.8]. Other things being equal, then, the greater the degree of technological interrelatedness, the less likely is the incumbent firm to adopt the new technology.

What this demonstrates is that with interrelatedness in the production process, technological change ceases to be the process of change at the margin that it is traditionally considered to be. With technological interrelatedness, it may be that the relevant comparison between the profitability of old and new methods of production is not on, say, a machine for machine basis, since existing plant may need to be overhauled if a new machine is to be utilized. In this way, the best technology available to a new industrial region (with a low degree of technological interrelatedness) may not be profitable in an established industrial region. The latter will thus become locked in to certain technological regimes, inherited as a legacy of the past.

A final point, with respect to the time horizon over which lock-in can occur, remains to be made. It may be argued that the problem outlined should only be temporary, simply calling for a delay in replacement investment in the established region until all existing plant wears out. In the example already developed, the investment decision of the incumbent firm would then be akin to that of the new entrant (equation [4.7]), and the new technology would unambiguously be adopted by both incumbent and new entrant alike. However, because investment is a continuous process, in the sense that different elements of the capital stock need to be replaced at different points in time, it need never be the case that existing plant and equipment will simultaneously wear out, and thus require wholesale replacement. The sequential nature of replacement investment may make it rational for an established region to continually replace elements of its original capital stock, which will entail continued use of an obsolete method of production. Hence the region may remain locked in to existing methods even in the long run.[5]

iii)   Technological Interrelatedness between Decision-Making Units

Technological interrelatedness can also occur between individual decision-making units. This inter-firm technological interrelatedness arises when there exist interconnections between the production processes of different firms. Such interconnections are likely to proliferate in the presence of uniform technical standards, which can exist throughout an industry/economy regardless of how much more or less well suited they are to the production plans of any particular, individual firm. For example, computer software that is 'IBM compatible' conforms to a uniform technical standard – in this case, the specifications of IBM computer hardware. Uniform technical standards are pervasive in advanced industrial economies, and are often efficiency enhancing. Hence in the previous example, if firms know that computer software is 'IBM compatible', this may reduce the transaction costs incurred in the process of purchasing such software. At the same time, however, uniform technical standards may create circumstances where changing some element of the production process of one firm would require complementary changes in the production processes of other firms, with which the former is interrelated by virtue of uniform technical standards. This may hinder technological change by making the size of the individual decision-making unit small relative to the size of the 'technological unit' that requires change. For example, as noted in Chapter 2, an individual firm may be constrained from upgrading its rolling stock if this would require complementary changes to the uniform standard gauge of railway tracks, which are in turn owned by different firms, and which are consequently beyond the range of its control. Essentially, in the absence of a central planning mechanism, what exists here is a form of coordination failure between decentralized decision-making units. If this type of problem prevails, we may once again observe the phenomenon of lock-in to existing methods of production.

III TECHNOLOGICAL INTERRELATEDNESS, TECHNOLOGICAL LOCK-IN AND THE PROCESS OF CUMULATIVE CAUSATION

Having developed the concepts of intra- and inter-firm technological interrelatedness and lock-in, it remains to be seen how these phenomena can cause the technological evolution of a region to become inefficient, in the sense of its becoming dysfunctional to the maintenance of the dynamics of relatively high growth. In other words, we wish to show how technological interrelatedness and lock-in might influence long-run relative growth outcomes in the model of cumulative causation developed in Chapter 3. In order to pursue this issue, we will reconsider the structural stability of the model developed earlier by examining the impact on key coefficients (such as α_j in equation [3.1] and γ_j in equation [3.3]) of technological interrelatedness and lock-in brought about by a prior period of relatively fast growth.

i) Technological Interrelatedness and Lock-In: The Impact on Verdoorn's Law

In equation [3.1], the coefficient α_j captures the extent to which output growth stimulates subsequent productivity growth through the realization of dynamic increasing returns. As discussed in Chapter 3, these dynamic increasing returns accrue through a variety of channels, some of which are intangible (such as learning by doing). However, other channels may involve the accumulation of specific types of tangible fixed capital if scale economies are to be realized. This is significant, because to the extent that new types of fixed capital must be accumulated in the pursuit of economies of scale, the ability of a region to realize dynamic increasing returns (reflected in the size of α_j) may be impaired if it suffers from technological interrelatedness. Since this phenomenon makes technological change a non-marginal process which can therefore become prohibitively costly and/ or subject to coordination failures, and because this can give rise to lock-in to a previously existing technological regime, the ability of a region to transform its stock of productive assets in a manner in keeping with the realization of dynamic increasing returns may suffer accordingly. More specifically, since interrelatedness (and hence the probability of lock in) varies directly with the level of development,[6] this suggests that the faster is growth within the context of a specific technological regime, the faster interrelatedness will proliferate and the higher the likelihood that the region will experience lock-in to this specific regime. Consequently, an initial period of high relative growth may, by generating interrelatedness and lock-in, impair the subsequent ability of a region to realize dynamic increasing returns based on changes in the technological regime. Formally, this will lower the value of α_j in equation [3.1].

ii) Technological Interrelatedness and Lock-In: The Impact on the Income Elasticity of Demand for Exports

As intimated in Chapter 3, the importance of inflation differentials in generating cumulative causation in equations [3.1]–[3.4] does not indicate that price competitiveness is the only determinant of a region's competitiveness in this model. The value of γ_j, the income elasticity of demand for exports in equation [3.3], can be thought of as reflecting a region's success in non-price forms of competition. As emphasized by Dixon and Thirlwall (1978) and McCombie and Thirlwall (1994, pp. 463–4), γ_j plays a key role in the determination of relative growth outcomes in the process of cumulative causation. Indeed, even casual inspection of equation [3.10] reveals that, *ceteris paribus*, the higher the value of γ_j, the higher the value of $\dfrac{\dot{Y}_{jt}}{\dot{Y}_w}$ will be.

What remains to be established, however, is the relationship between a region's prior growth trajectory, the phenomena of technological interrelatedness and lock-in and the size of γ_j. Recall that, according to Cornwall (1977), the growth of consumers' income propels their movement through a 'commodity hierarchy' in which different goods appear as luxuries or necessities (that is, have high or low income elasticities of demand) at different levels of income. This suggests that in order for its output to remain highly tradeable (that is, in order for it to have a high income elasticity of demand) a region must be able to transform the composition of its output in the course of growth to match the progression of its markets through the commodity hierarchy. However, such transformational growth may be difficult to achieve if technological interrelatedness promotes lock-in to a certain stage of the commodity hierarchy. This may arise if technological interrelatedness between existing ('old') industries and complementary capital comprising the physical and human resource infrastructure of a region deters the accumulation of complementary capital functional to the emergence of 'new' industries.[7] If the degree of technological interrelatedness between 'old' industries and a region's infrastructure varies directly with the level of development, then fast growth based extensively on the output of these 'old' industries will promote technological interrelatedness and increase the probability of lock-in to a certain stage of the commodity hierarchy. In this case, initially high relative growth may, by generating technological interrelatedness between a region's traditional industrial base and its infrastructure, become inimical to the subsequent ability of a region to realize transformational growth. Failure to transform the composition of its final output in a manner which conforms to the progression of its markets through the commodity hierarchy will depress the income elasticity of demand of a region's tradeable output. Formally, this will depress the value of γ_j in equation [3.3].

iii) The Consequences of Technological Interrelatedness and Lock-In for the Process of Cumulative Causation

The possibilities of technological interrelatedness and lock-in already discussed can be incorporated into the model of cumulative causation developed in Chapter 3, as follows. First, following the methodology discussed in Section III(v) of Chapter 2, consider the disequilibrium time paths $(\dot{Y}_{j0}^a, \ldots, \dot{Y}_{jt-1}^a)$ and $(\dot{Y}_{j0}^b, \ldots, \dot{Y}_{jt-1}^b)$.[8] Now define $d\dot{Y}_{ji} = \dot{Y}_{ji}^b - \dot{Y}_{ji}^a$ for all $i = 0, \ldots, t-1$, and suppose that $d\dot{Y}_{ji} \geqslant 0$ for all $i = 0, \ldots, t-1$. In other words, we assume that $(\dot{Y}_{j0}^b, \ldots, \dot{Y}_{jt-1}^b)$ represents a strictly higher growth trajectory than $(\dot{Y}_{j0}^a, \ldots, \dot{Y}_{jt-1}^a)$. What we now wish to discover are the consequences of following the higher rather than the lower growth trajectory for long-run relative growth outcomes in equation [3.10], which can be restated as:

$$\frac{\dot{Y}_{jt}}{\dot{Y}_w} = (\lambda_j \alpha_j \beta_j)^t \frac{\dot{Y}_{j0}}{\dot{Y}_w} + \lambda_j(\gamma_j - \alpha_w \beta_j)\sum_{i=0}^{t-1}(\lambda_j \alpha_j \beta_j)^i \qquad [3.10]$$

Suppose that:

$$\alpha_{jt} = f_j(\dot{Y}_{j0}, \ldots, \dot{Y}_{jt-1}) \qquad [4.9]$$

where:

$$f_{ji}' \neq 0 \quad for\ some \quad i = 0, \ldots, t-1$$

EXPEDITED

Items: **1**
Date: 04-Nov-2002

Order # 2006-**597**

Title # 3816338

Qty:

1

Rapid Growth & Relative Decline: Modelling Macroeconomic
Setterfield, Mark
ST MARTINS PRESS @
0312172680
$23.00 (USED MARKDOWN, **HARDCOVER**, HOYT)

Received Date: 23-May-1999
Condition: Standard Condition

[V-ECONOMICS]
Locator Code: **352D2**

Ship to:
Randa Alhegelan
1716 Strine Drive
Mclean, VA 22101
United States

powells
.com

40 NW 10th Avenue
Portland, OR 97209
800-291-9676

*Free shipping for North American orders $50 or more
placed directly through powells.com!*

and:

$$Da = \sum_{i=0}^{t-1} f'_{ji} \cdot d\dot{Y}_{ji} \neq 0$$

Equation [4.9] captures the sensitivity of α_j – the ability of region j to realize dynamic increasing returns from a given rate of output growth – to the prior growth path of region j. Most importantly, Da captures the cumulative effect on α_j of region j following the higher $((\dot{Y}_{j0}^b, \ldots, \dot{Y}_{jt-1}^b))$ rather than the lower $((\dot{Y}_{j0}^a, \ldots, \dot{Y}_{jt-1}^a))$ growth trajectory, suggesting that this effect is non-zero. The question is whether the higher prior growth path will enhance or reduce the long-run value of α_j – that is, whether $Da \lessgtr 0$ in equation [4.9]. On one hand, a sustained period of faster economic growth may increase opportunities for the realization of dynamic scale economies ($Da > 0$), as activities associated with learning and innovation become more specialized at higher levels of development. For example, separate research and development departments may be set up within firms. This will result in a higher proportional change in q_{jt} in response to a given proportional change in Y_{jt} – that is, an increase in the size of α_j.

However, what Sections II, III(i) and III(ii) illustrate is that as an economy grows, it may begin to experience technological interrelatedness and hence lock-in to a previously existing technological regime. Given that a sustained period of faster economic growth increases the level of development and hence the degree of interrelatedness in an economy, and in so doing raises the probability of lock-in, the cumulative effect of an initial phase of faster growth may be to impede the process of technological change and reduce the subsequent ability of the economy to realize dynamic increasing returns associated with technological change ($Da < 0$).

Suppose, then, that this second effect dominates, so that an initial period of faster growth in region j leads to $Da < 0$ in equation [4.9] with the result that the value of α_j now falls. Then the cumulative effect of initially faster growth will be to lower the subsequent relative growth rate of region j. This can be seen by inspection of equation [3.10], from which it follows that:

$$\frac{\partial \left(\dfrac{\dot{Y}_{jt}}{\dot{Y}_w} \right)}{\partial \alpha_j} = t\alpha_j^{t-1}(\lambda_j \beta_j)^t \cdot \frac{\dot{Y}_{j0}}{\dot{Y}_w} + \lambda_j(\gamma_j - \alpha_w\beta_j) \cdot \sum_{i=0}^{t-1} i\alpha_j^{i-1}(\lambda_j \beta_j)^i \geq 0$$

since α_j, β_j, λ_j and α_w are all positive by assumption and inspection of equation [3.8] reveals that we must have $(\gamma_j - \alpha_w\beta_j) > 0$ to satisfy the assumptions made earlier that $\dot{Y}_{jt}, \dot{Y}_w > 0$ for all values of t. In other words, if $D\alpha < 0$, region j will experience a climacteric – a deceleration of its trend rate of relative growth. In terms of the causal chain:

$$\text{high } \dot{X}_t \rightarrow \text{high } \dot{Y}_t \rightarrow \text{high } \dot{q}_{t+1} \rightarrow \text{high } \dot{X}_{t+1} \rightarrow \text{and so on}$$

$$b$$

we have identified a weak link at point b, emanating from the supply side of the economy. This illustrates the possibility of an economy experiencing inefficient technological evolution in the course of growth, and hence the possibility that high growth dynamics may ultimately sow the seeds of their own long-run destruction.[9]

Alternatively, we can write:

$$\gamma_{jt} = g_j(\dot{Y}_{j0}, \ldots, \dot{Y}_{jt-1}) \qquad [4.10]$$

where:

$$g'_{ji} \neq 0 \quad \text{for some} \quad i = 0, \ldots, t-1$$

and:

$$D\gamma = \sum_{i=0}^{t-1} g'_{ji} \cdot d\dot{Y}_{ji} \neq 0$$

Equation [4.10] expresses the income elasticity of demand for exports, γ_j, as a function of the prior growth trajectory of region j. Recalling that $d\dot{Y}_{ji} = \dot{Y}^b_{ji} - \dot{Y}^a_{ji} > 0$ for all $i = 0, \ldots, t-1$, $D\gamma$ now captures the cumulative impact on γ_j of following the higher rather than the lower growth trajectory, suggesting that this effect is non-zero. Once again, the issue as to whether $D\gamma \lesseqgtr 0$ is of critical importance. The arguments in Section III(ii) suggest that lock-in to a previously existing technological regime may entail lock-in to a certain stage of the commodity hierarchy. Hence a sustained period of faster growth which promotes technological interrelatedness and lock-in may obstruct the emergence of 'new' industries in a region. This will impede the region's ability to realize transformational growth and hence depress the income elasticity of demand for its tradeable output, as the region fails to match its markets' progress through the commodity hierarchy. This outcome is captured by the case where $D\gamma < 0$ in equation [4.10]. In this case, the cumulative effect of initially faster growth will be, once again, to lower the relative growth rate of region j. Inspection of equation [3.10] reveals that:

$$\frac{\partial\left(\dfrac{\dot{Y}_{jt}}{\dot{Y}_w}\right)}{\partial\gamma_j} = \lambda_j \cdot \sum_{i=0}^{t-1}(\lambda_j\alpha_j\beta_j)^i \gg 0$$

since λ_j, α_j and β_j are all positive by assumption. In terms of the causal chain:

$$high~ \dot{X}_t \rightarrow high~ \dot{Y}_t \rightarrow high~ \dot{q}_{t+1} \rightarrow high~ \dot{X}_{t+1} \rightarrow and~ so~ on$$

$$a$$

we have identified a second 'weak link' at point a – but this time, one which emanates from endogenously induced changes on the supply side of the economy (increases in the degree of technological interrelatedness) in the course of growth. Once again, this illustrates the possibility that a relatively fast growing region may eventually experience a relative growth climacteric – that is, the possibility that an initial period of relatively fast growth will bequeath the conditions for a subsequent relative growth slowdown.

Of course, should this slowdown extend to the case where $\dfrac{\dot{Y}_{jt}}{\dot{Y}_w} < 1$, then it may be accompanied by a second effect. Specifically, if $\dot{Y}_w > \dot{Y}_j$ in all future periods, the 'rest of the world' may begin catching up with region j's *level* of per capita income.[10] Indeed, if the 'rest of the world' can maintain its competitive advantage and avoid a breakdown of its own virtuous circle, it may even *overtake* region j's per capita income level. In this case, we will observe a change in the international ranking of economies by per capita income, which is akin to what Maddison (1991) defines as a change in 'economic leadership'.[11]

iv) Summary

The relative reversal of region j's fortunes already discussed is induced by the virtuous circle in this region ultimately creating conditions which are dysfunctional to the maintenance of high growth dynamics. Because the ability of an economy to undergo technological change depends on the degree of technological interrelatedness it experiences, fast growth which induces increases in interrelatedness may promote lock-in to a pre-existing technological regime. This will reduce an economy's ability to realize dynamic increasing returns and/or transformational growth. The technological evolution of the economy will therefore be inefficient, in the sense that it will not be functional to the maintenance of the high growth dynamics associated with a virtuous circle. Instead of success breeding success indefinitely in region j, allowing for the possibility of induced supply side effects such as technological interrelatedness and lock-in suggests a way in which the dynamics of a virtuous circle of cumulative causation may endogenously break down.

IV   CONCLUSION

The foregoing analysis, based on the extended model of equations [3.10] and equations [4.9] and/or [4.10], is thoroughly in keeping with the methodological spirit of hysteresis on which our modelling exercise purportedly rests. The supply side effects that are held to pose potential problems for the dynamics of cumulative causation arise endogenously, as a result of the prior historical time path of the economy. In the terminology developed in Chapter 2, the coefficients α_j and γ_j are conceived as being deeply endogenous to the prior growth trajectory of the economy. Furthermore, these coefficients are subject to adjustment asymmetries, since the effects of growth on technological interrelatedness and the probability of lock-in are asymmetrical. Hence, as illustrated earlier, an initial period of relatively high growth may promote technological interrelatedness and lock-in, resulting in a subsequent transition to a lower relative growth path. However, the latter will not automatically reverse the effects of lock-in, since slower but trend positive growth will sustain a level of development above the 'threshold' level assumed to trigger lock-in.[12] The effects on long-run growth of a decline in α_j or γ_j as postulated are therefore, *ceteris paribus*, generally permanent rather than transitory. In connection with these claims, note that the limit outcome associated with equation [3.10], which may be restated as:

$$\frac{\dot{Y}_j^*}{\dot{Y}_w} = \frac{\lambda_j(\gamma_j - \alpha_w\beta_j)}{1 - \lambda_j\alpha_j\beta_j} \qquad [3.8]$$

is also affected by equations [4.9] and [4.10]. More specifically, if α_j and/or γ_j are deeply endogenous and subject to adjustment asymmetries, this limit outcome can no longer be defined without reference to the path taken towards it. For example, if $D\alpha < 0$ in equation [4.9], it is clear by inspection that this will reduce the value of $\dfrac{\dot{Y}_j^*}{\dot{Y}_w}$ in equation [3.8]. The limit outcome in [3.8] therefore depends on the path taken towards it, so that when the model in equations [3.1]–[3.4] is augmented by equations [4.9] and/or

[4.10], it becomes hysteretic *regardless* of assumptions, such as those made in Chapter 3, about the relative speed of disequilibrium adjustment. Apart from its consistency with the methodology espoused in Chapter 2, the modelling exercise in this chapter, which generates a broader conception of cumulative causation taking into account the significance of induced supply side changes in the course of growth and development, is valuable for two main reasons.

i) The Increased Influence of History in the Extended Model

The first valuable feature of the extended model is that it increases the influence of history in the process of cumulative causation. No longer is it the case that success breeds success and failure begets failure indefinitely; the dynamics of cumulative causation may be affected by induced supply side changes. These arise in the long run as an endogenous response to the process of growth as cumulative causation itself. The technological evolution of an economy is influenced by technological interrelatedness and lock-in arising in the course of growth. Hence the ability of an economy to realize dynamic increasing returns (reflected in the size of α_j) and/or transformational growth (which affects the size of γ_j), both of which are sensitive to the 'technological regime' within which growth is occurring, must be treated as deeply endogenous. They will vary with the precise growth path of the economy over time. As a result, long-run relative growth outcomes no longer depend solely on the initial conditions prevailing in competing regions. Instead, a successful region may sow the seeds of its own future decline, as an initial phase of relatively high growth gives rise to the subsequent diminution of its virtuous circle, and possibly even a relative reversal of its comparative growth performance.

The extended model of cumulative causation developed in this chapter thus generalizes Kaldor's model of cumulative causation into a more generally hysteretic form, where successive changes in the variables of interest (export, output and productivity growth) need not be positively correlated over an indefinite time horizon.

ii) Polarization versus Emulation

The second valuable feature of the extended model of cumulative causation developed earlier relates to Kaldor's (1981) distinction between 'polarization' and 'emulation' in the course of growth. Kaldor argues that the type of model developed in Chapter 3 involves a 'polarization process', in which growth is inhibited in some regions and highly concentrated in others. However, he argues that throughout economic history, this polarization process has, to some extent, been counteracted by the spread of industrialization between regions. This point is illustrated by Cornwall's (1977, pp. 97–121) analysis of technology transfers between regions and their impact on the rate of growth. It has also become a central feature of the literature that seeks to explain relative growth rates in terms of technological convergence or 'catch up' (see, for example, Baumol *et al.*, 1989). Kaldor is therefore led to conclude that:

> The interaction between these forces – i.e., that of polarization which leads to concentration of development in successful areas, and of imitation or emulation which leads to the spread of industrialization into a wider range of areas – has never . . . been properly explored.
>
> (Kaldor, 1981, p. 206)

It is an interaction of this nature that the model developed in this chapter seeks to capture. Analysing the growth of technological interrelatedness within the context of cumulative causation suggests one way of analysing the processes of both polarization and emulation in the context of a single, long-run growth model, as an initially self-reinforcing virtuous circle (and so growth polarization) gives way to subsequent relative growth retardation (and so growth emulation). As indicated earlier, the advantage of this extended model over the traditional Kaldorian model of cumulative causation is that it does not predict that initial relatively high/low growth will necessarily propagate subsequent relatively high/low growth indefinitely. The extended model of cumulative causation also has several advantages over explanations of relative decline based solely on the notion of technological 'catch up'. First, it takes into account salient structural features of the comparative growth process, such as difficulties that may be associated with undergoing technological change and/or moving through the commodity hierarchy in economies constrained by the legacy of an early start, and the concomitant possibility that the technology of old industrial regions will, to use Kaldor's distinction again, be *emulated* rather than simply *imitated* by late starters. These features, which are omitted from discussions of 'catch up', appear to have played an important part in actual historical experiences of relative economic decline. Hence, as will be illustrated at length in Chapter 7, the technology in key nineteenth century British industries such as cotton textiles was emulated rather than simply imitated by late developing economies, who made extensive use of new technologies that Britain struggled to adopt. Meanwhile:

... increasingly towards the end of the nineteenth century, foreign economic advances ... rested ... heavily on industries which had never been important in Britain and which in some cases – such as electrical engineering, telephone communications and dyestuffs – Britain appeared almost incapable of sustaining.

(Kennedy, 1987, p. 5)

Second, the extended model of cumulative causation developed in this chapter explicitly allows for the possibility of changes in international economic rankings by per capita income or 'changes in economic leadership', rather than simply convergence towards the per capita income level of some contemporary technological leader (see also Cornwall and Cornwall, 1992). This income 'leapfrogging' rather than just 'catch up' seems to be more broadly in keeping with the stylized facts of long-run growth (see, for example, Maddison, 1991).

5 The Supply Side and Macroeconomic Performance II: Institutional Evolution

In recent years, renewed interest has been shown in both the importance of institutions for the functioning of capitalism, and the impact of capitalism's dynamics on the nature of institutions.[1] However, the common interests of this literature conceal profound methodological differences, which in turn give rise to substantially different conclusions with regard to the origins, nature and role of institutions in a capitalist economy.

This chapter considers the nature of institutional evolution, and its consequences for the growth dynamics of a capitalist economy. By illustrating the potential for the emergence and persistence of inefficient institutions, its development parallels that of Chapter 4, insofar as inefficient institutional evolution is identified as a potential 'weak link' on the supply side of the economy that may cause a virtuous circle of cumulative causation to break down.

I DEFINING INSTITUTIONS

Before proceeding, it is important to define what we mean by the term 'institutions' in the context of a capitalist economy. Economic institutions constitute 'any correlated behavior of agents . . . that reoccurs under the same or similar conditions' (Dopfer, 1991, p. 536). Institutions are 'proceduralist' rather than 'consequentialist', influencing the type of behaviour that occurs in a particular situation independently of the goal orientation of the individual actor (Elster, 1989a).[2] As social relations that frame the activities of production, consumption and exchange, institutions can be thought of as a structure within which individual action in the economy takes place.

Institutions thus defined possess a number of salient features. First, they are distinct from organizations (Bromley, 1989). The existence and operation of organizations depends on institutions, but the two are not equivalent.

For example, in the labour market, both trade unions and firms are examples of organizations whose internal structure depends on institutions (rules and norms concerning the appointment of officials, decision making processes, and so on) and whose relationship to each other is governed by a set of institutions (the industrial relations system).

Second, following Basu *et al.* (1987), the definition of institutions used earlier allows us to subsume under a single heading what are variously referred to in institutional analysis as institutions, conventions, norms, rules and customs. Finally, the definition is suggestive of arrangements and patterns of behaviour which do not originate from the actions of one individual alone, and/or which affect the actions of more than one individual; that is, institutions are collective rather than individualistic in nature.[3]

Having defined the term 'institution', we can now define what we mean by an 'institutional regime', the analogue of the technological regime discussed in Chapter 4. An institutional regime is simply a collectivity or matrix of institutions, which forms the current socio-economic environment within which individual agents act, and which helps define relations between these agents.

In the analysis that follows, we will implicitly distinguish between institutions and institutional regimes on one hand, and basic features of capitalism such as the price mechanism and private property on the other. From a broader historical perspective, these 'basic features of capitalism' may themselves be regarded as historically specific institutions, whose origins and role require analysis. Whilst the importance of this argument is not denied, its implications are held to be beyond the scope of the present analysis; our interest in the functioning of capitalist economies is assumed to justify a distinction between these intrinsic features of capitalism and what have been defined earlier as institutions.

II   IS THE PRICE MECHANISM ENOUGH? EARLY VIEWS ON THE ROLE OF INSTITUTIONS

Institutional analysis is by no means a new field of research. However, neither has there always been universal acceptance of the importance of institutions for the functioning of a capitalist economy. Hayek (1945) argues that the price mechanism alone is sufficient to ensure that an economy operates efficiently.[4] For Hayek, the basic economic problem facing society is how to organize the economy so that widely dispersed, individual specific information can be used in such a way that the economic system as a whole functions efficiently. He argues that whilst most events in an economy might be seen as having some bearing on the decisions a particular individual has to make, individuals do not need to be aware of all these events, nor all their effects. Instead:

> [i]t does not matter for him [her] (the individual decision maker) *why* at the particular moment more screws of one size than another are wanted . . . all that is significant for him [her] is *how much more or less* difficult to procure they have become compared with other things with which he [she] is also concerned.
>
> (Hayek, 1945, p. 525, emphasis in original)

Hayek argues that the key feature of the price mechanism is that it embodies exactly this information; prices consist of 'rates of equivalence' which attach an index to each scarce resource reflecting its significance in the economy as a whole. Thus for Hayek, all relevant information is concentrated in prices.[5] By adjusting to price signals, individuals are seen to be able to organize their behaviour without having to 'solve the whole puzzle of the economy', and in such a way that their actions are consistent with the efficient functioning of the system in aggregate.

The Hayekian view that 'the price mechanism is enough' takes a classically liberal view of the market as a 'state of nature'. Institutions have no role in this view; they enter only as un-natural imperfections which impair the operation of the market and which are therefore best eliminated. A modern variant of this hypothesis, which also has a direct bearing on the topic of long-run growth outcomes, is found in the work of Olson (1982). Olson's argument is couched in terms of the neoclassical theory of public choice. It suggests that periods of political stability foster the emergence of special interest groups. These are, in turn, capable of successfully lobbying for institutions, such as industrial and financial regulations, protectionism and so on, which satisfy their special interests but which are inimical to the dynamic efficiency and hence the long-run growth rate of an economy. Furthermore, these institutions tend to become entrenched, so that major political disruptions (such as foreign occupation) are necessary for their (otherwise desirable) removal.[6] The essentially Hayekian nature of Olson's conception of institutions is, perhaps, best illustrated by his admission that there may emerge 'encompassing' interest groups capable of acting in the collective interest. At first, this appears to shift the theory away from a conception of institutions as universally bad, towards a view in which different *types* of institutions may be better or worse at facilitating economic activity. However, Olson's 'encompassing' interest group serves mainly to keep other, special interest groups at bay – it even leads him to entertain a potentially positive role for totalitarian political regimes. The 'encompassing' interest group can therefore be likened to a Hobbesian 'Leviathan', whose duty is to supervise an otherwise 'natural' market order in such a way as to prevent the latter from becoming tainted by institutional 'imperfections' (Hodgson, 1989, p. 91).

The view that 'the price mechanism is enough' and that institutions are a superficial imperfection in a capitalist economy is challenged by Richardson (1959). Richardson argues that prices do not embody sufficient information to facilitate the functioning of an economy with decentralized decision making. According to Richardson, the configuration of an economic system at any point in time depends on both a set of economic actions, and an accompanying set of beliefs or expectations concerning economic conditions. Two different types of economic conditions may be identified: 'primary' conditions, which correspond to the data of traditional equilibrium analysis (preferences, technologies etc.) and 'secondary' conditions, which refer to the projected activities of other agents in the system. Richardson argues that the price mechanism may embody sufficient information to facilitate the formation of expectations concerning primary conditions. However, he argues that expectations concerning secondary conditions are a different matter, since the price mechanism cannot tell us exactly how other agents in the system will react to its signals.[7]

These considerations lead Richardson to conclude that in practice, a variety of institutional factors usually considered as 'frictions' or 'imperfections' actually play a vital role in transmitting important secondary information to individual agents. For example, 'goodwill' (that is, consumer loyalty, which may be identified as a behavioural norm) may provide information to firms concerning the likely future behaviour of their customers in the event of price fluctuations. Other product market institutions such as formal or implicit market sharing and barriers to entry may provide an indication to firms as to how actual or potential competitors will react in a particular economic environment. In short, Richardson contends that institutions are sources of important secondary information which is not embodied in price signals. The procedural nature of institutions allows agents operating under conditions of uncertainty to anticipate the likely future behaviour of other agents in the economy. As such, institutions are instrumental in the operations of a decentralized market economy.

III COMPETING CONCEPTIONS OF INSTITUTIONAL EVOLUTION: THE 'OLD' AND 'NEW' INSTITUTIONAL ECONOMICS

An increasing acceptance of Richardson's position – that 'the price mechanism is not enough' – has played an important part in provoking much of the current interest in institutional economics.[8] However, this emerging consensus that institutions matter belies the significant disagreement between different schools of thought as to why this is so. This conflict of opinions is illustrated by the contrast between two highly influential methodologies in institutional economics – what may be referred to as 'old' institutional economics (OIE) and the neoclassical 'new' institutional economics (NIE).[9]

i) The OIE

The OIE, associated with authors such as Commons (1961), Ayres (1962) and Veblen (1975) explains institutions in terms of a historical mode of analysis. By tracing institutions from one period to the next, their existence is accounted for on the basis of the principle that earlier states account for later ones. The OIE pursues a holistic methodology, postulating that the economy cannot be understood as a set of separable parts. Holism implies that individual phenomena cannot be explained without reference to the whole of which they form a part – that the characteristics and functioning of the part depend on its relations with other parts, and hence its place in the whole. For example, in the OIE the behaviour of individual agents in the economy is seen as a function of existing institutions, which form an environment to which individuals become socialized over time.

   That institutions influence individual behaviour should not be misconstrued as suggesting that institutions simply *constrain* individual behaviour in the OIE. For example, the discussion of Richardson (1959) in Section II draws attention to economic institutions which *facilitate* individual behaviour under conditions of uncertainty. Even institutions which appear explicitly prohibitive may, in fact, facilitate action. Hence a law which arbitrarily decrees that drivers must keep to the left hand side of the road appears to limit individual behaviour. However, by promoting safe travel, it arguably facilitates individual action by making otherwise monumental decisions (whether to risk life and limb by driving to a local store) relatively trivial. The 'situated action' of a socialized individual may be, therefore, both constrained and facilitated by the institutional regime within which he/she acts.[10]

The holistic methodology of the OIE does, however, lead to an emphasis on structure (that is, institutions) over action (that is, the choices and activities of individuals) in the determination of economic outcomes. One potential shortcoming of this 'structuralism' is that it can lead to a de-emphasis of the role played by goal oriented individuals, both in determining economic outcomes, and in shaping the institutional environment itself to meet their own ends (Brunner, 1987). This is particularly true of the Veblen/Ayres tradition, in which institutions are treated as constraints inhibiting technologically determined social and economic progress. In these circumstances, the individual is easily caricatured as a 'plaything of social forces or the passive executor of inherited standards' (Elster, 1989b, p. 97).

A related problem, as Brunner (1987), Basu *et al.* (1987) and Rutherford (1989) argue, is that the OIE often attributes the existence of current institutions to their history as if this in and of itself explains their origins and persistence. For example, Gordon (1980, p. 17) asserts that a basic characteristic of institutions is that they are inherited as a legacy of the past. The problem with this argument is that it suggests that contemporary institutions can be taken as given from the past. This precludes a proper explanation of institutional evolution since, devoid of any theoretical or historical dynamics, it provides no indication of what types of institutions will survive over time, or why an institution's demise should occur when it eventually does.[11] Although Gordon argues that technological change provides the imperative for institutional change, this simply replaces one autonomous, supraindividual force (institutions) with another (technology) (Rutherford, 1989).

ii)   The NIE

It is perhaps ironic that in attempting to overcome the problems associated with the OIE, many authors have pursued the opposite methodological extreme and based their analysis of institutions entirely on the self interested behaviour of individuals. These theories, associated with authors such as Schotter (1981) and Williamson (1985), make up the NIE.[12]

The central contention of the NIE is that institutions arise spontaneously in the course of market activity.[13] The core of this analysis is a model of rational economic behaviour on the part of individuals, who are defined by psychologically given preference structures, and whose key feature is that they are evaluative – that is, they are willing to make trade offs between things that they value positively in order to achieve the greatest personal benefit. Proponents of the NIE argue that the application of this model is not limited to some narrowly defined 'economic sphere' of activity.[14] Rather, they suggest that it characterizes all social behaviour. Hence they arrive at the notion of a 'generalized trade off' in which social arrangements such as institutions are seen to arise essentially because they are positively valued by rational maximizing individuals.[15]

Of course, this still leaves us to explain precisely how social arrangements which are extraneous to the individual come about. The emphasis in NIE analysis is on 'invisible hand' mechanisms; it is argued that interaction between rational individuals produces social patterns of behaviour without any one individual directing the results. The most common invisible hand mechanisms appealed to are repetition in game theoretic models (for example, Schotter, 1981),[16] and evolutionary selection processes (for example, Alchian, 1950).[17]

The NIE infers that the institutions of a capitalist economy are completely endogenous to market behaviour, in the sense that they are constantly evolving in response to rational individual actions. In other words, it pursues a reductionist methodology; the explanation of the institutional structure of an economy is entirely subsumed within an individualistic, choice theoretic framework. Causality is strictly uni-directional, with institutions arising solely in response to the current maximizing behaviour of rational individuals. In the NIE, individual action gives rise to structure (that is, institutions) and any reverse line of causality is denied.[18]

However, if, as the OIE argues, institutions form a 'social environment' to which individuals are socialized, the preferences and goals of individuals on which their actions are based can no longer be treated as 'psychological givens'. Instead, they can only be interpreted within a particular institutional context (Hodgson, 1986). Rutherford (1989) suggests that this criticism leaves the reductionist with two options. The first is to deny that existing institutions can significantly affect current behaviour and hence the development of new institutions. However, Rutherford argues that it is hard to avoid the notion that existing institutions can be conservative, resisting change and hence influencing the subsequent development of the institutional structure. There may be vested interests in pre-existing institutions which will deliberately resist change.[19] Alternatively, institutional inertia may arise spontaneously if the cost of enforcing compliance to rules increases substantially when institutions are changed frequently.

The second option identified by Rutherford is for the reductionist to accept that pre-existing institutions do affect current behaviour and hence the development of institutions in subsequent periods, but to argue that it is possible to trace institutional evolution back to some original, 'pre-institutional' starting point. This approach is popular in game theoretic strands of the NIE. The caveat in this argument is that it does not avoid the necessity of taking *some* initial set of rules or norms of behaviour as exogenously given (Field, 1984). For example, the emergence of cooperative solutions in game theory depends vitally on games being repeated. This in turn requires that no party can simply exit the game or inflict catastrophic damage on others that prevents retaliation (Rutherford, 1989). In other words, the games have a prior structure that is not explained by individual self interested behaviour.[20]

These criticisms suggest that it is not possible to conceive individual action as being independent of the institutional context within which it occurs. The methodological individualism of the NIE is flawed in that, by seeking to explain institutions wholly in terms of individual behaviour, it overlooks the reverse line of causality (attributable to the OIE) through which individual behaviour is influenced by institutions.

IV   TOWARDS A NEW CONCEPTION OF INSTITUTIONAL EVOLUTION: HYSTERESIS AND INSTITUTIONAL STRUCTURES

The criticisms outlined earlier suggest that neither the structuralist approach of the OIE nor the reductionism of the NIE offer truly satisfactory methodologies for institutional analysis. What is needed is an approach which captures the dynamic interaction between institutions and activity – one which recognizes the importance of current behaviour in shaping future institutions, but which at the same time takes account of the extent to which this behaviour is constrained by pre-existing institutional arrangements.

These considerations suggest that the institutional structure of an economy may be best conceived in terms of a process of hysteresis. In an institutional context, hysteresis can be thought of as existing when current institutions influence the nature of current economic activity, which in turn influences subsequent institutional forms.

The joint interaction between institutions and economic activity in a process of hysteresis has previously been considered by Cornwall (1990) and Cornwall and Cornwall (1987). However, these authors are primarily concerned to illustrate the implications of this joint interaction for the unemployment–inflation trade off, rather than the intrinsic nature of institutions themselves. To illustrate the process of 'institutional hysteresis' when the latter is of primary concern, suppose initially that the choice sets of individuals and groups are defined by currently existing institutions.[21] These institutions will consequently exert a straightforward influence on current economic activity. This activity in turn gives rise to economic outcomes, which may be judged by individuals and groups as either good

Figure 5.1   A Model of Institutional Hysteresis

Institutions → Definition of individ./ group choice sets → Economic activity → Outcomes and their evaluation → Institutions → and so on

or bad. Depending on this evaluation, individuals and groups will then attempt to either modify existing institutional arrangements or retain the status quo, which will in turn affect the form of future institutions and hence future choice sets and activities and so on. The essence of this model of institutional hysteresis is summarized by the causal chain in Fig. 5.1.

The central feature of the proposed model is that institutions act as exogenous 'data' in the short run, but in the long run, they are endogenous to the workings of the economy. The short-run exogeneity derives from the OIE, where institutions are not assumed to display the 'putty like' malleability necessary for their moment by moment renegotiation, as in the NIE. Instead, some degree of inertia is postulated, which will give rise to an institutional environment framing current economic activity.

However, the possibility that pressure for institutional change will arise from individuals' and groups' evaluations of current economic outcomes is not overlooked; hence the long-run endogeneity of the institutional structure, which derives from the NIE, allows economic outcomes to have feedback effects on the form of institutions. Unlike most branches of the reductionist NIE, however, there is no necessary tendency towards some determinate long-run 'institutional equilibrium' in the current model. Rather, long-run institutional changes can only be interpreted in terms of the sequence of short-run patterns of economic activity leading up to them – patterns of activity which are themselves influenced by previously existing institutions. In other words, long-run institutional changes are path dependent, deriving from the specific adjustment path the economy takes towards them. This is a fundamental difference between the way in which the endogeneity of the institutional structure is conceived in a model of institutional hysteresis, and the way it is conventionally conceived by the NIE.

The short-run exogeneity/long-run endogeneity of institutions in the model of institutional hysteresis gives rise to a second important feature of this model. Specifically, it is consistent with a view of institutional evolution which foresees periods of institutional stability (deriving from the short-run exogeneity) punctuated by substantial institutional change (the manifestation of the long-run endogeneity.)[22] According to this view, whilst economic outcomes, their evaluation, and subsequent pressures for institutional change may arise continuously, there is some extent to which this is counterbalanced by forces of institutional inertia. Hence unlike the NIE, which suggests that institutional evolution is a continuous process, the model of institutional hysteresis allows for the possibility of different institutional forms persisting over time in an episodic fashion.

V HYSTERESIS AND THE EFFICIENCY OF INSTITUTIONS

The model of institutional hysteresis previously developed combines exogenous and endogenous aspects of institutions in a historically consistent manner. It reconciles some of the most valid methodological contentions of the OIE and the NIE, whilst avoiding their worst excesses.

However, an important feature of the NIE that has so far been overlooked is its claim that institutions are functional to the dynamics of capitalism. In fact, according to the NIE, the 'invisible hand' coordinates the activities of rational individuals in such a way as to give rise to institutions that are *socially efficient*.[23] Is it the case, then, that a hysteretic theory of institutions subscribes to the view that evolving institutional structures are efficient? The answer to this question is in the negative, for a number of reasons connected with their path dependency.[24]

i) The Persistence of Inefficient Institutions

As previously intimated, the distinction between short-run exogeneity and long-run endogeneity in the model of institutional hysteresis permits a further distinction between the emergence of institutions, and their persistence over time once they have become the dominant form of procedure in a particular situation. This distinction is not immediately apparent from the moment by moment renegotiation of institutions in the NIE. Its importance, however, is that it gives rise to the possibility of institutions persisting over time even when they have ceased to be efficient.

As with the case of technology discussed in Chapter 4, one way in which this can occur is if an economy experiences lock-in to a pre-existing, but now inefficient institution. Once again, it is precisely this type of problem to which interrelatedness between and within institutions can give rise. By definition, institutions imply a degree of connectedness between individual behaviours in an economy – that is, there exists interrelatedness *within* any institution. Because of this, an inefficient institution may persist by virtue of a 'mutually sustaining structure of sanctions' (Akerlof, 1976; Basu *et al.*, 1987). The self interested individual will comply with the behaviour implied by an institution, even if it is inefficient, in order to avoid being ostracized. Meanwhile, others in society will continue to ostracize deviants fearing that if they do not, they will in turn be socially sanctioned. The changes necessary to rectify this situation are of a non-marginal nature. They require a restructuring of the institution as a whole which, as illustrated, cannot be brought about by incremental changes in the behaviour of any one individual who is currently held in compliance with the institution. On the contrary, no one individual has an incentive to deviate from the institution given the behaviour of all others. As a result, the system will become locked in to this institution. Lock-in arising in this manner may help explain the persistence of a variety of economic behavioural norms, such as the tendency of businessmen to wear ties even on hot days. A further example is provided by Akerlof (1976), who argues that continued racism in a firm's hiring practices may arise from the fear of ostracism by others which would result if the firm hired a worker from the 'wrong' racial group. At the same time, other firms would systematically punish any such deviance, for fear of the sanctions that would be consequent upon their failure to do so.

Alternatively, when an institution has distributive consequences – as when the institution is devised initially as a procedural resolution to some form of distributional conflict – and when changing the institution may therefore induce some form of redistribution, attempts to deviate from and hence change the institution by some parties may be resisted by others (Lorenz, 1991, pp. 124–6). This is likely to occur whenever there is difficulty in disseminating general welfare enhancing from purely redistributional institutional changes.[25] Furthermore, the problem is likely to be exacerbated if behaviour in the context of the current institution has fostered a lack of trust (that is, growing suspicion) between parties to the institution. As a result, it may be difficult for any one individual to deviate from the behaviour implied by the institution given the compliance of others, so that the system as a whole becomes locked in to the institution. The essence of the problem in this case, as in the case of mutually sustaining sanctions already discussed, is that the size of the decision making unit (the individual) is small relative to the scale of the unit of change required (the entire institution) due to the interrelatedness between individuals which is naturally implied by the institution.

Interrelatedness may also exist *between* institutions. For example, Elbaum and Lazonick (1986) and Zeitlin (1987, pp. 174–5) argue that Britain's industrial relations system and its pattern of industrial organization at the turn of the century were highly interrelated. To the extent that this is the case, and changes in one institution require complementary changes to a second with which it is interrelated, connectedness between institutions will clearly compound the type of problem, already identified, concerning the size of the decision making unit relative to that of the 'institutional unit' which requires change. Again, the possibility arises that faced with non-marginal changes beyond the control of any one individual decision making unit, the economy will experience lock-in to an inefficient institution.

When interrelatedness exists between institutions, a second potential problem arises. Even if the decision making unit is relatively large, changing an inefficient institution may be prohibitively costly due to the changes that would be required in other institutions with which it is interrelated. This is despite the fact that net benefits would accrue to changing the inefficient institution itself, and that such changes might actually occur in a competitor economy which suffers a lower degree of institutional interrelatedness. Even though the economy would be acting rationally on a cost benefit basis by not changing the inefficient institution, it may nevertheless experience 'regret', resulting from the knowledge that it is locked in to an institution which is demonstrably inferior to an available alternative that is being adopted elsewhere.[26]

ii) The Dynamics of Institutional Hysteresis and the Emergence of Inefficient Institutions

There are two ways of conceiving the emergence of institutional structures: by considering a competitive struggle between existing institutions on the basis of the assumption that one will emerge as dominant, or by considering the processes leading up to the very genesis of a particular institutional form. We will examine each of these conceptions in turn, illustrating that in both cases, the dynamics of path dependence inherent in the model of institutional hysteresis suggest mechanisms which may lead to the emergence of inefficient institutions.

As noted earlier, an emphasis on the role of 'natural selection' in the emergence of dominant institutional forms is common in some variants of the NIE. The natural selection mechanism conceives institutional outcomes as arising over time, as a result of a sequential, competitive struggle for survival between pre-existing institutions.[27] Usually, the outcomes of this process are held to be efficient. However, as Langlois (1986) notes:

. . . organizations well designed to economize on transaction costs in the long run may find themselves selected out by a very inhospitable selection

Figure 5.2   Path Dependent 'Natural Selection'

| Nature of Economic Environment | $\longrightarrow$ | Survival of Particular Organizational Forms | $\longrightarrow$ | Nature of Economic Environment | $\longrightarrow$ | and so on |

environment in the short run, leaving behind an observed population of relatively ill adapted forms.

(Langlois, 1986, p. 21)

The causal chain underlying this reasoning is of the form in Figure 5.2. This path dependent process contains no necessary implication that surviving organizations (and hence the institutions they embody) will be efficient. On the contrary, as Langlois effectively argues, a hostile short-run selection environment may mean that institutional forms which are efficient in some long-run sense are 'selected out' in the short run, the bequest to the future of this process being a collection of inefficient institutional forms. If this creates a subsequent selection environment which is again hostile to efficient institutions, then the process will become self reinforcing over time. As efficient institutions are repeatedly selected out, so inefficient institutional forms will emerge as dominant.

To illustrate this, consider the following example adapted from Hodgson (1991). Suppose there exist two types of firms, Type I and Type II, in an expanding market which is attracting new entrants. The profits, π, earned by these firms are described as follows:

$$\text{Type I: } \pi = \pi_I \qquad\qquad\qquad [5.1]$$

$$\text{Type II: } \pi = \pi_{II} = 40 + \frac{1}{2} \cdot \pi_I \qquad [5.2]$$

where π_I denotes the percentage of Type I firms in the market. The difference in the profit structures of these firms is intended to capture differences in their internal organization. Hence Type I firms engage in knowledge sharing, and their profit structure reflects the fact that such firms are highly interdependent. Meanwhile, Type II firms do not share knowledge, although they benefit partially from the existence of Type II firms due to knowledge 'spillovers' from the latter. Suppose we choose an initial environment in which Type I firms account for less than 80 per cent of all firms in the market. Inspection of the profit functions in [5.1] and [5.2] reveals that there exists an incentive for each new entrant to be of Type II.[28] Furthermore, as the proportion of Type II firms in the market increases, so the selection environment will become less and less favourable to Type I firms over time. Eventually, Type II firms will entirely dominate the market, despite the fact that the average profitability of these firms will be just 40 units, compared to average profits of 100 units that would be realized if Type I firms gained total market domination. The selection path emerging from the chosen initial conditions will therefore routinely select out the efficient practice of knowledge sharing, and form a 'groove' dominated by an inferior institution. If the economy subsequently becomes locked in to this self-selecting inefficient institution, then as was demonstrated earlier, it will persist over time.

The preceding arguments suggest that the process of 'natural selection' amongst competing alternatives envisaged by authors such as Alchian (1950) and Friedman (1953) may not give rise to the emergence of efficient institutions if the process of selection is path dependent. This relationship between hysteresis and inefficient outcomes is analogous to a process of selection between exogenously given, Pareto rankable multiple equilibria. However, the type of path dependence inherent in the model of institutional hysteresis affects more than simply the process of selection between *pre-existing* institutional forms. Implicit in this model is the notion that the set of existing institutional forms is not static, but is itself path dependent. This property derives from the principle that past institutions are instrumental in creating a subsequent economic environment from which new institutions originate. In other words, the model involves an endogenous process of institutional *creation* (rather than simply *selection*); it conceives society as endogenously creating its own set of future institutional possibilities.

The notion of institutional creation is omitted from the Alchian/Friedman concept of evolutionary natural selection, which, as noted earlier, concentrates on the competition for survival amongst pre-existing institutional forms. However, institutional creation is vital to the process of institutional evolution, not least because it may, in and of itself, be responsible for the emergence of inefficient institutions. Hence note that in the model of institutional hysteresis, prior institutions create an environment in which economic behaviour takes place, and from which new institutions may subsequently emerge. The question that arises, then, is whether this environment is conducive to the creation of efficient institutions. Just as the *selection* environment may be hostile to the selection of efficient institutions, so now the *creation* environment may be hostile to their very origination. For example, the type of institutions that are created in a particular economic environment may depend more on the ease with which they can be created than on their efficiency properties (Hodgson, 1991). To see this, reconsider the earlier example involving Type I and Type II firms. Suppose now that a new industry is emerging in an initial economic environment characterized by decentralized decision making and adversarialism. Under these conditions, which are antithetical to the cooperation required for knowledge sharing, it may be easier for individuals to create 'closed' firms than ones which engage in knowledge sharing. Hence only Type II firms may ever be created in the new industry, regardless of the existence of any efficiency gains that would result from externalities associated with the institution of knowledge sharing.

It is even conceivable that initially efficient institutions may bequeath an evolutionary time path which ultimately results in the creation of inefficient institutions. This point can be illustrated by the following example. Both Cornwall (1990) and Bowles *et al.* (1990) argue that the post-war (1945–c.1966) institutions of social cooperation in advanced capitalist economies, which included the rise of the welfare state and greater acceptance of the labour movement, were functional to the dynamics of the post-war 'golden age' of macroeconomic performance in these economies.[29] However, they argue that this economic environment fostered new demands from labour which were beyond the domain of the original capital–labour consensus.[30] Hence the latter was replaced by a newly created (path specific) set of labour market institutions based on adversarial industrial relations, which both Cornwall and Bowles *et al.* identify as having been dysfunctional to advanced capitalist macroeconomic performance since the late 1960s. The 'efficient' capital–labour consensus therefore ultimately gave rise to the subsequent creation of new, but inefficient, labour market institutions.[31]

The consequences of path dependence for the processes of institutional selection and institutional creation clearly illustrate that the dynamics of the model of institutional hysteresis are fundamentally incompatible with the notion that emerging institutions are always efficient.

VI INSTITUTIONS IN AN EVOLVING HYSTERETIC ECONOMY

The preceding analysis creates a picture of capitalism as a system which is dependent on institutions for its successful operation, but which contains no mechanism to ensure that efficient institutions will automatically emerge and persist. On the contrary, we have seen that conceiving institutional evolution in terms of a model of institutional hysteresis is immediately suggestive of mechanisms which will give rise to the emergence and persistence of inefficient institutions. These mechanisms arise from the sequential nature of the joint interaction between institutions (structure) and economic activity (action). They suggest that in the course of its development, an economy will endogenously generate institutional changes and/ or institutional inertia which may be either more or less functional to its macroeconomic performance.

There are obvious parallels between these considerations and those developed in Chapter 4 – especially insofar as we have now seen that institutional evolution, as with technological evolution, can be influenced by the problem of lock-in. Bearing this parallel in mind, it is not surprising that the potential consequences for relative growth of institutional evolution in the presence of lock-in mirror the potential consequences of technological evolution in the presence of lock-in as discussed in Chapter 4. In short, the maintenance of high growth dynamics depends in part on the maintenance of an institutional regime conducive to these dynamics. Inefficient institutional evolution may cause a virtuous circle of cumulative causation to break down. In order to see why this is so, it is instructive to concentrate on the institutions of the labour market.[32]

i) Labour Market Institutions and Their Effects on Growth

An important basic assumption in the model developed in Chapter 3 is that there exists a stable wage distribution and a variable productivity growth distribution across regions. This, in turn, gives rise to a varying efficiency wage distribution. It is self reinforcing changes in the efficiency wage distribution due to increasing returns which underlie the dynamics of the model. Suppose, however, that we now allow institutional changes in the labour market induced in the course of a virtuous circle to affect the nominal wage distribution between regions. Specifically, suppose that these institutional changes can give rise to upwardly flexible wages in a virtuous circle economy, which capture an increasing share of the productivity gains arising from dynamic increasing returns. Then the ability of this region to maintain a relatively favourable rate of inflation, on which the subsequent growth of exports and hence the furtherance of the virtuous circle itself depend, will be impaired. This 'Kaldor effect', so named because it emphasizes the impact of institutional changes on nominal wage relativities and hence the efficiency wage distribution central to the model of Chapter 3, suggests that induced institutional changes may cause the dynamics of a virtuous circle to break down.

Alternatively, suppose that institutional changes induced in the course of a virtuous circle lead to money wage inflation, but this time policy authorities respond by deflating the domestic economy in an attempt to 'discipline labour' and purge the economy of cost based inflation. This 'Cornwall effect', so named because following Cornwall (1990) it emphasizes the impact of institutional change on macroeconomic policy, will depress domestic autonomous demand, which has hitherto been held constant. This will have a direct adverse affect on an economy's short-run rate of growth of output, since growth is proportional to the expansion of autonomous demand by hypothesis (equation [3.4]). However, this demand shock would have to be repeated over time in order for a region to experience a growth climacteric – that is, a deceleration of its trend rate of long-run growth.

Both the Kaldor and the Cornwall effects can be described as 'indirect effects' of institutions on the dynamics of a virtuous circle as previously modelled. They affect the cumulative interaction of export, output and productivity growth via the prior effect of institutions on either nominal wage relativities or macroeconomic policy, which hitherto, we have either treated as constant or else overlooked. Without extending the formal model to incorporate these insights, however, and following Weisskopf *et al.* (1983) and Bowles *et al.* (1990), it is possible to identify mechanisms through which institutions may have a *direct* effect on the dynamics of cumulative causation as modelled in Chapter 3. What may be identified as the 'Bowles, Gordon and Weisskopf (BGW) effect' suggests that labour market institutions may be more or less functional to the rate of productivity growth.

According to the BGW effect, productivity is influenced by the way in which labour resources are utilized at the point of production. Hence an industrial relations system which results in less capital–labour cooperation may affect worker morale and hence work effort, and may also result in an increase in the incidence of disruptions to the production process, such as absenteeism or strikes. This will in turn have an adverse affect on the intensity with which labour resources are utilized over time, and hence retard the rate of productivity growth.

More importantly, the BGW effect also recognizes that productivity growth is vitally dependent on the ability of firms to undergo changes in their processes of production which allow them to reap the advantages of embodied technological progress.[33] Because they have a substantial impact on issues such as control over the labour process, the de- and/or re-skilling of labour, and labour displacement, the ease with which such changes can be made depends significantly on the compliance of labour in the production process. The less compliant labour is, the slower will be the pace of technological change within the firm, which will adversely affect the rate of productivity growth.

ii) Inefficient Institutional Evolution in the Labour Market and its Consequences for Cumulative Causation

In order to illustrate the possible implications of the BGW effect for cumulative causation, consider once again the extended model of this process developed in Chapter 4. Recall that we define $d\dot{Y}_{ji} = \dot{Y}_{ji}^b - \dot{Y}_{ji}^a$, with $d\dot{Y}_{ji} \gg 0$ for all $i = 0, \ldots, t-1$, where $(\dot{Y}_{j0}^b, \ldots, \dot{Y}_{t-1}^b)$ and $(\dot{Y}_{j0}^a, \ldots, \dot{Y}_{t-1}^a)$ represent 'higher' and 'lower' prior growth trajectories respectively. Once again, our concern is with the implications of following the higher growth trajectory for long-run relative growth outcomes given by the equation:

$$\frac{\dot{Y}_{jt}}{\dot{Y}_w} = (\lambda_j \alpha_j \beta_j)^t \frac{\dot{Y}_{j0}}{\dot{Y}_w} + \lambda_j(\gamma_j - \alpha_w \beta_j) \cdot \sum_{i=0}^{t-1} (\lambda_j \alpha_j \beta_j)^i \qquad [3.10]$$

Suppose, then, that:

$$\alpha_{jt} = f_j(\dot{Y}_{j0}, \ldots, \dot{Y}_{jt-1}) \qquad [4.9]$$

where:

$$f'_{ji} \neq 0 \quad \text{for some} \quad i = 0, \ldots, t-1$$

and:

$$D\alpha = \sum_{i=0}^{t-1} f'_{ji} \cdot d\dot{Y}_{ji} \neq 0$$

Once again, the key relation is equation [4.9], which captures the cumulative effect on α_j, and hence the ability of region j to realize dynamic increasing returns, of following the higher rather than the lower growth trajectory, suggesting that this effect is non-zero. In order to parallel the argument developed in Chapter 4, suppose that a sustained period of higher growth in region j promotes institutional interrelatedness and, as a result, lock-in to an institutional regime in the labour market (that is, an industrial relations system) which has ceased to be functional to technological change and hence the realization of dynamic increasing returns and productivity growth. The consequences of this will be reflected in equation [4.9] when $D\alpha < 0$, resulting in a fall in the value of α_j. Other things being equal, this will have implications for the dynamics of region j's virtuous circle identical to those previously identified in Chapter 4. Specifically, since:

$$\frac{\partial \left(\frac{\dot{Y}_{jt}}{\dot{Y}_w} \right)}{\partial \alpha_j} = t \cdot \alpha_j^{t-1} (\lambda_j \beta_j)^t \cdot \frac{\dot{Y}_{j0}}{\dot{Y}_w} + \lambda_j (\gamma_j - \alpha_w \beta_j) \cdot \sum_{i=0}^{t-1} i \cdot \alpha_j^{i-1} (\lambda_j \beta_j)^i \gtrless 0$$

then under the hypothesized conditions, the cumulative effect of initially faster growth will be to lower the subsequent relative growth rate of region j. In other words, given that $D\alpha < 0$, region j will experience a climacteric – a deceleration in its trend rate of relative growth.

The hysteretic nature of institutions, coupled with the fact that hysteretically evolving institutions need not be efficient, therefore suggests a further mechanism whereby supply side changes endogenous to the process of growth and development can cause the breakdown of a virtuous circle. In terms of the causal chain:

$$high \; \dot{X}_t \; \rightarrow \; high \; \dot{Y}_t \; \rightarrow \; high \; \dot{q}_{t+1} \; \rightarrow \; high \; \dot{X}_{t+1} \; and \; so \; on$$

$$b$$

the possibility of inefficient institutional evolution once again implies a 'weak link' at point b, on the supply side of the model of cumulative causation. As before, this 'weak link' implies that comparative long-run growth performance arising from a process of cumulative causation no longer depends only on the initial conditions prevailing in competing regions. And as before, because the effects of growth on institutional interrelatedness and lock-in are asymmetrical, the breakdown of a virtuous circle as hypothesized will be, *ceteris paribus*, permanent rather than transitory.[34]

VII CONCLUSION

Chapters 4 and 5 have shown how a model of cumulative causation can be extended to give rise to a more general, hysteretic model of long-run growth which links Kaldorian dynamics based on increasing returns to dynamics which affect the technological and institutional regimes in an economy, within which growth occurs. In this extended model, success need not generate success indefinitely – it may bequeath the conditions for subsequent relative economic failure. Indeed, current success will only give rise to future success as long as the institutional and technological regimes in the economy remain conducive to the continuance of a virtuous circle.[35]

These results have a number of interesting implications for the evolution of a capitalist system characterized by interregional trade. In particular, they indicate that there are conflicting forces in development, which mean that the growth and accompanying structural change of an economy can at once both stimulate (through the realization of dynamic increasing returns) and hinder (by inducing inefficient technological and/or institutional evolution) its future growth and development. The historical balance of these conflicting forces will govern the long run competitive fate of an initially fast growing region – a balance which, rather than being determinate, can be conceived as depending on a dialectical interaction of these forces.[36] Ultimately, then, the (hysteretic) realized growth path of a capitalist economy can be thought of as just one history out of many possible histories that remain unrealized.

PART III
The Evolution of a Macroeconomy: Growth and Structural Change in the British Economy since 1780

Introduction

In Part II, it was argued that the rates of growth of exports, output and productivity in an economy jointly interact in a self-reinforcing process of cumulative causation. However, it was suggested that success need not create success indefinitely in this framework; a virtuous circle of cumulative causation may induce inefficient technological and/or institutional evolution, leading to the breakdown of high growth dynamics. Augmenting the process of cumulative causation to take account of the evolution of the technological and institutional regimes within which cumulative causation takes place leads to a model with more generally hysteretic properties. The pattern of initial relative success and subsequent relative failure in the same region to which this model can give rise suggests the possibility of 'leapfrogging' in the international ranking of economies by per capita income.

The purpose of Part III is to illustrate the workings of the long-run theory of capitalist development modelled in Part II by reference to the experience of the British economy since 1780. As the 'first industrial nation', Britain enjoyed unprecedented prosperity in the nineteenth century, and dominated the global political economy. However, as early as 1870–1914, Britain's relative economic performance began to falter. In the twentieth century, this relative decline accelerated, and Britain surrendered its pre-eminence in the world economy. Of course, it is by no means unimportant that a number of Britain's competitors experienced industrial revolutions of their own during this period.[1] As illustrated in Chapter 4, autonomous changes in the 'rest of the world' can impact on a region's relative growth experience through either supply or demand side channels. However, it will be argued in what follows that Britain's experience of initial relative success and subsequent relative failure can be understood partly as a path dependent outcome, brought about by sequential patterns of economic activity that have characterized the British economy since its initial industrialization. In particular, we will argue that the period of relative success in the eighteenth and nineteenth centuries bequeathed the conditions for the subsequent period of relative economic failure.

I AN EMPIRICAL METHODOLOGY BASED ON ECONOMIC HISTORY

Throughout Part III, extensive use is made of historical evidence, which is sometimes qualitative in nature. Three important considerations recommend this empirical methodology over an approach based on econometrics. First, as was pointed out in Chapter 3, the model we have used to characterize macroeconomic evolution is not a fully specified model of the macroeconomy, of the type which might be suitable for econometric estimation. Second, given the long-run nature of the study, the lack of continuous (and consistent) data series forms a practical obstacle to econometric analysis. Finally, the emphasis of the theoretical model developed in Part II on the endogenous structural transformation of capitalist economies suggests that the macroeconomic 'data generating process' underlying capitalism is endogenously evolving, at least in the long run, or between what may be identified as different epochs in the history of an economy. This theoretical consideration implies that the classical statistical assumption of a stable population distribution will be violated in long-run time series analyses of capitalism, invalidating econometric results based on this assumption. Furthermore, statistical modelling of the endogenously transforming macroeconomic population distribution underlying the British economy is held to be beyond the scope of the current analysis.

The preceding considerations demand that we eschew econometrics in favour of an alternative empirical methodology. Throughout Part III, we therefore rely on the use of historical evidence. We proceed on the assumption that such evidence is capable of providing a valid indication of the explanatory power of the theory of capitalist development expounded in Part II.

II ORGANIZATION OF PART III

Part III is organized as follows. Chapter 6 provides a brief outline of the history of the British economy since 1780, highlighting the cumulative nature of Britain's rise and subsequent decline. Chapters 7 and 8 then concentrate on the years of relative failure after 1870, arguing that a combination of inefficient technological and institutional evolution help explain Britain's relative economic retardation in the late nineteenth and twentieth centuries.

6 A Brief History of the British Economy since 1780

The history of the British economy has drawn the attention of many leading scholars. Interpretations of distinct sub-periods of this history have been extensively debated – for example, the notion of a 'Great Depression' versus that of an 'Edwardian climacteric' in the late nineteenth century (Richardson, 1965b; Saul, 1969; Matthews *et al.*, 1982) and the role of new industries in the 1930s economic 'recovery' (Richardson, 1962; Dowie, 1968). Others have devoted attention to the formidable task of compiling accurate data to facilitate the economic interpretation of British history (for example, Deane and Cole, 1962; Feinstein 1972; Mitchell, 1988).

There is little that a brief survey of British economic history can add to debates over specific incidents such as the Great Depression. Any such survey is also necessarily limited by the adequacy of available data. These qualifications aside, the purpose of this chapter is to outline the history of the British economy since 1780, showing how the initial relative success and subsequent relative decline of the British economy over this period conforms broadly to the pattern of the hysteretic dynamics discussed in Part II. In keeping with the theoretical analysis of Part II, we will chiefly emphasize the rates of growth of exports, output and productivity when evaluating macroeconomic performance. For expositional purposes, we will divide the period since 1780 into three sub-periods: 1780–1870, 1870–1950, and 1950–89. These correspond respectively to the period of Britain's initial industrial dominance, the period during which its relative decline first became apparent, and the period during which this decline became pronounced.

I 'THE FIRST INDUSTRIAL NATION', 1780–1870

The period 1780–1870 was one of growth and prosperity for the British economy, which culminated in the great Victorian boom between 1850 and 1873 (Church, 1975). During this time, Britain established a dominant position in the global political economy, not least in terms of its levels of per capita income and productivity, and share of world exports.

Table 6.1   Average Annual Rates of Growth of Real GDP, 1700–1870

	1700–80	*1780–1820*	*1820–70*
UK	0.74	1.62	2.0
Netherlands	0.06	0.06	–
France	n.a.	n.a.	1.2
Germany	n.a.	n.a.	1.6
Italy	n.a.	n.a.	1.2
Japan	n.a.	n.a.	0.3
USA	n.a.	n.a.	4.5
ROW simple average	–	–	1.8
ROW weighted average[a]	–	–	1.4

Note: [a] Weights given by level of real GDP at start of period
Source: Maddison (1991, p. 50, pp. 198–9, p. 207)

Table 6.2   Average Annual Rates of Growth of Real GDP
per Capita, 1820–70

	1820–70
UK	1.2
France	0.8
Germany	0.7
Italy	0.4
Japan	0.1
USA	1.5
ROW simple average	0.7
ROW weighted average[a]	0.8

Note: [a] Weights given by level of real GDP per capita at
start of period
Source: Maddison (1991, pp. 6–7, p. 49)

From 1780–1870, Britain experienced rates of growth of output, exports, and productivity which were high relative to the rest of the world (ROW).[1] This is borne out by Tables 6.1–6.4. Tables 6.1 and 6.2 demonstrate the high rates of growth of real GDP and real GDP per capita experienced by Britain relative to the Netherlands prior to 1820, and relative to the rest of the world between 1820 and 1870. According to Church (1975, p. 20), peak rates of output growth during this era were realized during the great Victorian boom, 1850–73. Table 6.3 illustrates Britain's high rate of productivity growth relative to the Netherlands (the technological leader, in terms of its level of productivity, prior to 1820) even

Table 6.3   Average Annual Rates of Productivity Growth, 1700–1870[a]

	1700–80	1780–1820	1820–70
UK	0.27	0.43	1.15
Netherlands	−0.05	−0.05	1.06

Note: [a] Productivity is measured as GDP per person hour (US $, 1985 prices)
Source: Maddison (1991, pp. 276–7)

Table 6.4   Average Annual Rates of Growth of Exports, 1720–1870

	1720–90	1790–1820	1820–70
UK	1.6	2.9	4.9
Netherlands	−0.2	−0.2	–
France	1.2	0.7	4.0
Germany	n.a.	n.a.	4.8
Italy	n.a.	n.a.	3.4
Japan	n.a.	n.a.	n.a.
USA	n.a.	2.4	4.7
ROW simple average	0.5	1.0	4.2

Source: Maddison (1991, p. 75, pp. 311–23)

before 1780. Finally, Table 6.4 draws attention to Britain's superior rate of export growth relative to the rest of the world, the peak rate of growth of 5.6 per cent per annum occurring between 1830 and 1857 (Lee, 1986, p. 117). By the 1870s, Britain's share of total world exports of manufactured goods was 38 per cent, and this had probably been higher in earlier periods (Harley and McCloskey, 1981, p. 51).[2]

The expansion of overseas markets and relatively high (by contemporary international standards) trend rates of productivity and output growth were thus confluent in the British economy during the late eighteenth century and the first three quarters of the nineteenth century. As the 'first industrial nation', Britain achieved international economic pre-eminence, and established itself as technological leader in the world economy by 1820 (Maddison, 1982, 1991). This is illustrated by Tables 6.5 and 6.6, which compare British levels of income per capita and productivity with those of the rest of the world before 1870.

These Tables bear out the fact that by 1820, Britain was both the richest and the most productive nation amongst our comparison group, having

Table 6.5 Levels of Real GDP per Capita, 1820–70 (US $, 1985 Prices)

	1820	1870
UK	1405	2610
Netherlands	1307	2064
France	1052	1571
Germany	937	1300
Italy	960	1210
Japan	588	618
USA	1048	2247

Source: Maddison (1991, pp. 6–7)

Table 6.6 Levels of Productivity, 1700–1870[a]

	1700	1780	1820	1870
UK	0.78	0.97	1.15	2.15
Netherlands	1.14	1.10[b]	1.07	1.82
France	n.a.	n.a.	n.a.	1.15
Germany	n.a.	n.a.	n.a.	1.04
Italy	n.a.	n.a.	n.a.	0.85
Japan	n.a.	n.a.	n.a.	0.39
USA	n.a.	n.a.	n.a.	2.06

Notes: [a] Productivity measured as GDP per person hour (US $, 1985 prices)
 [b] Calculated using average annual rate of productivity growth of −0.05
     per cent, 1700–80
Source: Maddison (1991, pp. 272–7)

surpassed Dutch productivity levels by 1820. However, the dynamic success of the British economy on which this economic supremacy was based, along with its unrivalled dominance of world markets, proved to be of limited duration.

II EMERGING SIGNS OF RELATIVE DECLINE, 1870–1950

The period 1870–1950 itself comprises two distinct sub-periods: 1870–1913, and 1913–50. Between 1870 and 1913, Britain lost the unchallenged international position it had established as the 'first industrial nation'. It is important not to overstate the extent of Britain's relative decline during this period. Its export, output and productivity growth performance were

Table 6.7   Average Annual Rates of Growth of Real GDP, 1870–1950

	1870–1913	1913–50
UK	1.9	1.3
France	1.5	1.1
Germany	2.8	1.3
Italy	1.9	1.5
Japan	2.3	2.2
USA	3.9	2.8
ROW simple average	2.5	1.8
ROW weighted average[a]	2.7	2.2

Note: [a] Weights given by level of real GDP at start of period
Source: Maddison (1991, p. 50, pp. 198–9)

Table 6.8   Average Annual Rates of Growth of Real GDP per Capita,
1870–1950

	1870–1913	1913–50
UK	1.0	0.8
France	1.3	1.1
Germany	1.6	0.7
Italy	1.3	0.8
Japan	1.4	0.9
USA	1.8	1.6
ROW simple average	1.5	1.0
ROW weighted average[a]	1.5	1.1

Note: [a] Weights given by level of real GDP at start of period
Source: Maddison (1991, p. 50, pp. 198–9)

not vastly inferior to that of the emerging new industrial nations (Floud, 1981), nor to Britain's own prior historical record.[3] Furthermore, with approximately a one third share of the world export market for manufactures, Britain continued to dominate world trade. However, Britain's grip on this position of dominance was clearly slipping.

After 1870, Britain was unable to maintain the rates of growth of output that it had achieved earlier in the nineteenth century (Floud, 1981). Tables 6.7 and 6.8 illustrate not only this point, but also that Britain's rate of growth of real income and real income per capita were now slower than the average rates experienced by the rest of the world. In particular, at a rate of 1.9 per cent per annum, Britain's annual average rate of real GDP growth 1870–1913 was lower than that in both the USA (3.9 per cent per

Table 6.9   Average Annual Rates of Productivity Growth, 1870–1950[a]

	1870–1913	1913–50
UK	1.2	1.6
France	1.6	1.9
Germany	1.9	0.0
Italy	1.7	2.0
Japan	1.9	1.8
USA	1.9	2.4
ROW simple average	1.8	1.8
ROW weighted average[b]	1.8	1.9

Notes: [a] Productivity measured as GDP per person hour (US $, 1985 prices)
         [b] Weights given by level of productivity at start of period
Source: Maddison (1991, p. 50, pp. 274–5)

annum) and Germany (2.8 per cent per annum), who were rapidly emerging as Britain's main industrial competitors.[4] Britain's rate of productivity growth also suffers by comparison with the rest of the world after 1870. Table 6.9 suggests that Britain's productivity growth rates 1870–1913 were unfavourable compared with all the countries in our reference group.

The decline in Britain's relative rate of productivity growth after 1870 appears to be robust with respect to changes in the definition of productivity. According to Floud (1981, p. 22), the growth of total factor productivity in Britain averaged just 0.4 per cent per annum 1873–1914. This compared unfavourably with the average rates of productivity growth in both the US (1.2 per cent per annum) and Germany (0.9 per cent per annum).

The geographical distribution of British overseas trade was also transformed after 1870, as Britain's traditional markets became self sufficient in goods such as textiles, which dominated British exports (Floud, 1981; Kaldor, 1981). In some instances (for example, the US) countries which had formerly been traditional markets for British goods actually began to compete with Britain as exporters in their own right. Thus accompanying the changing geographical pattern of its overseas trade, after 1870 Britain experienced a decline in both its absolute and relative rate of growth of exports, and its share of world exports of manufactured goods. These developments are clearly illustrated in Tables 6.10 and 6.11.

In sum, between 1870 and 1913, Britain experienced a decline in its relative rates of growth of exports, output and productivity. This relative decline was exacerbated by the 'Edwardian climacteric' – a historical deceleration in Britain's trend rates of growth of output and productivity

Table 6.10   Average Annual Rates of Growth of Exports, 1870–1950

	1870–1913	1913–50
UK	2.8	0.0
France	2.8	1.1
Germany	4.1	−2.8
Italy	2.2	0.6
Japan	8.5	2.0
USA	4.9	2.2
ROW simple average	4.5	0.6
ROW weighted average[a]	3.2	0.6

Note: [a] Weights given by level of export volume at start of period
Source: Maddison (1991, p. 75, pp. 312–323)

after 1899.[5] Meanwhile, the loss of international markets to Germany, the USA and Japan, and the loss of technological leadership to the USA by 1890 (Maddison, 1982, 1991), were symptomatic of the gradual weakening of Britain's dominant international economic position during the late nineteenth and early twentieth centuries.

Ironically, Britain's relative economic decline was attenuated somewhat during the period 1919–50. This is illustrated in Tables 6.7, 6.8 and 6.9, which indicate no worsening of Britain's relative rate of growth of real output, and some improvement in its relative rate of growth of real output per capita and productivity 1913–50, as compared with the period 1870–1913. Trends in export statistics also reflect some arrest in the pace of Britain's relative economic decline between 1915 and 1950. Although Table 6.10 suggests a further slowdown in Britain's rate of growth of exports after 1913, this occurred in the context of a general and, indeed, more pronounced export growth slowdown in the rest of the world. Moreover, the trend decline in Britain's share of world exports of manufactured goods was (albeit modestly) reversed towards the end of the period. As illustrated in Table 6.11, despite falling rapidly from 31.8 per cent in 1913 to 23.8 per cent in 1929, by 1937 Britain's export share was still as high as 22.3 per cent and had actually risen to 24.6 per cent by 1950.

The deceleration or even reversal of Britain's declining relative economic fortunes between 1913 and 1950 has received widespread attention in the economic history literature, and a number of theories intended to explain this phenomenon have been forwarded. Some authors concentrate on developments in the domestic economy, arguing, for example, that the

Table 6.11   Shares of World Exports of Manufactures, 1899–1950 (per cent)[a]

	1899	1913	1929	1937	1950
UK	34.5	31.8	23.8	22.3	24.6
France	14.9	12.8	11.6	6.2	9.6
Germany	16.6	19.9	15.5	16.5	7.0
Italy	3.8	3.5	3.9	3.7	3.6
Japan	1.6	2.5	4.1	7.4	3.4
USA	12.1	13.7	21.7	20.5	26.6

Note: [a] 'World' excludes small manufacturing countries and the post WWII
        Soviet bloc
Source: Matthews *et al.* (1982, p. 435)

new industries (such as motor vehicles and chemicals) formed a 'development block' which spurred a trend acceleration of British economic growth
during the 1930s (Richardson, 1967). Others have emphasized developments
in the external sector, arguing that Britain's improving fortunes were a
response to changes in commercial policy after 1930, which became
increasingly orientated towards protectionism (Kaldor, 1981; Kitson and
Solomou, 1989).

It is important, however, not to exaggerate the extent of Britain's relative economic 'recovery' after World War I. Britain's real output, real
output per capita, export and productivity growth performance 1913–50
remained inferior to the average performance of the rest of the world
during this period. Britain's performance also lagged considerably behind
the achievements of at least one of the economies – the USA – that by
the turn of the twentieth century had begun to emerge as major threats
to British international pre-eminence.[6] Meanwhile, the inter-war years were
marred by unprecedented social strife which culminated in the equally
unprecedented mass unemployment of the Great Depression. They also
proved to be a period of 'interregnum' in international affairs. With the
end of 'Pax Britannica', the US became poised to replace Britain as the
dominant power in the global political economy.

On the whole, then, the years 1873–1950 can be regarded as a period
of transition for the British economy. Its dynamic macroeconomic performance was, on the whole, worse than it had been between 1780 and
1873, and worse than that of the economies which had begun to emerge
as its chief rivals – but not greatly so. Britain experienced something of
a 'genteel decline'; it remained a major participant in the global economy,
and suffered less from the ravages of the monetary instability of the 1920s
and the Great Depression of the early 1930s than did some of the newer

Table 6.12   Average Annual Rates of Growth of Real GDP, 1950–89

	1950–73	1973–89
UK	3.0	2.0
France	5.0	2.3
Germany	5.9	2.1
Italy	5.6	2.9
Japan	9.3	3.9
USA	3.6	2.7
ROW simple average	5.9	2.8
ROW weighted average[a]	4.5	2.6

Note: [a] Weights given by level of real GDP at start of period
Source: Maddison (1990, p. 50, pp. 198–9)

industrial economies (most notably, Germany and the USA). However, whilst by no means disastrous, Britain's faltering relative economic performance and loss of international pre-eminence during this era appear, in retrospect, to have been clear indications of what lay ahead.

III   THE CONTINUANCE AND EXACERBATION OF RELATIVE DECLINE, 1950–89

The continuance and, indeed, exacerbation of Britain's relative economic decline between 1950 and 1989 is clearly illustrated by a comparison of its export, output and productivity growth performance with that of the other countries in our comparison group. Table 6.12 suggests that although Britain's post-war rates of real output growth were historically high (at least up until the 1970s), they were relatively low compared with those rates achieved by the rest of the world. These trends are also reflected in Britain's relative rate of real per capita output growth, as illustrated in Table 6.13.

Britain's relatively poor output growth performance after 1950 was matched by relatively poor productivity growth performance. Table 6.14 illustrates that between 1950 and 1989, Britain's rate of productivity growth was worse than the average rate experienced by the rest of the world. Moreover, as with output growth performance in Tables 6.12 and 6.13, Table 6.14 reveals that Britain's productivity growth performance was worse than that of any of its major competitors, with the exception of the USA.[7]

Table 6.13   Average Annual Rates of Growth of Real GDP per Capita, 1950–89

	1950–73	1973–89
UK	2.5	1.8
France	4.0	1.8
Germany	4.9	2.1
Italy	5.0	2.6
Japan	8.0	3.1
USA	2.2	1.6
ROW simple average	4.8	2.2
ROW weighted average[a]	3.8	2.2

Note: [a] Weights given by level of real GDP per capita at start of period
Source: Maddison (1991, pp. 6–7, p. 49)

Table 6.14   Average Annual Rates of Productivity Growth, 1950–89[a]

	1950–73	1973–89
UK	3.2	2.3
France	5.0	3.2
Germany	5.9	2.6
Italy	5.8	2.6
Japan	7.6	3.5
USA	2.5	1.0
ROW simple average	5.4	2.6
ROW weighted average[b]	3.1	2.4

Notes: [a] Productivity measured as GDP per person hour (US $, 1985 prices)
           [b] Weights given by level of productivity at start of period
Source: Maddison (1991, p. 51, pp. 274–5)

Meanwhile, as Table 6.15 shows, Britain's rate of growth of exports 1950–89 suffers by comparison with the rates of growth achieved by the rest of the world. Britain's export growth during this period was slower than that achieved in every country in our reference group. It is not surprising, in light of this, to find that Britain's share of world trade in manufactured goods declined monotonically after 1950. This is captured in Table 6.16. During the post-war years, Britain's share of world exports has been surpassed not only by the USA, but also by France, Germany and Japan. Indeed in 1983, Britain became a net importer of manufactures for the first time in its history (Rowthorn and Wells, 1987, p. 98).

Table 6.15   Average Annual Rates of Growth of Exports, 1950–89

	1950–73	1973–89
UK	3.9	3.9
France	8.2	4.6
Germany	12.4	4.7
Italy	11.7	4.9
Japan	15.4	6.8
USA	6.3	4.7
ROW simple average	10.8	5.1
ROW weighted average[a]	10.4	6.0

Note: [a] Weights given by level of export volume at start of period
Source: Maddison (1991, p. 75, pp. 312–23)

Table 6.16   Shares of World Exports of Manufactures, 1950–85 (per cent)

	1950[a]	1962[b]	1970[b]	1980[b]	1985[b]
UK	24.6	15.9	10.8	9.7	7.9
France	9.6	9.2	8.7	10.0	8.4
Germany	7.0	19.9	19.8	19.8	18.6
Italy	3.6	6.0	7.2	7.9	7.7
Japan	3.4	7.4	11.7	14.8	20.0
USA	26.6	20.2	18.5	16.9	16.8

Notes: [a] 'World' excludes small manufacturing countries and the post-WWII
Soviet bloc
[b] 'World' defined as listed countries plus Belgium, Luxembourg,
Netherlands, Canada, Sweden and Switzerland
Sources: Matthews et al. (1982, p. 435); Handbook of International Economic
Statistics (1986)

Whilst the OECD economies as a whole experienced periods of both sustained growth and stagnation between 1950 and 1989, one constant feature of this era was the relatively poor dynamic performance of the British economy. In terms of its export, output and productivity growth performance, Britain was surpassed not only by the US (which finally assumed Britain's former position of world hegemonic power) but also by a number of its European and Asian competitors. In the course of the post-war years, Britain established itself within the OECD as a 'growth laggard'.

IV   THE SIGNIFICANCE OF BRITAIN'S RELATIVE ECONOMIC DECLINE

The figures presented clearly illustrate the decline in Britain's relative dynamic macroeconomic performance since the late nineteenth century. However, it is important to put this decline into context. For example, becoming a 'growth laggard' is of less obvious consequence if a region's competitors only succeed in achieving faster growth through the expansion of resources – especially labour inputs, in which case faster output growth may be offset by faster population growth. Under these circumstances, variations in relative growth performance reveal little about variations in the relative rates of growth of efficiency and living standards between regions. Furthermore, slow growth in and of itself need not imply a relative decline in either absolute standards of living or levels of productivity, if the output/productivity base from which fast growing regions are expanding is small. Similarly, relatively fast export growth may only be achieved by competitors whose initial export base is relatively small, and whose total share of world trade therefore remains small.

In fact, as the tables illustrate, none of these considerations offset our concern with the decline of Britain's relative dynamic macroeconomic performance. As has been amply illustrated in Sections II and III, the relatively slow rate of growth experienced by the British economy since the late nineteenth century has, indeed, been accompanied by relatively slow productivity and per capita income growth. It is also clear from Tables 6.10, 6.11, 6.15 and 6.16 that countries experiencing faster rates of export growth than Britain have generally succeeded in surpassing Britain's share of world exports of manufactures, and have subsequently maintained or further increased their export share whilst Britain's has continued to decline. This illustrates that the decline in Britain's export share has not just occurred as a result of competitors experiencing faster export growth from a smaller initial export base; many of these competitors have surpassed the absolute level of British exports and have continued to achieve faster rates of export growth thereafter.

Slower growth has also acted to the detriment of Britain's relative standard of living and level of productivity. For example, in 1950, output per capita in the UK was higher than in any EEC economy apart from Belgium.[8] By 1973, it was lower than in any EEC economy with the exception of Italy (Cairncross, 1981). Tables 6.17 and 6.18 illustrate more comprehensively the decline of Britain's relative standard of living and level of productivity since the late nineteenth century. These tables suggest that the superior growth performance of Britain's competitors has not merely reflected 'catching up'. On the contrary, by 1989, only Italy and

Table 6.17 Levels of Real GDP per Capita, 1870–1989 (US $, 1985 Prices)

	1870	1913	1950	1973	1989
UK	2610	4024	5651	10063	13468
France	1571	2734	4149	10323[a]	13837
Germany	1300	2606	3339	10110[a]	13989
Italy	1210	2087	2819	8568	12955
Japan	618	1114	1563	9237	15101[a]
USA	2247	4854[a]	8611	14103	18317

Note: [a] Denotes date by which country has overtaken UK
Source: Maddison (1991, pp. 6–7)

Table 6.18 Levels of Productivity, 1870–1989[a]

	1870	1913	1950	1973	1989
UK	2.15	3.63	6.49	13.36	18.55
France	1.15	2.26	4.58	14.00b	21.63[c]
Germany	1.04	2.32	3.40	12.83	19.53[b]
Italy	0.85	1.72	3.52	12.82	18.25[c]
Japan	0.39	0.86	1.69	9.12	15.18
USA	2.06	4.68[b]	11.39	19.92	23.87

Notes: [a] Productivity measured as GDP per person hour (US $, 1985 prices)
       [b] Denotes date by which country has overtaken UK
       [c] Figures are for 1987
Source: Maddison (1991, pp. 274–5)

Japan had failed to surpass Britain's level of productivity, whilst Italy alone continued to lag Britain's level of output per capita (see also Matthews et al., 1982, pp. 29–33). The decline in its relative dynamic macroeconomic performance has clearly relegated Britain to a lower position in the international ranking of economies by per capita income, as the living standards achieved in the 'first industrial nation' have steadily been surpassed by its later industrializing competitors.

V BRITISH ECONOMIC HISTORY SINCE 1780: AN INTERPRETATION

The brief outline of British economic history provided above is congruent with the model of capitalist development outlined in Part II. The period of complementary, relatively high export, output and productivity growth between 1780 and 1870, which established Britain as an international per capita income and productivity leader, was not sustained. Instead, what ensued were subsequent periods of relative economic decline which were at first moderate (1870–1913) and later, more pronounced (the post-war years), and which saw Britain become an export, output and productivity growth laggard.

This pattern of development is consistent with an interpretation of British economic history in terms of the cumulative interaction of export, output and productivity growth in an initial virtuous circle, which subsequently gave rise to the conditions for its own breakdown and hence Britain's relative economic decline. As intimated earlier, external factors certainly influenced Britain's relative economic performance after 1870. However, internal factors were also important. In particular, we will argue that Britain's virtuous circle of relatively high export, output and productivity growth could not be sustained because it occurred in the context of specific technological and institutional regimes – regimes to which Britain was effectively locked in by the end of the nineteenth century, but which were, by that time, unsuitable for the maintenance of relatively fast growth. Britain's inability to switch between technological and institutional regimes helps to explain its relative economic decline after 1870.

The notion that British competitive success in the nineteenth century resulted from a process of cumulative causation is supported by Elbaum (1990). Elbaum argues that examining the structure of British industry and British trade patterns in the nineteenth and early twentieth centuries reveals that Britain's nineteenth century prosperity and dominance of the world economy are best explained by cumulative advantages related to its status as the 'first industrial nation'. First, he points to the concentration of British exports in a small number of traditional staple industries with strong interconnections (for example, textiles and textile machinery.)[9] Second, Elbaum points out that these sectors built and retained a dominant position in the British (and indeed world) economy despite lacking any distinctive 'comparative advantage' in technology or factor endowments. For example, they were extensive employers of low skilled labour in what was essentially a high wage economy.[10]

This leads Elbaum to suggest that Britain's export and output growth success in the staple industries was related to cumulative competitive advantages arising from economies of scale. For example, the cotton industry enjoyed external economies of scale arising from the combination of its vertical and horizontal specialization with its geographical concentration in Lancashire (Lazonick, 1983, 1986; Farnie, 1979). Individually, small and specialized British cotton firms achieved long production runs, whilst as a whole they produced a wide variety of products. The local development of an organized commodity market for raw cotton allowed spinning firms to keep small inventories and transferred the risks associated with the importing of raw cotton to specialized traders. Finally, the growth of the textile machinery industry in Lancashire reduced the cost of capital for the British cotton industry, and eliminated the need for spinning and weaving firms to hire their own maintenance staff.

Scale economies resulted in efficiency gains for British textile firms which offset their relatively high wages (Elbaum, 1990) and contributed to the low costs per efficiency unit of labour in the British cotton industry (Clark, 1987). This in turn contributed to the export success of the industry, which, if it could not always undersell its competitors (particularly those in the Far East), was consistently able to supply a more varied and higher quality product (Farnie, 1979). Furthermore, it is important to acknowledge the role of expanding external markets in promoting and reinforcing output and productivity gains in the British cotton industry during the nineteenth century. Hence export success encouraged entry into the cotton industry, which, in turn, tended to reinforce the geographical concentration and specialization of the industry – precisely the sources of its external economies of scale (Lazonick, 1983, 1986). The success of the British cotton industry, then, seems to have been directly influenced by exactly the sort of cumulative process propagated by growing demand and increasing returns to scale that was modelled in Chapter 3.

Evidence also suggests that returns to scale, and hence the cumulative interaction of output growth and efficiency gains, were instrumental in the success of a number of other British industries which grew to dominate world markets during the nineteenth century, such as shipping and shipbuilding (Elbaum, 1990). The British shipbuilding industry became internationally dominant between 1860 and 1880, during which time the industry experienced a technological transition from sail to steam power, and from wooden to iron hull construction (Elbaum, 1990; Lorenz, 1991, p. 5). Instrumental in this expansion was the growth of the industry's domestic market, coupled with the simultaneous growth of export demand (Pollard, 1957). These developments were concomitant with the realization by British shipbuilders of economies of scale, which accrued in two ways. First, the growth and consequent extent of their markets enabled British shipbuilders to achieve a degree of specialization which was unprecedented in other maritime nations (Pollard, 1957; Pollard and Robertson, 1979; Lorenz, 1991). This specialization occurred primarily at the yard level, different individual shipyards specializing in the production of different classes of vessels. Second, the growth of the industry coupled with its geographical concentration resulted in external economies of scale. The British shipbuilding industry was concentrated on the Clyde river of Scotland and in the north-east of England, the former accounting for 30–35 per cent and the latter for 50–55 per cent of total mercantile tonnage by the end of the nineteenth century (Lorenz, 1991, pp. 25–6). The importance of this geographical concentration lay in the labour intensive methods of British shipyards.[11] British firms relied on the 'squad system', whereby skilled workers who were not permanently attached to the firm were contracted for specific jobs (Elbaum, 1990). According to Elbaum:

> British employment arrangements were made possible by the size and regional concentration of the British (shipbuilding) industry, which created well articulated labour markets for apprenticeship-trained craftsmen.
>
> (Elbaum, 1990, p. 1265)

Hence the growth of the shipbuilding industry after 1860, spurred by the growth of its internal and external markets, facilitated specialization and resulted in external economies of scale which, in turn, '. . . assured it (the shipbuilding industry) of a dominant position in world markets' (Elbaum, 1990, p. 1264). By the 1890s, Britain accounted for 80 per cent of the world's mercantile tonnage (Elbaum, 1990, pp. 1264–5) and achieved levels of labour productivity substantially greater than those of its foreign rivals (Pollard, 1957). Clearly, the development of the British shipbuilding industry in the mid-Victorian era is confluent with the pattern of cumulative export, output and productivity growth emphasized in Chapter 3.

Another pertinent example of cumulative processes influencing Britain's relative economic success is provided by the textile machinery industry, an important branch of British engineering. Britain's initial technical superiority in the production of textile machinery, established in the eighteenth century and prompted by demand from the domestic cotton textile industry, was subsequently reinforced by the expansion of the industry's overseas markets (Elbaum, 1990).[12] This gave rise to dynamic economies of scale within the firm based on learning by doing and specialization (Saul, 1968; Farnie, 1979). Hence:

> [t]he market for textile machinery became large enough to permit the separation of the industry both from the cotton industry and from general engineering. [This] reduced the industry's costs by providing full employment for highly skilled and specialized workers and enabled it to

supply machinery of the highest quality and the lowest price in the shortest time.

(Farnie, 1979, p. 55)

As late as 1914, the largest of the six Lancashire firms that dominated the British textile machinery industry still produced an output equal to that of the entire US textile machinery industry (Saul, 1968, pp. 191–192).

The preceding evidence suggests that the competitive success of a number of key British industries in the nineteenth century was directly related to the cumulative export, output and productivity growth mechanism based on increasing returns to scale that was identified in Part II. However, if Britain's nineteenth century prosperity can be understood in terms of a virtuous circle of cumulative causation, the question arises as to how this growth dynamic might have broken down, giving rise to Britain's subsequent relative economic failure. In keeping with the model developed in Part II, the argument that we will pursue is that Britain's virtuous circle of export, output and productivity growth prior to 1870 was affected by mechanisms endogenous to the dynamics of this virtuous circle itself. It will be contended that Britain provides a striking example of the notion that success need not breed success indefinitely, but may instead sow the seeds of its own long-run destruction.

In order to develop this argument, we will concentrate on two processes which have been instrumental in determining the evolution of the British economy since 1870. The first of these is the problem of technological interrelatedness and hence lock-in to certain regimes of interrelated technologies and lines of production. This phenomenon was especially evident during the period 1870–1930, having both intra and inter firm dimensions. Technological interrelatedness and lock-in affected both the choice of technology and hence the rate of productivity growth in British industry, and the sectoral composition of Britain's output, to which its export success was partially linked in a growing world economy progressing through a commodity hierarchy.

The second process is institutional hysteresis, especially as it has affected the evolution of institutional regimes in the British system of industrial relations. This factor has been particularly significant throughout the twentieth century,[13] and has again had two dimensions, related this time to the persistence and creation of inefficient institutions. Together, these aspects of institutional evolution have tended to be dysfunctional to British economic performance during the twentieth century.

The remaining chapters of Part III are devoted to investigating these causes of Britain's relative economic decline in detail. Chapter 7 examines the prevalence of technological interrelatedness and lock-in in British industry at the turn of the century, and the extent to which this caused inefficient technological evolution in the British economy. Chapter 8, meanwhile, develops a causal chain designed to illustrate the process of institutional hysteresis as it has affected the British industrial relations system in the course of the twentieth century. Once again, emphasis is placed on the extent to which factors such as lock-in generated inefficient institutional evolution, and how this contributed to Britain's long-run relative economic decline.

7 Technological Interrelatedness and Lock-In in the British Economy, 1870–1930

By the turn of the twentieth century, the resources of the British economy were concentrated in the production of a narrow range of output emanating from staple industries such as cotton and coal, and in traditional (that is, mid nineteenth century) techniques of production. In 1907, 46 per cent of Britain's net industrial output was accounted for by just three industries – coal, iron and steel, and textiles (Aldcroft, 1968, p. 23).[1] As was noted in Chapter 6, the same industries also dominated Britain's exports. For example, cotton textiles alone made up 25 per cent of Britain's total visible exports in 1910, whilst textiles as a whole accounted for fully 37 per cent (Elbaum, 1990, p. 1257). At the same time, Britain's manufacturers were slow to adopt new technology. By 1913, for example, new ring frame technology accounted for 87 per cent of all spindles in the US cotton industry, compared to just 19 per cent in the British cotton industry (Lazonick, 1986, p. 19).

The explanation for and implications of this industrial structure – what brought it about and how it affected the British economy – are controversial subjects. One popular thesis concentrates on the failings of British entrepreneurship in the late Victorian era. It is argued that the maturing of British firms bred an inertia that accounts for the continued use of traditional technologies and the continued production of staple commodities after 1870 (see, for example, Aldcroft, 1964). However, the idea that Britain suffered an 'entrepreneurial malaise' during the late nineteenth century, as a result of which the propensity of British firms to undergo changes in their methods and lines of production was significantly weakened, is by no means universally accepted (see, for example, Payne, 1974 and Sandberg, 1981).

An alternative to the theory of entrepreneurial failure is based on the notion that at the turn of the century, the British economy was 'over committed' to the industrial structure that had provided the wellsprings of its nineteenth century success (Richardson, 1965b; Aldcroft, 1968). The term 'over commitment' is intended

... to convey the impression that once resources are tied up in certain sectors (technologies) ... there are high costs involved in releasing them for other uses ... ; ceteris paribus, the greater the proportion of resources 'committed,' the more inflexible the economy's structure.

(Richardson, 1965b, p. 238)

As illustrated in Chapter 3 and again in Chapter 6, specialization can be advantageous if it yields increasing returns to scale. However, as illustrated in Chapters 4 and 5, sustained growth within a particular technological and/or institutional context can become disadvantageous. Richardson's hypothesis suggests that by the early twentieth century, Britain's resources were *too* concentrated in a nineteenth century industrial structure. The commitment of British producers to a narrow range of staple industries and traditional techniques of production is seen to have been symptomatic of an inflexibility in the British economy, which thwarted technological and structural change and was thus instrumental in Britain's relative economic decline around the turn of the century.[2]

Richardson's concept of over commitment is clearly similar to the concept of lock-in developed in Part II. Both are intended to capture the notion that technological and structural change in an economy may be constrained by features of the production process inherited from the past. Furthermore, in their accounts of technological and structural change, neither concept relies on the idea of 'entrepreneurial failure' which, as reasonable as this idea might actually be, is especially difficult to verify empirically.[3]

Building on Richardson, then, in what follows, we will concentrate on the possibility that even if Britain's entrepreneurs were individually rational and well motivated, British firms were locked in to a prior industrial structure which was no longer functional to the maintenance of high growth dynamics. In keeping with the analysis of Chapter 4, we will stress the role of technological interrelatedness in generating this lock-in. Hence we proceed on the hypothesis that technological interrelatedness and lock-in constrained the processes of technological and structural change in the British economy. This adversely affected Britain's productivity and export growth rates, causing the cumulative export, output and productivity growth dynamics which had characterized Britain's relative economic success prior to 1870 to break down. These developments, in turn, contributed to the period of relative economic decline that Britain experienced thereafter.

I TECHNOLOGICAL INTERRELATEDNESS, LOCK-IN AND OVER COMMITMENT IN THE BRITISH ECONOMY

As intimated earlier, two aspects of over commitment or lock-in affected technological and structural change in the British economy after 1870. The first aspect relates to the continued use of certain *methods* of production, and the second to the continued manufacture of certain *lines* of production. The first of these two aspects involves the problem of lock-in to outmoded technologies and techniques of production.

In Chapter 4, it was demonstrated that technological interrelatedness within and between firms can give rise to this type of problem.[4] Hence if the technical components of the production process are interrelated, the introduction of a new technology may involve non-marginal changes which it is rational for the individual firm to avoid within any given period. As a result, firms will become locked in to pre-existing methods of production.

If lock-in impairs the rate of adoption of a new technology, and hence the realization of dynamic scale economies accruing to it, the rate of productivity growth within an economy may be arrested. This will retard the cumulative dynamics of export, output and productivity growth. Furthermore, if the new technology is adopted faster in competing regions, these may subsequently realize a relatively higher rate of productivity growth. Technological interrelatedness and lock-in, which will be manifest in the form of an over commitment to traditional and obsolete technologies, may then result in the displacement of a virtuous circle of export, output and productivity growth by a vicious circle of cumulative relative economic decline.

To what extent do the theoretical dynamics outlined above provide insights into Britain's relative economic decline after 1870? One way in which to pursue this question is to examine the structure of British industry 1870–1930 in search of examples of technological obsolescence, and identify the ways in which this was related to the phenomena of technological interrelatedness, lock-in and poor productivity performance. This approach is not without difficulties, not least because technological interrelatedness is not itself a quantifiable variable. It is also difficult to procure comparative cost data to prove conclusively that the technological interrelatedness of existing plant and machinery was a source of cost disadvantage to British producers operating in an environment of technological change. However, a substantial body of historical evidence points to the importance of technological interrelatedness in British industry. Furthermore, it seems reasonable to assume that costs will increase monotonically with the scale of the changes to existing plant and machinery which are necessary to accommodate a new technology. This suggests that where technological interrelatedness proliferates, it will be a source of relative cost disadvantage to producers faced with the prospects of technological change.

The following examples provide a pertinent illustration of the extent to which technological interrelatedness and lock-in at the industry level contributed to the relative decline of the British economy after 1870. Whilst the number of examples provided may at first appear quantitatively small, recall that the British economy was highly concentrated in a narrow range of industries. Hence it is not unreasonable to draw conclusions about the state of the British economy at this time by examining some of the small number of industries which so dominated its industrial structure.

II THE COTTON TEXTILE INDUSTRY

The experience of the cotton industry provides what is perhaps the best example of technological interrelatedness and lock-in in the British economy. Although Britain continued to dominate world trade in cotton 1870–1914, the growth of the British cotton industry declined markedly after 1870, and this was coupled with the loss of traditional overseas markets and a decreasing share of world trade in cotton goods (Tyson, 1968).[5] After 1914, the decline of the cotton industry continued apace, with Britain initially losing lower quality markets to Japan and India, and subsequently losing higher quality markets to the producers of Europe and the US (Lazonick, 1986).

One reason for the climacteric and decline experienced by the British cotton industry relates to the technical obsolescence of the industry dating from the late nineteenth/early twentieth centuries, and its subsequent loss of relative efficiency. Even as late as the 1950s, the dominant technologies in the British industry were the spinning mule and the plain or power loom. These technologies were dominant despite the availability, by the mid to late nineteenth century, of technically superior alternatives – the ring frame and the automatic loom.

The spinning mule comprised a fixed bank of rollers and a movable carriage.[6] Spinning took place as the carriage moved away from the rollers, and stopped as the carriage returned to its original position, winding the yarn onto a bobbin as it did so. On the ring frame, yarn passed through a bank of rollers and then around a ring fixed about a rotating bobbin. The ring frame stretched and twisted the yarn into its final form as it was being wound onto the bobbin at the centre of the ring. The advantage of the ring frame over the mule was that it spun continuously, whereas the latter spun only intermittently due to its separation of the spinning and winding processes.

The power loom was originally designed to mechanize the process of weaving, but in fact required close manual supervision for two reasons. First, if a warp thread broke, the power loom continued to work.[7] It had to be stopped manually and the break repaired to prevent serious deterioration in the quality of the final cloth. Second, when the shuttle of a power loom exhausted its yarn, the loom had to be stopped and the yarn manually replaced and rethreaded. The automatic loom was purposely designed to overcome these problems. It stopped automatically in the event of warp breakage, and automatically changed and rethreaded the shuttle. These improvements not only meant that automatic looms were required to stop less frequently than power looms, but also that they required less intense manual supervision. Hence a single loom operator could tend more automatic looms than power looms.

The failure of the British cotton industry to adopt newly emerging ring frame and automatic loom technology, in spite of its relative efficiency, is illustrated by the fact that by 1913/14, only 19 per cent of all spindles in Britain were ring spindles (compared to 87 per cent in the US), and only 1–2 per cent of all looms were automatic looms (compared to 40 per cent in the US) (Lazonick, 1986, p. 19). Indeed, as late as 1954/5, ring spindles still accounted for less than half of Britain's spinning capacity, and automatic looms only 12 per cent of its weaving capacity, whereas the spinning mule and power loom on which Britain continued to rely had completely disappeared from the US cotton industry (Lazonick, 1986, p. 20).

Britain's adherence to obsolete spinning and weaving technology involved substantial drawbacks. By 1900, the mule and power loom had essentially been perfected (limiting the extent to which learning by doing could subsequently raise the productivity of this technology), whereas the ring frame and automatic loom constituted an untapped source of technological improvement (Tyson, 1968). Consequently, deprived of the source of dynamic scale economies that were accruing to its competitors, Britain's rate of productivity growth declined relative to that of countries such as the US even before 1914 (Tyson, 1968, p. 123). By 1960, labour productivity in the French, German and Dutch cotton industries was 30–60 per cent higher than in the British industry (Lazonick, 1986, p. 20).

If one source of the competitive decline of the British cotton industry was thus its technical obsolescence and consequent inefficiency, the question arises as to why the industry continued to rely on obsolete technology?

Why was the adoption of the ring frame and the automatic loom so slow in Britain relative to the rates of adoption achieved by its emerging competitors such as the US? Historical evidence suggests that one factor contributing to the continued use of the spinning mule and power loom was technological interrelatedness, which subsequently locked the British cotton industry in to its nineteenth century technological structure.

i) Technological Interrelatedness within Cotton Firms

Both Frankel (1955) and Tyson (1968) suggest that technological interrelatedness within the firm were responsible for the slow adoption of the automatic loom in the British cotton industry. The substitution of automatic looms for power looms entailed not just the replacement of one machine with another, but usually involved the complete redesign of weaving sheds (Tyson, 1968). For example, the introduction of automatic looms required the strengthening of flooring, the elimination of pillars, and the respacing of other machinery (Frankel, 1955). This suggests that the changes necessary within established British weaving firms to accommodate the automatic loom were of a non-marginal nature, requiring complementary changes in the other components of nineteenth century plant and equipment in which the British cotton industry had invested heavily. Other things being equal, technological interrelatedness may thus have made automatic loom technology prohibitively expensive for British weaving firms to adopt. The consequent lock-in of British firms to a prior (and obsolete) technology would help explain the slow rate of adoption of the automatic loom, and hence the declining relative efficiency of the British cotton industry.

ii) Technological Interrelatedness between Cotton Firms

Even if *existing* British cotton firms were locked in to obsolete technology due to intra-firm interrelatedness, this cannot explain why *new entrants* into the industry were not faster in the adoption of new technology. For this reason, it is important that it is also possible to identify *inter*-firm dimensions of technological interrelatedness within the British cotton industry. This source of interrelatedness would have affected the choice of technology of both new and existing firms.

The nineteenth century industrial organization of the cotton industry was typified by a high degree of both horizontal and vertical specialization (Lazonick, 1983). This high degree of specialization appears to have hindered the introduction of new spinning and weaving technology in the late nineteenth and early twentieth centuries. For example, because mule yarn was wound on lightweight paper tubes whereas ring frame yarn was wound on heavier wooden bobbins, the latter was more expensive to ship between geographically separate spinning and weaving firms (Lazonick, 1986). Given the industrial organization peculiar to the British cotton industry, then, ring frame technology may not have been the least cost method of production for individual British spinning firms.

More importantly, the introduction of new weaving technology required complementary changes in spinning firms (and vice versa) if the industry as a whole was to successfully convert from its traditional low throughput to the new high throughput technology (Frankel, 1955; Lazonick, 1986). For example, automatic looms required weft yarn in larger packages than spinning mules, the dominant technology in spinning firms, were able to produce (Frankel, 1955).

Furthermore, Lazonick (1981) argues that vertical specialization may have deterred investment in high throughput weaving technology by creating uncertainty about the supply of and demand for yarn of differing qualities. An important feature of the Lancashire cotton industry was that spinning firms purchased raw cotton week by week as orders for finished yarn were placed. This, coupled with the fact that the spinning mule was capable of spinning cotton of a wide range of different qualities, allowed British spinning firms to take advantage of even short term changes in the relative prices of cotton of different qualities.[8] Uncertainty in the short term concerning the quality of yarn may therefore have deterred weavers from investing in the automatic loom, which required yarn of a high quality for its successful operation. The consequent continued demand for mule yarn by British weavers may, in turn, have deterred spinners from investing in ring frame technology, due to the lack of any apparent market for yarn of a consistent high quality (Lazonick, 1981).

The technology of spinning firms was obviously beyond the control of individual weaving firms, and vice versa. Hence regardless of the cost efficiency of the new versus the old technology, the small size of the individual decision making unit (the individual spinning/weaving firm) relative to the size of the technological unit which required change (current weaving *and* spinning technology) hindered the adoption of new technology (ring frames and automatic looms). In this case, then, inter-firm technological interrelatedness locked the British cotton industry into obsolete nineteenth century technology by virtue of the absence of a centralized decision making authority amongst vertically specialized spinning and weaving firms.

iii)   Inter-Firm Interrelatedness and the Issue of Consolidation

The disadvantages of horizontal and vertical specialization in the cotton industry raise the question as to why spinning and weaving firms *were* so specialized. One reason for this was specific to the structure of the cotton industry itself. By the mid-nineteenth century, the extensive degree of existing specialization inherited as a legacy of Britain's early industrialization afforded considerable external economies of scale. These, in turn, encouraged new nineteenth century entrants into the cotton industry to replicate the existing pattern of specialization (Lazonick, 1983). Hence the prior structure of the Lancashire cotton industry seems to have discouraged the formation of integrated firms in the nineteenth century, regardless of the fact that subsequently, such firms would have proved to have been better suited to the adoption of new spinning and weaving technology. This is not to suggest that mid-nineteenth century cotton firms suffered from entrepreneurial failure, however; firms cannot reasonably be criticized for failing to organize in anticipation of technological innovations which had yet to occur.

Even so, none of these would seem to explain why the cotton industry *remained* specialized even after the advantages of integration became apparent. From a Coasian perspective, it appears that integration should have followed automatically under these circumstances.[9] Why did British cotton firms not imitate trends in the German and US economies towards the consolidation and rationalization of industry? The answer – which applies not just to the cotton industry but to the entire British economy – would appear to be that consolidation is not the simple process of substituting organization for markets at the margin that the Coase theorem suggests it is. First, there may be unique problems associated with amalgamating *existing* enterprises as opposed to forming new, integrated firms. Such amalgamation may not be costless, and so integrated production may be more attractive and, therefore, more frequently observed in new industrial centres (such as late nineteenth century Germany and the USA) than in older ones (such as late nineteenth century Britain). Furthermore, amalgamating existing concerns involves organizational changes which may conflict with vested interests within these concerns, again thwarting the pace of integration (Lazonick, 1983).

Second, a concern for both new and existing firms is the nature of capital markets, and the consequent availability of finance to support the objective of integration. It is questionable as to whether, by the late nineteenth century, the British financial sector was oriented towards facilitating the type of industrial consolidation activity we are contemplating. Best and Humphries (1986) argue that whether or not the British financial sector differed from its US and German counterparts with respect to its attitudes towards risk and uncertainty, anti-industrial biases, or lack of information, it did differ by failing to participate directly in the restructuring of domestic industry in the late nineteenth century. Whilst German credit banks and US investment banks promoted combination and rationalization in the German and US manufacturing sectors, British financial developments in the late nineteenth century provided no such spur for integration. On the contrary, Best and Humphries argue that by providing easy access to funds for new capacity, the British financial sector encouraged entry, thus exacerbating competitive pressures in product markets. This forced existing firms to increase dividends in the short term in order to attract new external capital, thus preventing them from amassing retained earnings which might otherwise have accumulated into a viable source of internal financing for acts of consolidation.

Similar themes are emphasized by Kennedy (1987), whose account is couched in terms of Akerlof's (1970) theory of asymmetric information, the existence of 'lemons' and the consequent 'thinning' of markets. Kennedy emphasizes the role played by financial intermediaries in reducing Akerlofian informational obstacles, and so facilitating trades (in this case, long-term finance) which would not otherwise occur. He argues that British financial intermediation was deficient by comparison with that found in both Germany and the USA. Hence by the last quarter of the nineteenth century, British banks had become specialists in short term finance, and were unwilling to participate in the long run financing of industry. Meanwhile, the stock exchange specialized in government debt, foreign loans and public or semi-public utility securities – but not the finance of domestic industry. Whilst it is beyond the scope of this analysis to fully examine the controversial relationship between British finance and industry, the preceding arguments do suggest that the failure of the British financial sector to play as active a role in the reorganization of domestic industry as its US and German counterparts may have been a key factor inhibiting widespread consolidation in British industry.

Finally, it is important to bear in mind the dynamics of the consolidation issue in the context of the process of cumulative causation. Specifically, if consolidation does not occur *instantaneously* when inter-firm lock-in thwarts technological change, the initial failure to adopt a superior new technology may quickly result in competitive failure and the decline of output growth. In keeping with our interpretation of the Verdoorn Law, if this growth slowdown is sufficient to deter the subsequent adoption of the new technology, the issue of consolidation becomes mute. The industry will enter a self-reinforcing vicious circle in which slow growth deters investment and technological change. The objective of integration, therefore, loses its importance, its *raison d'être* having effectively disappeared.

Clearly, the problem of integration is rather more complicated than the Coase theorem leads us to believe. This, in turn, may explain the continued high degree of specialization exhibited by certain British industries (such as the cotton textile industry), and hence the continued problems of inter-firm technological interrelatedness suffered by these industries.

III THE COAL INDUSTRY

Although an extraction rather than a manufacturing industry, evidence suggests that the application of new technology played an important role in the late nineteenth/early twentieth century development of the coal industry. Furthermore, the adoption of this new technology in Britain again appears to have been impaired by technological interrelatedness and lock-in.

Despite unprecedented growth in the exports of British coal between 1875 and 1913, the factors which would subsequently lead to the diminution of Britain's share of world coal exports in the face of US and German competition were already evident during this period. Taylor (1968) argues that Britain's initial dominance of world trade in coal was based largely on geographical chance,[10] and that even as it enjoyed its greatest successes as an exporter, Britain's relative efficiency as a coal producer was being eroded. This trend is most evident after 1885, when the British coal industry experienced a negative trend rate of productivity growth (Taylor, 1968, p. 46). This loss of efficiency cannot be explained by the underemployment of mining capacity, as the years in which it was chiefly sustained correspond to periods of heavy demand for coal (Taylor, 1968).

However, it may be explained by the failure of the industry to adopt new technology. Coal mining comprises four main operations: the hewing of coal at the face; the conveying of coal to the main roadways; the carrying of coal to the pit bottom; and the raising of coal above ground. In the mid-nineteenth century, the chief technological advances made by the industry were in the carrying of coal to the pit bottom, and British mines were amongst the foremost innovators during this period (Taylor, 1961). However, in the late nineteenth century, the main technological advances took place at (or near) the coal face – the development of the mechanical cutter and conveyor. British mines were slow to adopt this technology. Indeed by 1913, only 7.7 per cent of Britain's total coal output was mechanically cut (Taylor, 1968, p. 57).[11]

Why was the British coal industry slow to adopt mechanical coal cutting technology? Evidence suggests that part of the explanation is that technological interrelatedness in the coal extraction process locked the industry in to its existing technique of production. Hence:

the efficient large scale use of cutters and conveyors demanded a reorganization of activity not only where the coal was hewn but throughout the cycle of operations from face to surface.

(Taylor, 1968, p. 58)

For example, the mechanization of coal cutting required the retraining of labour (Taylor, 1968), and so the abandonment of workers' existing skills, in which mine owners had previously invested. Furthermore, there existed problems with the supply of power. Up to 1905, compressed air was the most common form of power employed underground in British coal mines (Taylor, 1961). This created problems for mechanization of any kind, since transmission of this source of power was difficult, and the pressure achieved was often below necessary requirements (Taylor, 1961). The adoption of mechanical coal cutters and conveyors in British mines therefore required not only investment in the relevant machinery, but also an accompanying change in power generating technology from compressed air to electricity.

These details suggest that the technical changes required to accommodate mechanical cutters and conveyors were non-marginal in nature, necessitating accompanying changes in other components of existing plant and equipment, and in the human capital of workers. The costs associated with these changes may have made them appear unprofitable compared with continued use of the existing (obsolete) technological regime. This is despite the fact that the adoption of mechanized technologies appears to have been the most profitable option in less highly developed economies such as the US, which would have suffered less technological interrelatedness as a legacy of past mining activity.

It is important not to overlook factors such as geological difficulties in the twentieth century decline of the British coal industry. In the Lancashire coalfield, for example, where thinning seams were otherwise appropriate for the application of the mechanical coal cutter, geological faults and the pitch of the seams made mechanization at the coal face impossible (Taylor, 1968). However, there is evidence to suggest that lock-in to an outmoded technological regime, which was a legacy of Britain's early start as an industrial nation, contributed to the decline of British coal mining.

IV THE CHEMICAL INDUSTRY

The problems of technological interrelatedness in the British economy emerged not only in traditional staple industries such as cotton and coal, but also in new industries such as chemicals.[12] Again, the legacy of an initial technology selection appears to have been a crucial factor in the subsequent development of certain of these industries.

Richardson (1968, p. 278) suggests that whereas before 1880, Britain had been the dominant producer of chemicals, by 1913 it ranked only third in terms of its share of world production, well behind the USA and Germany.[13] Britain's declining fortunes as a chemical producer in the late nineteenth and early twentieth centuries are illustrated by the loss of its pre-eminence as an alkali producer. This branch of the industry was characterized by competition between the Leblanc and Solvay processes. The Leblanc process involved the oxidization of hydrochloric acid into chlorine using manganese dioxide. The Solvay process, meanwhile, involved the passing of carbon dioxide into salt and ammonia in order to precipitate sodium bicarbonate, which was subsequently converted into soda.

Throughout the late nineteenth and early twentieth centuries, British alkali firms relied largely on the Leblanc process, despite the fact that as early as the 1870s, alkali produced by the newly emerging Solvay process could undersell Leblanc output by up to 20 per cent (Richardson, 1968, p. 284). Once again, the competitive decline of a British industry can be linked to its continued use of an obsolete technology; and once again, this may in turn be explained by technological interrelatedness and lock-in. The Leblanc process emerged historically prior to the Solvay process, so that by the time the latter did emerge, Britain already had a sizeable alkali industry based on Leblanc technology. In contrast, the German and US industries developed largely after the Solvay process became available. Switching from the Leblanc to the Solvay process would have necessitated the complete reconstruction of existing British chemical plant. Such non-marginal changes for British chemical producers would, in turn, have necessitated the large scale scrapping of existing (and relatively new) plant. This would likely have made the costs of switching between processes prohibitively high for existing British manufacturers, effectively locking them in to an obsolete technology inherited as the legacy of an early start, and which constituted an obstacle to technological change that did not exist for late starting US and German producers.

The lock-in of existing British chemical producers to the Leblanc process was partially offset by the adoption of the Solvay process by 'new entrants' into the industry. For example, in 1893 the United Alkali Company, a Leblanc combine, opened a new plant utilizing the Solvay process (Richardson, 1968, p. 282). Nevertheless, adoption of the Solvay process in Britain was extremely slow. In 1883, Solvay output accounted for just 12 per cent of UK alkali production, compared with 44 per cent in Germany and 100 per cent in the USA. British Leblanc producers prolonged their survival by improving their production process to reduce costs,[14] and most importantly, by specializing more in the production of bleaching powder and caustic soda.[15] However, with the rise of the electrochemical industry, the loss of its markets for caustic soda sent the British Leblanc industry into terminal decline. The industry had closed down completely by 1920.

V TECHNOLOGICAL INTERRELATEDNESS AND LOCK-IN TO THE PRODUCTION OF CERTAIN COMMODITIES

The second aspect of over commitment, and the one given primary emphasis by Richardson (1965b), relates to the narrow range of output produced by the British economy and its concentration in traditional staple industries such as cotton and coal.

Lock-in to the production of certain commodities can occur if the initial commitment of resources to specific interrelated lines of production subsequently retards the reallocation of resources towards newly emerging industries. For example, suppose that a region's transport system and/or its geographical distribution of labour have evolved in such a way as to cater for the needs of a specific block of existing industries (in other words, its industry, physical infrastructure and stock of human capital are technologically interrelated). Then reallocating resources towards new industries with different transport and labour requirements will involve both investment in these industries, and changes to the existing infrastructure and stock of human capital – changes which may, of course, affect the existing industrial base. As such, the process of resource reallocation will require non-marginal changes in the structure of a region's economy, which may make it prohibitively expensive compared to the alternative of continuing to work existing lines of production. Alternatively, the type of resource reallocation necessary for the growth of new industries may be beyond the control of individual decision making units within these industries. Either way, a region may become locked in to its existing industrial structure, committing resources to new industries at a slower pace than regions with a previously less developed industrial structure, where any necessary adjustments to the infrastructure and/or the technologies of existing traditional industries are easier and/or cheaper to accommodate. This time, lock-in will manifest itself in the form of an over commitment to 'traditional' industries within a region.

Lock-in to traditional industries may have adverse effects on the growth dynamics of a region. Recall from Part II that the growth of a capitalist economy can be conceived as a process of structural transformation, involving progression through a 'commodity hierarchy'. If a region becomes locked in to certain traditional industries, its ability to realize transformational growth (that is, to progress through the commodity hierarchy) will be hindered. The composition of its output and hence exports will become dominated by 'necessities', and tend not to reflect those commodities with the highest income elasticities of demand. The region will effectively be producing the 'wrong' goods, in the sense that the demand for what it does produce will not be growing as rapidly as the demand for the output of newer industries to which it is failing to commit resources. As was illustrated in Chapter 4, this will lower the income elasticity of demand for the region's tradeable output, thus lowering its long run relative growth rate. Hence lock-in to traditional lines of production in a world economy which is moving through a commodity hierarchy may cause the high growth dynamics of a virtuous circle to break down.[16]

i)   Over Commitment to Traditional Industries in the British Economy

In order to determine whether these mechanisms influenced Britain's relative economic decline after 1870, we need to identify to what extent Britain was producing the 'wrong' goods – that is, to what extent it was over committed or locked in to the production of goods emanating from a narrow range of traditional (staple) industries.

The commitment of the British economy to a narrow range of output has already been remarked upon at the beginning of this chapter. In the early twentieth century, three industries (coal, iron and steel, and textiles) accounted for almost half of Britain's net industrial output, whilst textiles alone made up 37 per cent of total visible exports (Aldcroft, 1968; Elbaum, 1990). Whilst industrial concentration is not, in and of itself, indicative of structural weakness in an economy, evidence suggests that the narrow range of industries which dominated the output of the British economy were concentrated in declining sectors of the international economy (Aldcroft, 1968). Hence in 1913, contracting export industries accounted for 62.5 per cent of Britain's total manufactured exports, compared to just 49.5 per cent in Germany and 37.3 per cent in the US (Svennilson, 1983, p. 295).[17]

Furthermore, there is evidence to suggest that over commitment to declining industries played a direct role in diminishing Britain's share of world trade in manufactures. Tyszynski (1951) argues that a country's share of world trade is determined by both the relative importance in world trade of the commodity bundle that it exports, and its competitiveness in individual product markets. Hence it is possible to decompose any change in a country's share of world trade into that part which is due to changes in the structure of world trade, and that part which is due to changes in the country's international competitiveness. Utilizing this 'export accounting' framework, Tyszynski (1951, p. 289) finds that between 1899 and 1937, declining international competitiveness in all industries provides the chief explanation for Britain's declining share of world trade. However, he finds that the composition of British output during this period (reflecting the concentration of Britain's productive resources in traditional industries) reduced Britain's share of world trade in manufactures by 1.5 percentage points.[18] This suggests that the composition of Britain's export commodity bundle contributed directly to its declining importance in world trade in the late nineteenth/early twentieth centuries – that is, that Britain was effectively producing the 'wrong' goods.

ii) Lock-In to Traditional Industries: Interrelatedness between Industry and Infrastructure

Evidence also suggests that lock-in provides at least part of the explanation for Britain's continued devotion to traditional industries in the late nineteenth/early twentieth centuries. Richardson (1965b) argues that there existed technological interrelatedness between Britain's staple industries, and its power and transport facilities. The latter, as a result of Britain's early start to industrialization, chiefly comprised coal, steam and gas, and railways respectively. Hence the development of the electricity industry in Britain was retarded by the commitment of the country's existing industrial base to more traditional sources of power. This in turn impeded the development of new industries such as aluminium, which were dependent on electricity. The non-marginal changes necessary not only to Britain's infrastructure, but also to the plant of existing staple industries in order to make the new industries, the traditional industries, and the infrastructure of the British economy technologically compatible formed a barrier to the development of the new industries. Not only is it possible that changes of this magnitude would have been prohibitively costly for the British economy to undertake; it is also clear that they would have been extremely large relative to the size of the individual decision making unit in the British economy at that time. Meanwhile, Britain's late starting competitors developed staple and new industries simultaneously and, free of the legacy of an early start, an infrastructure well suited to both.[19]

iii) Lock-In to Traditional Industries: Interrelatedness between Industry and Labour Force

The transfer of resources from old to new industries in Britain was also complicated by interrelatedness between the location of the staple industries and the location of Britain's industrial labour force. The regional concentration of new industries in the Midlands and the South East meant that their development required not just the occupational transfer of labour, but also its geographical reallocation. This would not only have increased the costs associated with setting up new industries in Britain relative to continued investment in traditional industries. It would also have impeded the transfer of resources towards new industries in Britain by virtue of the fact that by the early twentieth century, labour was a far less geographically mobile factor of production than it had been when the staple industries were first expanding during Britain's initial period of industrialization.[20] Richardson (1965b) argues that despite extensive north–south migration, the location of the labour force hindered the physical transfer of labour resources from old to new industries in Britain. Once again this suggests that a form of technological interrelatedness – this time between the location of industry and the location of a key input (labour) in the process of production – may have resulted in Britain becoming locked in to its prior industrial structure. British industry remained concentrated in a narrow range of traditional lines of production at a time when the growth of world income, and hence movement through the commodity hierarchy, demanded structural change in the composition of final output as a necessary condition for competitive survival.

VI CONCLUSION

This chapter has emphasized the failure of the British economy in the late nineteenth/early twentieth century to undergo technological and structural changes related to methods of production, and the composition of final output. We have argued that the phenomena of technological interrelatedness and resultant lock-in help explain this failure. Furthermore, it has been suggested that structural weaknesses related to the methods and lines of production in which British productive resources were concentrated played a role in causing the dynamics of Britain's mid-Victorian prosperity to break down. This, in turn, suggests that these weaknesses contributed to Britain's relative economic decline after 1870.

The hypothesis already outlined is complicated in nature, and the preceding analysis cannot claim to have tested it exhaustively. Neither the descriptive statistics nor the qualitative historical evidence which have been called upon can be regarded as conclusive. Indeed, it cannot be overlooked that some authors have argued that the failures resulting from the slow pace of technological change in the British economy were of a modest nature. Hence Sandberg (1981) suggests that British firms' continued use of nineteenth century technology was rationally motivated, and that the resulting loss of efficiency in British industry relative to its US and German competitors was modest.[21]

However, none of the arguments presented in this chapter necessarily contradict the postulate that British firms acted in an individually rational manner. On the contrary, the chief determinant of British technological obsolescence is taken to be the *constraints* placed on firms by the prior industrial history of the British economy, rather than any shortcomings in the *motivation* of these firms. Furthermore, the evidence presented suggests that significant efficiency impairing failures related to the slow adoption of new methods of production *were* in evidence in the British economy after 1870.[22] Indeed, even if Sandberg were correct to argue that the extent of these failures and their impact on British economic performance was modest, it will be recalled from Chapter 6 that so, too, was the extent of Britain's relative economic decline during this period. With only a modest reversal of Britain's relative economic position to explain, it would still not be unreasonable to assert that modest failings relating to technological change may help account for this reversal.

Finally, Sandberg does not address the issue of the composition of Britain's output, which has been discussed earlier, and to which authors such as Richardson (1965b) attach primary importance in the explanation of Britain's relative economic decline. We may therefore conclude that the evidence presented in this chapter lends support to the idea that after 1870, Britain became over committed or locked in to methods and lines of production inherited as a legacy of the past, and that this had adverse implications for its relative economic performance.

8 Institutional Hysteresis and the Performance of the British Economy after 1914

Chapter 5 stressed that in a model of institutional hysteresis, institutions are best regarded as evolutionary, path dependent phenomena which may not be efficient in the sense of being functional to the growth dynamics of a capitalist economy. It was shown that inefficiency may arise due to either the persistence or creation of inefficient institutions over time.

In this chapter, we will argue that the evolution of institutions in the British economy has been a path dependent process which has displayed both of the sources of inefficiency already mentioned. This has contributed to the exacerbation of Britain's relative economic decline during the twentieth century.[1] In order to support this hypothesis, we will concentrate on the evolution of a set of institutions which, as was shown in Chapter 5, has a direct effect on the productivity and hence growth performance of a capitalist economy – the industrial relations system.[2]

Throughout the following analysis it is important to bear in mind the distinction made in Chapter 5 between *organizations* (such as firms and trade unions) and the set of *institutions* that defines the relationship between them (the industrial relations system). Following Dunlop (1958), the industrial relations system is identified as comprising three sets of actors – the state, employers and their associations, and employees and their associations. The interaction of these actors produces the 'web of rules' governing the employment relationship that is the essence of the industrial relations system. Our interest, then, is in the evolution of a set of *institutions* (the industrial relations system) which may be influenced by, but is nevertheless distinct from, the existence of certain labour market *organizations* (such as trade unions). Comments on the relative efficiency of the former should not, therefore, be misconstrued as comments on the desirability (or otherwise) of the latter.

What follows is a history (including industry level case studies) and analysis of twentieth century British industrial relations. This reveals that changes in the pattern of industrial relations in Britain during this period have been largely superficial. Systemic change has been lacking; instead, what we observe is the persistence of nineteenth century industrial relations practices, which have not been conducive to technological and organizational change, and hence the dynamic efficiency of British industry in the twentieth century. Evidence suggests that institutional interrelatedness and lock-in provide part of the explanation for this inefficient institutional evolution.

I A BRIEF HISTORY OF BRITISH INDUSTRIAL RELATIONS IN THE TWENTIETH CENTURY

In order to analyse the evolution of British industrial relations, it is necessary to first outline their history. The (brief) outline that follows can be broken down into three broad epochs: the pre-war and inter-war years; the post-war years up to the late 1960s; and the period since the late 1960s.

i) The Pre-War and Inter-War Years

The first two decades of the twentieth century were part of a period of consolidation for the British labour movement. This followed attacks on its very legitimacy at the turn of the century, such as the Taff Vale Decision (Pelling, 1972).[3] Between 1914 and 1920, trade union membership doubled. However, the evolution of the industrial relations system at this time was influenced less by the growing strength of labour than by the state of national emergency caused by World War I. The conditions emanating from the war heralded a brief phase of close cooperation between the state, labour and capital (Pelling, 1972). For example, Labour Party politicians held positions in the coalition governments during the war, including positions in the War Cabinet after 1916. In the industrial arena, tripartite agreements limited the number of trades disputes in key industries. In the 'Shells and Fuses Agreement' of 1915, unions permitted the introduction of unskilled labour on jobs traditionally reserved for skilled workers, in return for government and employer pledges that traditional practices would be restored in good faith after the war (Pelling, 1972, p. 151).

These conditions of cooperation did not extend into the inter-war period, which witnessed considerable social unrest. Heavy unemployment in the early 1920s was followed by the General Strike of 1926, which lasted nine days and involved one million miners and one and a half million transport workers, printers, construction workers, and iron and steel, chemical and power industry workers (Pelling, 1972, p. 175). In the aftermath of the

Table 8.1 Index of Relative Strike Volume in the UK,
1927–72 (1968–72 = 100)

	1927–32	1933–37	1948–52	1953–57	1958–62	1963–67	1968–72
Strike volume	80	35	25	45	60	35	100

Source: Shalev (1978, p. 15)

General Strike, the 1927 Trade Disputes and Trade Union Act curbed the power of unions to engage in sympathetic strike action, a measure which was resented within the labour movement as a curtailment of its rights. Furthermore, in light of the mass unemployment created by the Great Depression, trade unions became increasingly antagonistic to the orthodox (balanced budget) fiscal policies pursued by the state. On the whole, the period between 1920 and *circa* 1935 was not a good one for British industrial relations, characterized as it was by significant breakdowns such as the General Strike, and feelings of mutual hostility and suspicion between trade unions, employers and the government. This is partly reflected by the high value of Shalev's (1978) index of relative strike volume for 1927–32, as reported in Table 8.1.[4]

ii) World War II and the Emergence of the 'Post-War Consensus'

Ironically, it was once again the threat of a war which began to reverse these conditions of hostility and mistrust. As early as the mid-1930s, there is evidence of a growing acceptance of trade unionism in Britain, and a consequent willingness of employers to negotiate with labour. Pelling (1972, p. 211) accredits the growing 'respectability' of trade unions during the 1930s to the pragmatism and constitutionalism of prominent union leaders such as Ernest Bevin. Whatever the source of this growing toleration of trade unionism, it resulted in a significant reduction in the amount of time lost due to industrial disputes in the mid-1930s relative to the preceding era. This is reflected in the fall in the Shalev index in Table 8.1 for 1933–37, and by the fact that between 1934 and 1939, the number of working days lost to disputes only once exceeded two million, whereas it was never less than seven million between 1919 and 1926 (Pelling, 1972, p. 211).

By the late 1930s, the preparations for, and especially the outbreak of, World War II posed sufficient threat to national security to enforce cooperation in industrial relations. In 1940 the number of working days lost to strikes was the lowest since records began in the late nineteenth century (Pelling, 1972, p. 218).[5] However, cooperation was never absolute, even during the war. The growing number of unofficial strikes is illustrated by the fact that more working days were lost to strikes in 1944 than in any year since 1932 (Pelling, 1972, p. 221).[6]

Following World War II, the task of rebuilding the British economy and the austerity measures this necessitated led to renewed cooperation between capital, labour and the state. This spirit of cooperation, born partly of necessity and partly as a result of a rejection of the conditions of the 1930s,[7] came to characterize the social consensus which accompanied the post-war 'golden age' of growth and full employment. This is reflected in figures for relative strike volume between 1945 and 1960. The Shalev index in Table 8.1 falls to 25 and 45 during the periods 1948–52 and 1953–57 respectively, compared to an index of 80 for the strife torn years between 1927 and 1932. However, even during this era of cooperation in industrial relations, no form of 'social corporatism' emerged in Britain. Trade unions remained many and varied, and no strong, centralized, representative bodies of trade union and employer interests emerged to fully coordinate industrial relations at the national level. For example, within the labour movement, even individual unions within a specific industry frequently struggled to contain the strength, independence and militancy of shop stewards at the level of the firm (Pelling, 1972). The tradition of 'voluntarism' in industrial relations also remained (Pelling, 1972; Crouch, 1978), restricting the role of the state to conciliation rather than detailed coordination. The fragile nature of industrial relations, even during this era of increased cooperation, is illustrated in Table 8.1 by the general upward trend in relative strike volume throughout the post-war era. This was associated with uniformly upward trends in the incidence, median duration and median size of strikes, as indicated by Table 8.2.

Table 8.2   Incidence, Duration and Size of Strikes in the UK, 1959–73

	1950–58	1959–63	1964–67	1968–73
Incidence[a]	27	50	67	115
Median Duration[b]	1.3	1.5	1.7	2.6
Median Size[c]	n.a.	58	80	115

Notes: [a] Strikes per million employees, excluding mining
  [b] Number of man days lost per striker
  [c] Number of strikers per strike
Source: Shalev (1978, p. 17)

iii)   The Decline of the 'Post-War Consensus'

Although the objectives of British trade unions have traditionally been modest and narrow, the decade of the 1960s witnessed the emergence of new demands from the labour movement (Crouch, 1978). Whilst traditional concerns such as wage increases continued to dominate the agenda, trade unions began to show greater concern over issues such as the quantity of employment, resisting redundancies and demanding to negotiate the terms of layoffs. For example, by the late 1960s, most productivity agreements were negotiated to ensure no loss of manpower, or at least that redundancies would be voluntary and compensated (Crouch, 1978).[8]

New egalitarian concerns with the plight of low-paid workers also emerged. The notion of 'social justice bargaining', which originated within the Transport and General Workers Union and was based on demands for a £16 10s. minimum wage, was taken up by the Trades Union Congress (TUC) in 1969. The late 1960s also witnessed an increase in pay settlements which concentrated on the lowest paid, and 'tapered' as they progressed up the income scale (Layton, 1973). Finally, the campaign for the low paid was matched by an increase in the militancy and demands of these workers – especially in cases where low-paid workers comprised 'new' demographic groups within the labour force, such as women.

Trade unions also began to make new demands with respect to qualitative, non-wage aspects of the labour process – in particular, in connection with control over the organization of work (Brown, 1972). For example, in 1967 the TUC began formally advocating worker representation on company boards. Finally, the labour movement began to show an increased awareness of the broader political issues related to its actions. The traditional division between the 'industrial' and 'political' wings of the British labour movement began to fade, as the TUC engaged in such activities as the formulation of its own economic policies, complete with growth targets and policies designed to achieve them, and policy initiatives on matters such as the welfare state.

By the late 1960s and early 1970s, the decline of the post-war industrial relations consensus was becoming increasingly evident in the increased industrial conflict in the British economy. Indices of the number of strikes, the number of workers involved in strikes, and the number of working days lost all indicate an increase in industrial conflict occurring between 1966 and 1975 (Crouch, 1978, pp. 201–2). These trends are clearly reflected in Tables 8.1 and 8.2, which indicate that the periods 1968–72 and 1968–73 respectively were peak years for strike activity, whether measured by volume, size, incidence or duration.

The most significant response to these developments was that of the state, which Coates and Topham (1986) argue was conditioned by the rapid rise of the New Right in British politics. This led to the rejection of post-war efforts to assimilate and diffuse industrial conflict in the political arena. Following the General Election of 1979, a succession of legislation including the Employment Acts of 1980 and 1982 and the Trade Union Act of 1984 imposed an unprecedented degree of state control over internal union processes, by legislating rules for the election of union leaders, the decision to strike, and the accumulation and use of political funds.[9] Legislation of this nature, deliberately aimed by the state at the allegedly unrepresentative and unaccountable power of union leaders, brought about a further, dramatic breach in cooperation between labour, capital and the state, and constituted a total rejection of even the comparatively modest terms on which this cooperation had previously been based.[10]

II THE EVOLUTION OF THE INDUSTRIAL RELATIONS SYSTEM AND ITS EFFECTS ON BRITISH ECONOMIC PERFORMANCE

The preceding outline suggests that although there have been changes in the character of British industrial relations during the twentieth century, industrial relations in Britain have never been systematically resolved in a cooperative manner. In light of the BGW effect outlined in Chapter 5, according to which technological and organizational change in an economy depends on the compliance of labour in the production process, this suggests the possibility of inefficiency in the British industrial relations system. As illustrated later, industry level studies provide concrete examples of the inhibiting effects of the structure of industrial relations on technological and organizational change, and consequently on the relative efficiency of British industry. These provide evidence in favour of the notion that Britain has experienced inefficient institutional evolution in the sphere of industrial relations during the twentieth century.

i) Inefficient Institutional Evolution in the Cotton Industry

A central feature of industrial relations in the cotton industry during the early and mid-twentieth century was the system of wage lists. Negotiated at the district level, the wage structures enshrined in these lists were designed to adjust pay to compensate workers for the amount and difficulty of work done. For example, the Oldham list, first adopted in 1876, provided spinning mule minders with standard weekly earnings plus a 'quick speed' allowance, which compensated them for time during which the mules were operating faster than a negotiated standard speed (Lazonick, 1990). The Oldham and Bolton lists, the most important of the district wage lists, determined 75 per cent of mule spinners' wages in 1894, and 90 per cent by 1945 (Lazonick, 1979).

Although the wage lists tended to reflect the local balance of power between labour and firms at the time of their negotiation, there may be some extent to which they originally constituted 'efficiency wages' in the late nineteenth century. Cotton industry operatives constantly feared that higher output per man hour resulting from greater work intensity would lead management to cut piece rates. By guaranteeing piece rates for workers regardless of their productivity, the wage lists therefore reduced workers' incentives to shirk (Lazonick, 1986, p. 25).

However, the wage lists became dysfunctional to the British cotton industry in the twentieth century. By this time, the success of the US cotton industry based on ring frame and automatic loom technology necessitated changes in the technique of production employed in British cotton mills.[11] Such changes required the dismantling of the wage lists, and the relative pay scales and division of labour enshrined therein. Instead, the wage lists remained in place until after the Second World War, so that despite their being the basis for the growth and efficiency of the American cotton industry, technological and organizational change '[were] to find little application in the British cotton industry, where even into the 1960s management was constrained by industrial relations systems that had become entrenched in the late nineteenth century' (Lazonick, 1986 p. 28).

Why, then, did the wage lists remain in place for so long? One reason for their longevity was interrelatedness *within* these institutions, in the form of the connections which arise between individual decision making units whose behaviour is governed by the same institution. Hence it would have been difficult for spinning or weaving firms to deviate from an industrial relations practice common throughout the cotton industry, because of the conflict with organized labour that such deviance would have provoked. This is attested by the spate of industrial disputes in the inter-war period provoked by individual mill owners' attempts to reorganize working conditions and rewards. For example, an attempt by one large Burnley weaving firm in early 1931 to introduce an eight loom per weaver system (departing from an industry standard of less than six) resulted in a strike and subsequently an industry wide lock out from which mill workers emerged victorious (Lazonick, 1986, p. 29). Following the analysis of

Chapter 5, this behaviour can be explained by conceiving industrial relations systems – and in this case, the wage lists in particular – as procedural solutions to distributional conflict, which are difficult to change in an environment of mutual distrust. Hence labour may have resisted employer led attempts to change these institutions for fear of a resulting redistribution of value and/or power away from workers and towards firms. There is certainly reason to believe that workers may have lacked trust in firms' motives, given the repeated manipulation of piece rates by the latter in response to changes in worker productivity (see earlier and Lazonick, 1986). Interrelatedness within the wage lists seems, therefore, to have thwarted attempts by firms to change these institutions.

Whilst even concerted action by cotton firms may not have been sufficient to overcome the problem of interrelatedness already outlined, a further difficulty may help explain why firms in the cotton industry were unable to change the pattern of industrial relations by acting in unison. Recall from Chapter 7 that the British cotton industry was characterized by a high degree of horizontal and vertical specialization. Although employer associations did exist, attempts to assert their will in the conditions that specialization bred were typically ineffective. For example, even attempts at cartelization in order to control output prices by the Federation of Master Cotton Spinners Associations (FMCSA) in the 1920s were a failure (Lazonick, 1986, pp. 31–2). This was partly because of the degree of competition between spinners, and partly because of a basic division of interests between employers within the cotton industry; weaving firms were, of course, opposed to attempts to raise the price of one of their key inputs.[12] Hence there existed a source of interrelatedness *between* the institutions of industrial relations and industrial organization in the cotton industry; changing the former required accompanying changes in the latter, in order to increase cotton firms' degree of central co-ordination and hence their collective power *vis à vis* workers.

As early as the beginning of the twentieth century, the industrial relations system in the cotton industry required fundamental changes in order to remain functional to the development of the industry. However, the changes required (the replacement of the wage lists) were large relative to the size of the individual decision making unit (specialized spinning and weaving firms; individual trade unions). Because of this, the industry effectively became locked in to a system of industrial relations inherited from the nineteenth century. This system of industrial relations persisted into the twentieth century as an inefficient institution, inhibiting technological change in the cotton industry and thereby contributing to the industry's decline.

ii) Inefficient Institutional Evolution in the Shipbuilding Industry

As intimated in Chapter 6, prior to 1914, the British shipbuilding industry was largely comprised of small, specialized, independent shipyards. This corporate structure affected the initial technological and organizational development of the industry, and hence its system of industrial relations (Lorenz and Wilkinson, 1986).[13] The emergence of highly specialized trades in the shipbuilding industry resulted in the steady proliferation of trade unions, each one responsible for organizing a different trade. Even during the late nineteenth century heyday of British shipbuilding, this complicated pattern of labour representation hindered technological change. Changing production methods tended to blur traditional craft distinctions, something to which the many craft unions in the industry were opposed. However, these effects were compensated by the benefits of unionization, which aided the organization of work and the transmission of skills, and lent cyclical flexibility to the processes of hiring and firing (Lorenz and Wilkinson, 1986).

After 1920, and especially after World War II, the decline of British shipbuilding, which had first been evident at the turn of the century, took the industry to the brink of collapse.[14] This decline took place during a period of sustained expansion in the demand and output in the world shipbuilding industry, world tonnage launched rising from 3.25 to 21 million gross tons between 1950 and 1970 (Lorenz, 1991, p. 74).[15] More importantly, it took place during a period of qualitative changes in demand conditions, and of rapid technological change. With regard to the former, the world market for ships became increasingly oriented towards larger, standardized vessels after World War II (Lorenz, 1991, pp. 73, 76). With regard to the latter, more standardized vessels facilitated the adoption by shipyards of welding, burning and prefabrication techniques, which made traditional methods of riveting and plate working obsolete and so redefined the division of labour in shipbuilding. The British industry's failure to transform the nature of its product and to assimilate technological changes that were widely adopted by its competitors were instrumental in its decline. This failure may be explained, in part, by lock-in to a by now inefficient industrial relations system.

Changing the nature of its product and technology would have involved the shipbuilding industry in a change in its division of labour. But, as Lorenz and Wilkinson (1986) point out, trade unions were generally antagonistic to changes in craft demarcation lines, which a change in the division of labour would necessarily involve. This was, perhaps, hardly surprising in an industry characterized by high labour turnover, and where fears of structural unemployment resulting from demarcation changes consequently ran high. The shipbuilding industry therefore needed to change its industrial relations system, which was characterized by the proliferation of unions representing different trades and inflexible craft demarcation lines. However, it appears that institutional interrelatedness promoted lock-in to this dysfunctional institution within the shipbuilding industry. For example, interrelatedness existed *within* the industrial relations system, in the form of the connections which necessarily arise between individual decision making units who comply with the same institution. It would have been difficult for any firm to deviate from industrial relations practices common to the shipbuilding industry as a whole (that is, practices to which all other firms conformed) because of the conflict with organized labour that such deviance would have provoked. This is illustrated by the series of demarcation disputes that resulted from attempts in the 1930s and '40s by Clydeside shipbuilders to introduce and extend welding, burning and prefabrication techniques (McGoldrick, 1982; Lorenz, 1991, pp. 105–14). As in the case of the cotton industry, what this implies is that the basic interrelatedness existing between individuals whose behaviour is conditioned by a common institution created an obstacle to employer initiated changes to the industrial relations system in the shipbuilding industry. And as in the cotton industry, this can be interpreted in terms of the difficulties associated with delineating redistributive from general welfare enhancing changes to an institution designed as a procedural solution to distributional conflict. Hence workers in the shipbuilding industry resisted employer initiated changes in occupational boundaries for fear of a redistribution of control over the terms of employment and employment security towards firms. Once again, there is reason to believe that this situation was compounded by workers' lack of trust in firms' motives for institutional change. Reid (1991, p. 43) argues that whilst shipyards dominated whole neighbourhoods economically and socially, few workers were made to feel 'part of the firm'. Apart from the fact that labour turnover was high, company housing was provided only for foremen and a few technical workers, and company welfare provision was limited (most workers relied on their union and/or the state for the latter). Hence '. . . there was no effective basis for employers to establish a leverage of persuasion . . . outside the immediate relationship of the short-term employment contract' (Reid, 1991, p. 43).

Even if concerted action by employers had been sufficient to overcome these obstacles, the industry faced the further problem that concerted employer action was not easy because of the proliferation of small, specialized, independent shipyards. Whilst an employers' association existed (the Shipbuilding Employers Federation (SEF), founded in 1899) it was internally divided: first, divergent economic interests existed between independent merchant- and war-shipbuilders; second, divergent attitudes towards industrial relations existed between the Clyde shipbuilders and those located in the north-east of England; and finally, differences of opinion existed amongst employers on the very need for a radical reorganization of production (Reid, 1991, pp. 36–40). It appears, then, that interrelatedness existed *between* the patterns of industrial organization and industrial relations in shipbuilding – a pattern which is again similar to that found in the cotton industry. For shipyard owners to have changed the industrywide industrial relations system would have required accompanying changes in the pattern of industrial organization, away from small, specialized, independent firms towards a greater degree of central coordination.

Both the industrial relations system and the pattern of industrial organization in the shipbuilding industry therefore required non-marginal changes if new techniques of production based on the rationalization of existing craft methods were to be successfully introduced. The key problem for British shipbuilding was that the institutional units which required change (the pattern of industrial organization and the industrial relations system) were large relative to the size of decision making units in the industry (individual firms and unions). The difficulties associated with coordinating decentralized decision making units appear to have locked the shipbuilding industry in to an inefficient institutional structure, which thwarted technological change and contributed to the dramatic competitive decline of the industry during the post-war years.

iii)   Inefficient Institutional Evolution in the 'New' Industries: The Case of Motor Vehicles

The problem of inefficient institutional evolution in the British economy has not been confined to traditional industries. 'New' industries, which began emerging only in the late nineteenth and early twentieth centuries, *after* Britain's period of initial industrial dominance, inherited no early-mid Victorian institutional legacy. Nevertheless, in cases such as the motor vehicle industry, the evolution of industrial relations still proved inimical to long-run dynamic efficiency. What was common to the experience of both the new and traditional industries was that initial institutional selections proved critical in their subsequent development and decline.

The key technical feature of British motor vehicle firms in the late nineteenth/early twentieth centuries was their manufacture of virtually the entire vehicle. This was an important point of contrast with US producers, who were largely assemblers relying on outside supplies of finished components. It created a unique problem for British producers, who had to coordinate production units very much more complex than the US assembly shops, and bodies of labour which were much larger per unit of output.[16] These problems, in turn, contributed to the creation of a pattern of industrial relations in the motor vehicle industry characterized by 'labour independence', that is, weak control of management over the shopfloor and the supply of effort by labour (Lazonick, 1990; Lewchuk, 1986; Walker, 1981). This structure of industrial relations persisted well into the post-war era, until after the industry was nationalized in the 1970s. What the motor vehicle industry illustrates is the propensity of the British economy to *create* nineteenth century 'craft' type industrial relations in the twentieth century, even in industries which, due to their relative infancy, had neither extensive legacies of nineteenth century craft production, nor entrenched craft unions.[17]

Management's lack of control over the labour process resulted in the failure of the British motor vehicle industry, during the inter-war and especially the post-war years, to embrace the capital intensive, Fordist technique of production pioneered in the USA. Fordism involved use of the integrated assembly line, and an accompanying division of labour and degree of managerial control over the labour process that was antithetical to the type of craft control that had emerged in the British motor vehicle industry. Hence the pattern of industrial relations created by the early evolution of the industry, and which persisted thereafter, was inefficient; it obstructed the adoption of new techniques and was thus dysfunctional to the long-run dynamic efficiency of the motor vehicle industry. This is illustrated by the fact that between 1950 and 1965, a period of expansion for the world motor vehicle industry, the rate of productivity growth in the British motor vehicle industry was slower than that achieved by all of its major competitors (France, West Germany, Italy, Japan) except the USA (Pratten and Silberston, 1967).

Throughout this period, the British motor vehicle industry remained profitable only by virtue of the strong growth of world demand for motor vehicles, and because firms retained control over the setting of piece rates and were thus able to pay low wages (Lewchuk, 1986). By the late 1960s, however, declining demand conditions had provoked a crisis of profitability in the industry. Its failure to undergo technological and organizational change in the past, coupled with the hostile reaction of labour towards management efforts to finally convert to Fordism – both of which were products of the industry's inefficient industrial relations – created the conditions for the virtual collapse of the British motor vehicle industry after 1970. Inefficient institutional evolution in the British motor vehicle industry was, therefore, inimical to the dynamic efficiency of this industry, and contributed directly to its dramatic competitive decline in the late twentieth century.

III TWENTIETH-CENTURY BRITISH INDUSTRIAL RELATIONS: AN ANALYTICAL INTERPRETATION

Section I suggests that for analytical purposes, the history of British industrial relations during the twentieth century can be divided into three broad epochs. The first, running from 1918 to *circa* 1935, was characterized by adversarial industrial relations, accompanied by the depressed economic and social conditions of the inter-war years. The second, which encompasses both the late 1930s/World War II and the post-war years up to the mid-1960s, was characterized by more cooperative industrial relations. Many of the vestiges of Britain's historically decentralized and uncoordinated industrial relations system remained. However, in the context of twentieth century British industrial relations, the degree of cooperation between trade unions, employers and successive governments suggests that this period may be referred to as one of (albeit limited) capital–labour–state consensus. It was accompanied by the macroeconomic performance of the post-war 'golden age', which, as was illustrated in Chapter 6, saw Britain achieve historically high but relatively low (compared with its major competitors) rates of export, output and productivity growth.

The third epoch, which runs from the late 1960s to the present, represents a return to an adversarial pattern of industrial relations, marked initially by increased labour militancy and subsequently by the hostile response of the state to trade unions. Furthermore, at least since 1973, the macroeconomic performance of the British economy has compared unfavourably to that achieved during the preceding 'golden age'.[18]

Interpreting these developments in terms of the model of institutional hysteresis discussed in Chapter 5, it appears that the epochs identified and the economic conditions associated with them have been sequentially linked, with each epoch bequeathing the conditions for its successor. Hence negative social evaluations of the economic and social conditions during the inter-war years, coupled with the legacy of enforced cooperation between labour, capital and the state during World War II, resulted in the move towards increased cooperation associated with the post-war capital–labour–state consensus.[19] This appears to have been broadly complementary to the growth dynamics of the post-war British economy, accompanied as it was by the macroeconomic performance of the 'golden age'.[20] However, the capital–labour–state consensus only ever represented a partial change in the institutions of British industrial relations. Although the *attitudes* of trade unions, employers and especially governments appear to have been more favourably inclined towards the notion of a 'social partnership', there was no trend towards *systemic* change in the pattern of industrial relations after World War II. As is clear from Section I and the industry level studies in Section II, traditional structures and practices derived from earlier periods continued to dominate British industrial relations. Accompanying this, it is important to remember that Britain's dynamic macroeconomic performance, whilst satisfactory by historical standards, was relatively poor by contemporary international standards.

Furthermore, the economic conditions of the 'golden age' appear to have been responsible for generating a re-evaluation of and subsequent challenge to the capital–labour–state consensus by materially secure, organized labour. Many of the 'new demands' made by the labour movement in the late 1960s, such as those connected with control over the organization of work, pay equity and the quantity of employment, lay beyond the terms of the original post-war industrial relations consensus, which was essentially based on recognition of the rights of trade unions to bargain over their members' pay and the provision of state welfarism. This re-evaluation of the post-war 'social partnership', coupled with the hostile reaction (after 1979) of the state towards trade unions, signified a further institutional change which gave rise to a new epoch based on adversarial industrial relations. These institutions appear to have been broadly dysfunctional to the dynamics of the British economy, judging by its inferior macroeconomic performance since 1973 compared to the preceding quarter of a century.[21]

The interpretation of the evolution of British industrial relations outlined above can be summarized by the (annotated) causal chain in Fig. 8.1.

i) The Creation and Persistence of Inefficient Institutions

The causal chain in Figure 8.1 indicates that, in terms of the model of institutional hysteresis developed in Chapter 5, we can identify two key features of the evolution of British industrial relations in the twentieth century. First, it suggests that since World War I, the institutions of British industrial relations have followed an evolutionary time path along which they have transformed from being less functional (1918–c.1935) to more functional (late 1930s–mid 1960s) to less functional (late 1960s–present) to the dynamics of British capitalism. To some extent, then, the trajectory

Figure 8.1 The Historical Evolution of British Industrial Relations

CONDITIONS OF
INTER-WAR YEARS

- Legacy of social and economic strife

- Legacy of cooperation prior to and during WWII

↓

POST-WAR
INSTITUTIONAL
CHANGE

- Emergence of capital–labour–state consensus

- But institutional change only partial – *systemic* change lacking, so that traditional structures and practices persist

Institutions 'more' functional to macroeconomic performance

↓

POST-WAR
ECONOMIC
CONDITIONS

- 'Golden Age' of macro performance

- Generates new demands from labour movement beyond terms of original capital–labour–state consensus

↓

FURTHER
INSTITUTIONAL
CHANGE

- Late 1960s labour unrest; hostile response of state leads to demise of capital–labour–state consensus

Institutions 'less' functional to macroeconomic performance

↓

1970s/80s ECONOMIC
CONDITIONS

- Poor macro performance relative to prior epoch

of the British economy since World War I has involved the *creation* of different institutional structures in the sphere of industrial relations, which have been broadly more or less complementary to its macroeconomic dynamics. This interpretation of the British economy as having experienced different 'regimes' of industrial relations during the twentieth century, with each regime growing out of a set of economic conditions associated with its predecessor, has received widespread support (see, for example, Barkin, 1975; Soskice, 1978; Crouch, 1978; Cornwall, 1990).[22] Second, and more importantly, however, the causal chain indicates that even during the post-war 'golden age' of British capitalism, the British industrial relations system was highly imperfect. The capital–labour–state consensus involved only a partial institutional transformation. Many of the practices of the preceding period of industrial relations adversarialism, which the consensus might ideally have overcome, were retained as central features of the post-war industrial relations system. The limitations of the post-war capital–labour–state consensus are also illustrated by the fragility of this consensus in the face of new, non-wage demands from the labour movement, which it was unable to accommodate. Finally, although the period of adversarialism since the late 1960s has chiefly been characterized by the hostile attitude of the state towards *trade unions* during the 1980s, at least some of this hostility has been directed towards 'traditional practices' in the *industrial relations system*, such as the nature and legality of the closed shop.[23] Hence regardless of the causes of and underlying motives for the state's hostility towards labour, it is significant to note that even as late as the 1980s, traditional practices and forms of control over the shop-floor which, in many industries, had emerged more than a century earlier, were still an important issue in British industrial relations.

What all this suggests is that during the twentieth century, the British economy experienced the *persistence* of institutions, inherited as a legacy of the past, which were no longer functional to the dynamics of British capitalism. This phenomenon is clearly illustrated by the historical case studies in Section II. These case studies suggest that interrelatedness between and within institutions, and hence lock-in to prior institutional structures, helps explain the persistence of nineteenth century industrial relations practices in Britain.[24] Most importantly, they also illustrate the inhibiting effect of nineteenth century patterns of industrial relations on technological change, and hence the dynamic efficiency of British industry in the twentieth century.

What is also clear from Section II is that British industrial relations throughout the twentieth century have been synonymous with the persistence in Britain of the 'craft method' of production. Craft production relies heavily on the knowledge of skilled craft labour on the shop-floor. As such, it vests a relatively high degree of control over productive activity on the shop-floor in labour, but without treating labour as a long-term asset which is 'part of the firm'. Hence high rates of labour turnover and antagonism over the terms of remuneration are not uncommon within craft production, as the examples of the British cotton and shipbuilding industries attest. Craft production is therefore characterized by an industrial relations environment in which labour is granted little employment or income security by right, but is presented with the means to struggle for such security by manipulating its knowledge about and control over the production process.

Craft production is by no means always inimical to industrial development. During Britain's initial industrialization, one advantage of this technique was that skilled craft labour instilled discipline in the newly emerging factories. For example, in late eighteenth century spinning firms, skilled spinners were employed as subcontractors, who out of their piece rate wages paid time rate wages to assistants whom they themselves recruited and supervised (Lazonick, 1979). This gave the spinner a vested interest in intensifying the supply of effort by his assistants and maintaining shop-floor discipline. The subcontracting hierarchy was retained even after spinning became more capital intensive in the 1830s and 1840s (Lazonick, 1979). Indeed, even in the late nineteenth century, craft coordination of activity on the shop-floor in Britain entailed lower fixed costs than those associated with the organizational changes (heralding the advent of managerial capitalism) underway in the US (Lazonick, 1990), whilst the apprenticeship system ensured the continual (intergenerational) retraining of labour on the shop-floor.

However, the main disadvantage with the craft method of production also lies in its system of industrial relations – and this disadvantage was to become increasingly evident in British industry during the twentieth century. Craft type industrial relations vest a low degree of control over the shop-floor in management, and simultaneously create no incentive for labour to relinquish control over the production process.[25] They consequently create a poor environment for organizational and technological change in the context of a capitalist firm. Hence throughout the twentieth century, Britain has been forced to rely largely on intensifying the supply of effort by labour rather than undergoing technological change in order to remain competitive. Locked in to nineteenth century institutional structures, the British economy has been forced to grow *within* the craft technique of production. It has proved incapable of expanding *between* techniques, as evidenced by the failure of key British industries to convert to mass production during the middle of the twentieth century.[26] As the evidence presented in this and the preceding chapter suggest, Britain's failure to achieve 'extensive growth' – expanding between techniques of production by embracing technological and organizational change – helps to explain its relative economic failure since the late nineteenth century.

IV CONCLUSION

In this chapter, the evolution of British industrial relations in the twentieth century has been interpreted in terms of the model of institutional hysteresis developed in Chapter 5. Evidence has been provided to suggest that during the twentieth century, Britain has experienced inefficient institutional evolution in the sphere of industrial relations, in particular as a consequence of the persistence of industrial relations practices inherited as a legacy of the nineteenth century. This has been shown to have had a detrimental effect on the dynamic efficiency of key industries in the British economy, by undermining the ability of these industries to undergo technological and organizational change.

It is important to bear in mind that the nineteenth century craft technique of production and the system of industrial relations associated with it were not brought about by trade union power. On the contrary, as illustrated earlier in this chapter, eighteenth and nineteenth century factory proprietors were only too willing to utilize craft workers to hire and train labour, and maintain discipline on the shop-floor. Following from this, it is important to emphasize that it is not trade unions *per se* that have posed problems for the British economy, but rather the structure of the industrial relations system (that is, the institutional setting) in which these organizations have found themselves operating.

The evidence presented in this chapter illustrates that, as in the case of technological evolution discussed in Chapter 7, Britain has experienced inefficient institutional evolution since its nineteenth century industrial heyday. In terms of the model outlined in Part II, the development over time of key labour market institutions in the British economy can be interpreted as having proved dysfunctional to Britain's long-run growth dynamics. This suggests that inefficient institutional evolution has been instrumental in Britain's continued and exacerbated relative economic decline during the twentieth century.

Conclusion

I UNDERSTANDING THE EVOLUTION OF CAPITALIST ECONOMIES

This book has arisen from a discontent with the traditional equilibrium approach to economic modelling, especially as applied to the dynamics of long-run growth and development in capitalist economies. The alternative methodology that has been adopted – based on the importance of path dependency and, in particular, the concept of hysteresis – represents a major departure from traditional equilibrium analysis, especially in so far as it calls into question the very usefulness of equilibrium as an organizing concept when studying the evolution of an economic system.

Yet if an approach based on hysteresis constitutes a *major* departure from traditional equilibrium economics, several features of the preceding analysis suggest that it is nevertheless a *sensible* departure, in the sense that modelling with hysteresis provides a 'metaphor' for understanding capitalist dynamics that is superior to that of equilibrium constructs such as the steady state.

i) The Importance of Historical Time

As noted in the introduction to Part I, traditional equilibrium economics – whether of a formally static or dynamic nature – treats time as a mathematical space. The approach adopted here, on the other hand, attempts to take account of the fact that economies exist in historical time. Economic events occur in a uni-directional sequence, in the course of which any event occurring in the 'present' takes place in the context of a series of prior events corresponding to the periods which make up the past.

The importance of conceiving economic dynamics in this manner is that it rules out any approach to economic analysis which insists on interpreting the economy as a *tabula rasa* in each period. Rather, we are forced to take account of the elementary fact that in each period, the economy inherits the legacy of its own past. Once this is admitted, we are faced with the possibility that 'the past matters', in the sense that it may systematically influence subsequent configurations of the economy. If this is the case – and the analysis in this book is strongly suggestive of such a possibility – then long-run economic outcomes cannot be seen as determinate, depending only on exogenous 'data' imposed upon the economic system from without. Instead, they must be seen as path dependent, which places emphasis on the nature of adjustment processes endogenous to the economy in explaining these outcomes. The notion that 'the past matters' – that the *historical configurations* of an economic system can affect its evolution in a manner which is overlooked by traditional equilibrium analysis – and that this is something that economic models should strive to take account of is essentially what this book seeks to assert.

ii)   The 'Unsmooth' Process of Economic Change

A second important feature of the preceding analysis is its emphasis of the idea that economic change is not a smooth and continuous process. On the contrary, it is suggested that there may be important difficulties associated with effecting a transition between, for example, different technological or institutional regimes in an economy. In part, this is due to the influence of the past on current economic activity. However, it is also caused by the existence of important indivisibilities in economic variables, which frequently render change a non-marginal process. The possibility of interrelatedness between technological and institutional components of the production process has been shown to be an important source of these indivisibilities. As illustrated in Chapters 4 and 5, interrelatedness can make incremental changes at the margin a practical impossibility, giving rise to the phenomenon of lock-in. The elementary idea that not all of the activities or components which comprise the production process are continuously divisible, which implies that change is frequently a non-marginal and discontinuous process, can therefore have a major influence on the evolution of a decentralized economic system.

iii)   The Potential Inefficiency of Economic Outcomes

What follows naturally from consideration of the constraints of history and the difficulties associated with economic change is the possibility that economic outcomes in any period may be, by some definition, inefficient, and therefore could be improved upon to the net benefit of society as a whole. Allowing for the possibility of inefficient outcomes seems intuitively appealing – especially when compared with the alternative of arguing that anything *but* an efficient outcome is impossible. Yet this is a departure from at least some of the more casual interpretations of traditional equilibrium analysis, despite the association of specific branches of this methodology with the analysis of problems such as public goods and externalities (neoclassical welfare economics), multiple, Pareto rankable equilibria (game theory) and involuntary unemployment (conventional Keynesian macroeconomics). In the hands of its less careful practitioners, traditional equilibrium analysis can degenerate into a series of Panglossian assertions to the effect that the assumption of individual rationality *demands* that market outcomes be resolved in an efficient manner.

This assertion of the necessity of efficient market outcomes is highly unsatisfactory. As Elster (1989b, pp. 147–8) argues, we can only be truly confident that a particular outcome has been brought about by virtue of its efficiency if a process can be demonstrated which specifies how the good consequences of an outcome act so as to both give rise to and maintain it over time. In short, '[i]mputations of optimality require hard work, not just armchair speculation' (Elster, 1989b, p. 150).

An obvious corollary of Elster's argument is, of course, that imputations of inefficiency cannot be made casually, either. In view of this, taking as its point of departure the fundamentally historical nature of economic processes, one of the main aims of this book has been to specify processes which may create and sustain economic outcomes which are inefficient by virtue of their being inimical to the achievement of relatively rapid long-run growth.

iv) Capitalism as an Evolving System

Ultimately, the analysis in this book can be seen as working towards a conception of capitalism as an endogenously evolving system which, whilst continually subject to genuinely external influences, is nevertheless comprised of mechanisms whose very operation can influence the long-run configuration of the system as a whole. This conception is in keeping with the views expressed by Robinson (1974a, 1980) and Kaldor (1934, 1970, 1972, 1985) on the role of history in endogenously determining current economic outcomes, and following Kregel (1976), can also be seen as close to the views of Keynes himself. It suggests that there are no determinate 'laws of history' which govern the fate of a capitalist economy independently of its prior (historical) trajectory. Instead, it is held that '[t]he only truly exogenous factor is *whatever exists at a given moment of time*, as a heritage of the past' (Kaldor, 1985, p. 61 – italics in original), a heritage from which current and future economic activities will arise as part of a historical sequence of path dependent events.

II GROWTH AND DEVELOPMENT IN THE 'REAL WORLD'

To what extent does this conception of the historical process underlying capitalism contribute to our understanding of the growth and development experience of actual capitalist economies? One potential problem with the model developed earlier is that its evolutionary nature and insistence on the essential indeterminacy of historical time renders it useless as a tool for the prediction of future outcomes. Indeed, the underlying philosophical premise of the model is that the very act of prediction, at least as it is usually thought of by economists working within the traditional equilibrium approach to economic modelling, is, especially in the long run, a folly. However, it may still be possible to learn from the past and in particular, from understanding the processes which have been at work in capitalism and how they have affected actual capitalist economies – even if prediction of the future as conventionally conceived is not possible. In other words, economists can at least aspire to becoming good historians. To this end, Part III indicates the potential applicability of a hysteretic model of growth and development to the relative rise and decline of the British economy since 1780. In particular, the concept of lock-in to past technological and institutional 'regimes' – an important source of adjustment asymmetries in the model developed in Part II – has been found useful for explaining why Britain's initial phase of relative economic success bequeathed a subsequent phase of relative economic decline. Industry level studies suggest the persistence in Britain of nineteenth century techniques of production long after these had been rendered obsolete, and the contribution made by this inefficient technological and institutional evolution to declining relative efficiency and competitiveness.

i) Is the British Case Representative?

However, it is important to acknowledge that only so much can be learnt from studying the experience of one specific country. The evidence presented in Part III is therefore suggestive rather than conclusive. Whether the hysteretic model developed in Part II can explain the experience of other advanced industrial nations, and whether it is therefore more generally applicable to the evolution of capitalism than the evidence provided by the British experience is able to suggest, remains to be seen. To this end, it is perhaps reasonable to speculate that the trajectory of the US economy, which to some observers appears to have followed a developmental path not unlike that encountered by Britain before it,[1] is worthy of substantial future investigation. The tremendous contemporary significance of the relative decline of the US economy, as remarked in the introduction to this book, provides still further motivation for an investigation of this nature.

ii) The Neglected Roles of Money and Public Policy

As intimated in Chapter 5, apart from a simple form of 'horizontalism' (which can be thought of as an implicit feature of the model developed in Part II) we have engaged in no thorough discussion of money and monetary relations. Whilst this may be interpreted as an oversight of the highest order, it is, nevertheless, possible to see how a discussion of money could be integrated into the preceding analysis. Following the Post-Keynesian theory of money and monetary relations as institutional solutions to fundamental uncertainty, it is conceivable that money could be studied as an institution evolving according to principles similar to those advanced in Chapter 5. The further development of this idea would not only serve to complement the theory outlined in Part II, but would no doubt also contribute to the analytical insights rendered by the model when it is applied to the experience of actual capitalist economies – economies which have experienced frequently turbulent monetary histories in the course of their growth and development.

It is also important to note that one vitally important 'exogenous' variable that has not been discussed in the course of this book is public policy. For some authors writing on the recent East Asian experience, policy can be seen as a vital component in ensuring that the technological and especially the institutional preconditions for cumulative high growth emerge and are maintained over time (see, for example, Amsden, 1989, pp. 63–4).[2] Researching the influence of policy on path dependent growth dynamics would appear to be imperative if the British experience is to be successfully reversed. It may also lend vital insights into what is necessary to prevent economies such as the US following similar trajectories. Following authors such as Amsden (1989), it may prove fruitful for research of this nature to examine more closely the example of the 'East Asian model' of growth and development. Whatever, the preceding analysis presents clear challenges for policy. We have seen how cumulative high growth dynamics can endogenously break down, and how a period of relative economic success can consequently bequeath a subsequent period of relative economic failure. Is it possible, then, that policy can play a role in preventing such a breakdown, by successfully managing the fragile dynamic of cumulative high growth? Indeed, does the further possibility exist of utilizing public policy to reverse a given historical breakdown in this dynamic, permitting the renewed rise of a 'fallen', but once relatively successful, economy?

III SUMMARY

Taking as its starting point a methodology based on path dependency, the principal aim of this book has been to construct a long-run model of growth and development which takes account of the fact that economic activity occurs as a uni-directional sequence in historical time. The model that has been developed is of a simple form, and can by no means claim to account for all the features of growth and development in a capitalist economy. Furthermore, the model raises as many important questions about growth as it provides potential answers to others. In particular, the vital conundrum surrounding the role of public policy in influencing the course of capitalist development springs to mind. What this book can claim, however, is to have provided a step away from the theoretical straitjacket of equilibrium analysis, a methodology which attempts to characterize the history of capitalism – a history rich with change – as intrinsically unchanging. In so doing, the model that we have developed points towards the possibility of analysing economic dynamics 'as if history mattered', in a manner which takes account of both the nature and significance of change in the evolution of economic systems.

Notes

Introduction

1. There exists a voluminous literature relating to this concern. See, for example, Pollard (1962, 1989) and Eatwell (1984) for an introduction to the debates.
2. See Hont (1983) for an overview of this debate.

Part I Economic Modelling: Some Methodological Considerations: Introduction

1. There are, however, important differences between neoclassical theory and some branches of Keynesianism (such as Post-Keynesianism) as regards the treatment of equilibrium as an organizing concept. These differences will be discussed in due course.
2. This will be made clear in the discussion of hysteresis and persistence in Chapter 2.

1 Economic Modelling and the Concept of Equilibrium

1. This encompasses the preceding 'market clearing' definition, and also allows for stationary but non-market clearing configurations.
2. Specifically, individuals are in equilibrium in these models when they are forming the 'best' (that is, strong form rational) expectations on the basis of available information.
3. Prices are, of course, endogenous to the market process, but assuming perfectly competitive conditions, they are exogenous to the individual decision maker.
4. The notion of stability used here corresponds to the formal mathematical concept of asymptotic stability. This implies that following some initial disturbance, all subsequent motion will lead a system towards convergence, in the limit, with the equilibrium from which it was initially displaced.
5. Equation [1.5] follows from the homogeneous function derived from equation [1.3], which can be written:

$$Y_t = \alpha Y_{t-1}$$

Recalling that $Y_t = Ab^t$, this implies that:

$$Ab^t - \alpha Ab^{t-1} = 0$$

$$\Rightarrow \qquad b = \alpha$$

6. Again, equation [1.10] follows from the homogeneous function derived from equation [1.7], which can be written:

$$\dot{p}_t^e = (1 - \beta)\dot{p}_{t-1}^e$$

Recalling that $\dot{p}_t^e = Bd^t$, this implies that:

$$Bd^t - (1 - \beta)Bd^{t-1} = 0$$

$$\Rightarrow \qquad d = (1 - \beta)$$

7. Kaldor is quite explicit in identifying the variant he wishes to criticize as 'the general economic equilibrium originally formulated by Walras, and developed . . . by the mathematical economists of our own generation'. (Kaldor, 1972, p. 1237.) However, many of the criticisms he makes could be applied to neoclassical theory in general.

8. On the methodology of 'storytelling' in economics, see, for example, Wilber and Harrison (1978).

9. It is interesting to see how these ideas are beginning to permeate orthodox thinking. For example, while Romer (1994) avoids using the terms 'realism' and 'stylized facts', his concern is clearly with the use of both in the evaluation of models. Romer's explicit argument is that while both traditional neoclassical and new endogenous growth theories can be made consistent with empirical observations regarding cross country growth rates, 'non-standard' evidence (that is, descriptive, non-econometric evidence not associated with the prediction of final growth outcomes) can be drawn upon to support his intuition that new endogenous growth theories are 'richer' and 'more insightful' than their neoclassical predecessors. Romer's implicit argument, then, is that using stylized facts to evaluate the realism of models may encourage more satisfactory theory, in light of the fact that predictive ability alone cannot be relied upon to distinguish between alternative theories.

10. A strong association exists in economics between equilibrium and optimal outcomes, although it is well known from situations such as the static or 'one shot' prisoner's dilemma problem that this association does not necessarily hold.

11. This point pre-empts the notion that final outcomes may not be independent of the path taken towards them, which is dealt with at length in Section V and Chapter 2.

12. The Second Fundamental Theorem of Welfare Economics is a property of general competitive systems. The First Fundamental Theorem of Welfare Economics states that a Walrasian (market) equilibrium is Pareto efficient. See, for example, Varian (1984, pp. 220–1) for a standard exposition.

13. By 'restrictions on individuals' we mean conventional microeconomic axioms such as the strict convexity of agents' preferences.

14. It will be recognized, in light of this, that part of the significance of representative agent models in macroeconomics is that they bypass the Sonnenschein–Debreu–Mantel dilemma by treating the economy as if it were comprised of a single maximizing individual. Note, however, that the representative agent approach offers no *solution* to the problems of non-uniqueness and instability. Since it avoids, by construction, the crucial problem of aggregation, the representative agent approach simply assumes these problems away. Put differently, '. . . the "representative" individual is being used to *provide* the stability and uniqueness of equilibria which are not *guaranteed* by the underlying model' (Kirman, 1992, p. 120; emphasis in original).

15. Some rational expectations models attempt to circumvent the issues discussed here by conceiving the economy as a moving equilibrium, that is, as a system which never experiences disequilibrium. However, this still begs the question as to how the economy is supposed to have achieved equilibrium in some initial period. Hence see Setterfield (1995a, pp. 11–12) on the argument that *all* models postulate adjustment processes of some kind at some level, so that none can completely finesse the problem of disequilibrium adjustment.

16. The term 'equilibrium economics' used here may be thought of as referring broadly to the Walrasian and Marshallian traditions in neoclassical economics.

17. As a prominent neo-Walrasian, Hahn's scepticism makes all the more sense in light of the Sonnenschein–Debreu–Mantel 'impossibility theorem' discussed in the text, which questions the ability of the Walrasian paradigm to generate appropriate stability results solely on the basis of its microeconomic axioms concerning individual behaviour.

18. Although his/her role may be taken by strong form rational expectations, in which agents know the 'true' model of the economy and hence instantaneously adjust their behaviour to that which is compatible with equilibrium.

19. In view of this, and in light of the discussion in Section II, formal dynamic models are open to criticism as being 'unrealistic' in their representation of stability conditions. That such a criticism is possible is itself testimony to McCloskey's (1983) argument that mathematical economic reasoning is inherently metaphorical, and can therefore be questioned with regard to its aptness as a characterization of any given economic process.

20. For example, this problem will certainly arise in any model in which the process of production takes place, unless we assume that production decisions have no concrete manifestation in physical assets, that is, that we are working with 'putty capital.' See, for example, Robinson (1974b).
     Kaldor (1934) provides an early discussion of the importance of this point, arguing that 'constant carry over' from period to period is a necessary condition for the determinacy of any equilibrium which is not established instantaneously.

21. Tatonnement is a disequilibrium adjustment process in which agents 'grope' for an equilibrium outcome over time basing their demands and supplies in each period on the *same* initial endowment.

22. We may, however, postulate that disequilibrium adjustment occurs via a *non*-tatonnement process, where stocks of varying size are allowed to carry over from period to period. Under these circumstances, though, initial disequilibrium production, consumption and trade may affect stocks and hence alter individuals' 'endowments', so that in the next 'period', new disequilibrium production, consumption and trade will take place which will further alter individual 'endowments' and so on. As a result, because economic activity in non-tatonnement processes is a function of current rather than initial endowments, and because current endowments are influenced by past 'mistakes' made in the course of disequilibrium activity which cannot be predicted *a priori*, the outcomes of non-tatonnement processes cannot be specified *ex ante*. This suggests that non-tatonnement processes

do not give rise to determinate outcomes. In fact, the outcomes of non-tatonnement processes are subject to what will subsequently be identified as a process of hysteresis.

23. Note that this Keynesian critique relates primarily to the notion of adjustment towards the type of general equilibrium described by Walras, and in turn makes use of a new equilibrium concept – the short run under employment equilibrium. A simple interpretation of this concept has already been identified in Section I(i) as part of the traditional equilibrium approach; hence adjustment towards *it* may be subject to some of the criticisms previously outlined (for example, the problem regarding the speed of adjustment relative to the rate of change of the data of the model may be apposite.)

24. See Kirman (1989) and Ingrao and Israel (1990) for further discussion of this neo-Walrasian literature. Lavoie (1992, pp. 26–41) provides an overview from a Post-Keynesian perspective, which links developments in neo-Walrasian economics to the neo-Ricardian critique of aggregate neoclassical analysis.

25. In an environment of fundamental uncertainty, agents exist in a state of partial ignorance about the future. Some possible future outcomes and/or their relative probabilities are unknown in the present, either because agents suffer bounded rationality, or because these features are unknowable in principle due to the historical specificity of some information and hence knowledge. See, for example, Lawson (1985) and Davidson (1988, 1991).

26. There may, of course, be more than one admissible configuration if we allow for the possibility of multiple equilibria. In this case, of course, any individual equilibrium configuration can only be locally stable.

2 An Alternative approach – Modelling with Hysteresis

1. That it is necessary for the system always to achieve a state of long-run (as opposed to short-run) equilibrium can be illustrated by using the example of equilibrium business cycle models. It was noted earlier that models of this nature seem to circumvent the problems posed by the process of disequilibrium adjustment, by postulating that individuals are always in equilibrium by virtue of the fact that their conditional expectations are (strong form) rational. However, equilibrium business cycle models do not, in fact, avoid the problem of path dependency. This is because the sub-optimal *short-run* equilibria that they postulate as arising from conditional expectations formed in the presence of 'price surprises' will necessarily create a sub-optimal history of the economy in the short run. The 'mistakes' made during this period may influence the future behaviour of the economy – in particular, the nature of the *long-run* equilibrium about which it is presumed to oscillate.

2. This time path may take any one of a variety of forms, such as a stationary state, a steady state expansion path, a limit cycle, and so forth.

3. See Cross and Allen (1988) for further discussion of this and other points relating to the history of hysteresis.

4. Note that this definition of hysteresis is consistent with Elster's (1976) claim

that the past can only be seen to influence the present by virtue of the traces left by the past in the present. In the preceding definition, these 'traces of the past' are reflected by the sensitivity of the current structural model to past values of the variable of interest.

5. This point is illustrated in detail in Sections II(i) and II(ii).

6. Note that from [2.4], if $\mu = 1$, in the steady state:

$$X_t - X_{t-1} = 0 = v + \phi Z^*$$

$$\Rightarrow \qquad Z^* = -\frac{v}{\phi}$$

7. Note that if $Z_t = Z^*$ for all $i = 1, \ldots, t$, then equation [2.6] reduces to:

$$X_t = X_0 + tv + t\phi Z^*$$

Recalling the existence condition $Z^* = -\frac{v}{\phi}$, this implies that:

$$X_t = X_0$$

The long-run value of X will therefore conform to a steady state which depends entirely on the initial condition X_0.

8. Not all hysteretic systems are influenced by their entire past history, however. See Section III(ii) and Cross (1991, 1993).

9. The analogous condition in continuous time is that a system of differential equations possess a zero root. See Giavazzi and Wyplosz (1985).

10. Note that the case where $-1 < \eta < 0$ is not considered since, although mathematically admissible, it has no economic interpretation in equation [2.8] in terms of the theory of hysteresis in the labour market.

11. See, for example, Henin (1986). Attention is confined to the case of damped cycles to avoid the possibility of divergence in the multiplier–accelerator model, which cannot be interpreted as persistence. Indeed, such behaviour may be closer to the notion of hysteresis (see Cross (1987, p. 79) and Setterfield (1995a, p. 15)). However, it is important to note that hysteresis is not usually characterized in terms of model instability (in the sense of monotonic divergence from equilibrium), and indeed the two are not generally equivalent. Hence models displaying hysteresis may approach states of rest, although any such equilibria they reach will, of course, depend on the prior disequilibrium adjustment path taken towards them. See Section V for further discussion.

12. References to 'contemporaneous natural rates' and 'temporary equilibria' as in Section II(i) are really just rhetorical devices which give new names to the familiar outcomes associated with a process of non-instantaneous convergence towards a determinate long-run equilibrium.

13. Note that the homogeneous function derived from the general solution to [2.4] can be written as:

$$X_t - \mu X_{t-1} = 0$$

Recalling that $X_t = Ab^t$, this yields:

$$Ab^t - \mu Ab^{t-1} = 0$$

$$\Rightarrow \qquad b - \mu = 0$$

$$\Rightarrow \qquad \mu = b$$

14. Suppose, for example, that X is fixed capital of the 'putty-clay' variety which, once purchased, cannot easily be substituted for more or less of any other factor of production or remoulded into a different form representing the same 'quantity of capital.'

15. See Katzner (1993) and Setterfield (1993a, 1995a) for further discussion of this point.

16. Note that from equation [2.16]:

$$\left(\frac{X_t}{X_{t-1}}\right) = \lambda Z_t$$

$$\Rightarrow \qquad Z^* = \frac{1}{\lambda}$$

when $X_t = X_{t-1}$, as in the steady state.

17. Note that if $Z_i = Z^*$ for all $i = 1, \ldots, t$, equation [2.17] reduces to:

$$X_t = X_0 \cdot \prod_{i=1}^{t} \lambda Z^*$$

$$= X_0 \cdot (\lambda Z^*)^t$$

$$= X_0$$

recalling that $Z^* = \dfrac{1}{\lambda}$. Once again, this implies that X will conform to a steady state which depends entirely on the initial condition X_0.

Note that it is possible to conceive of instances when X_t in equation [2.17] will converge to zero regardless of its prior timepath (for example, if $-1 < \lambda < 1$ and $Z_i < 1$ for all values of $i = 1, \ldots, t$). These cases are overlooked as being of little general economic interest.

18. Note that equation [2.16] can be rewritten as:

$$x_t = \Lambda + x_{t-1} + z_t$$

where $x_i = \ln X_i$, $i = t, t-1$, $\Lambda = \ln\lambda$ and $z_t = \ln Z_t$. This equation is comparable, upon inspection, with equation [2.4] in the case where $\mu = 1$.

19. To clarify the terminology used here, note that Z_i (for all $i = 1, \ldots, t$) represents the 'input' of the system summarized in equation [2.17].

20. The discussion in Sections III(iii) and III(iv) follows that found in Setterfield (1994a, pp. 6–15).

21. See, for example, Georgescu-Roegen (1971), Arthur (1988), and Witt (1991).

22. Following the Lucas (1976) critique of econometric policy evaluation, as a result of which conventional 'data' such as tastes and technology have been referred to as 'deep parameters' determined outside the economy, the term deep endogeneity is deliberately contrived to suggest the potential sensitivity

of at least some conventional 'data' to the economic outcomes they are supposed to explain.

23. If we have $\delta_1 + \mu + \delta_2 = 1$ then there exists a unit root which, as we have already seen, will result in hysteresis.

24. Once again, this result is contingent on the existence condition $\mu + \delta_2 \neq 1$ – that is, on the absence of a unit root in equation [2.4b].

25. Equation [2.5] is used in the following analysis as a pedagogic device. It is not likely to represent the actual long-run value of X in the system we are considering at any point in time, since it omits the information about Z in equation [2.20]. However, it is *changes* in the long-run value of X that are of interest when considering the possibility of hysteresis. These changes (or the lack thereof) can be inferred by examining equation [2.5] in light of equation [2.20] without neglecting any information in the structural model we are considering. Ultimately, the changes we observe can be compared to those that would be observed by a researcher who overlooks the deep endogeneity of Z, and who interprets changes in the 'data' of equation [2.1] and [2.3] as exogenous shocks rather than as being systematically related to the disequilibrium behaviour of X. It is also useful from this point onwards to think of X^* in equation [2.5] as a *conditional* equilibrium or steady state. This is because, as will subsequently be demonstrated, its precise value will depend on the behaviour of over time of Z_t in equation [2.20], and it therefore lacks the traditional stability properties of a *conventional* equilibrium or steady state.

26. Obviously, since $X^* \neq X^{**}$, it must be that $DX = \sum_{i=1}^{n} dX_i \neq 0$, our original assumption that $DX = \sum_{i=1}^{t} dX_i = 0$ notwithstanding. This is, of course, because the convergence of X towards X^{**} postulated above implies that

$$DX = \sum_{i=t+1}^{n} dX_i \neq 0.$$

27. Both of these examples are developed in more detail in Setterfield (1994a).

28. Although Marshall is usually seen as the father of period analysis, Keynes provides a more appropriate starting point since Marshall's short and long runs are not sequential; the latter bears no strict intertemporal relationship to the former. Hence in Marshall, 'there is no analysis of a process which could generate long period equilibrium as the (asymptotic) result of a sequence of short period equilibria, just as the short period equilibrium is not explicitly constructed as the outcome of output adjustments in a sequence of ultra short period equilibria. . . . The problem (of the historically consistent aggregation of time) is ingeniously side stepped by the use of *ceteris paribus* clauses in a nested set of equilibrium concepts.' (Skott, 1983, p. 10)

29. The idea of cumulative causation was first introduced by Veblen (1919) and subsequently discussed by Myrdal (1957).

30. In fact, the notion that successive changes in a variable are positively correlated over time is a potentially serious shortcoming of cumulative causation in the long run. This issue is taken up in detail in Chapters 4 and 5, in the context of the growth model developed in Part II.

31. Indeed, cumulative causation might even be thought of as a special case of the set of all hysteretic outcomes. See Setterfield (1995a, pp. 17–18).
32. This example is discussed by Arthur (1988). For a formal characterization, see Setterfield (1995a, p. 20).
33. It might be objected that this result relies upon the individual in question having a finite time horizon. Otherwise, the realization that medicine is the superior option in the long run would presumably motivate a career change. The assumption of a finite time horizon is, however, clearly suitable for the example developed here, because of the strictly finite nature of the individual's working life. More generally, the suitability of this assumption will likely depend on the subsidiary hypotheses we prefer to entertain about the nature of the economic environment and/or individual agents' perception of it. For example, in a monetary production economy characterized by fundamental uncertainty, the finite time horizon would appear to be a highly plausible generalization.
34. Recall from Chapter 1 that problems of this nature are likely to persist even in the absence of vested interests and regardless of the existence and recognition of potential 'gains from trade' amongst interested parties, whenever signalling problems or the absence of appropriate co-ordinating mechanisms frustrate spontaneous co-ordination amongst decentralized decision making units.
35. It will be recognized immediately that Kaldor's concept of indeterminacy was a prototype of what we have defined as hysteresis.
36. Kaldor (1934, p. 125, footnote 4) implicitly defines equilibrium as a stationary state. However, any equilibrium concept – such as a steady state or a limit cycle – could be substituted for the stationary state in Kaldor's original definition.
37. What follows bears close resemblance to Kalecki's conception of the dynamics of a monetary production economy. See Targetti and Kinda Hass (1982).
38. A pertinent, if rather tangential, example that springs to mind is the behaviour of soldiers in war movies. A sustained lull in hostilities inevitably results in someone deciding that he/she 'doesn't like it'. A behavioural innovation results, provoking a reaction from the enemy, and the fighting resumes. The audience identifies with all this, despite the fact that the lull in hostilities represents a sort of 'peaceable equilibrium' which, if perpetuated indefinitely would, by its very nature, end the war altogether.
39. As has already been suggested, the term equilibrium means many different things in economics. The idea of conditional equilibrium defined here simply adds to the variety of conceptions of equilibrium that already exists.
40. In other words, as long as equilibrium is treated as an *ex post* position of rest rather than an *ex ante* centre of gravity as in traditional equilibrium economics.

Part II Modelling Macroeconomic Systems with Hysteresis: Growth and Structural Change in Capitalist Economies: Introduction

1. The 'long run' is defined here in essentially Marshallian terms, as a period during which the 'data' underlying short-run macroeconomic outcomes – the

level of autonomous demand, the quantity and quality of the capital stock and the institutional structure of the economy – are subject to endogenous revision in light of path dependence. The 'long run' during which path dependency effects prevail may represent a different period of calendar time, depending on what aspect of the economy we are considering as being path dependent. It will become apparent in Part III, and is consequently worth noting at the present time, that some of the effects of path dependency on economic growth and structural change may only take place over decades of calendar time.

3 A Model of Cumulative Causation

1. Note that an important assumption underlying this argument is that there exist indivisibilities in production which make the adoption of more capital intensive techniques of production a discontinuous process.
2. The role of knowledge in generating externalities is a particular emphasis of 'new endogenous' growth theory. See, however, Wulwick (1993) and Setterfield (1994b) for discussion of the differences between 'new endogenous' growth theory and models of cumulative causation, with regard to both their treatment of increasing returns and various other facets of macroeconomic dynamics.
3. See Hahn (1974) for further discussion of the importance of this assumption.
4. A similar point is made by Schumpeter (1942), who argues that there exists a potentially boundless scope for technological advance and hence increased productivity in production activities which rely on produced means of production. This theme has also been revisited more recently by 'new endogenous' growth theorists such as Grossman and Helpman (1991, p. 17), who argue that knowledge and hence the potential for its accumulation are unbounded.
5. A formal analysis of this argument, drawing on the model developed by Sundrum (1990), can be found in Appendix A of Setterfield (1992).
    Note that the arguments expressed implicitly assume that there exist commodities *throughout* the commodity hierarchy which can be produced under conditions of dynamic increasing returns, and that each successive commodity can be produced with a higher average productivity than its predecessor. These assumptions, which will be retained throughout the following analysis, attach special importance to the role of manufacturing activities in economic growth (see also Kaldor, 1970 and Cornwall, 1977). For an analysis of the limit effects of an economy whose commodity hierarchy becomes increasingly dominated by the output of the service sector, see Sundrum (1990, Chapter 3).
6. See Kaldor (1972) for a summary and appraisal of the demand side of Young's original model.
7. In his earlier models (see, for example, Kaldor, 1972) investment spending plays a more prominent role.
8. Note that this vision of production as a process of extending social cooperation is similar to Frankel's (1955) argument that the degree of interrelatedness between the components of the production process (machines,

firms, institutions and so on) increases as the economy grows. This idea is explored more fully in Chapter 4.

9. This assumption is in keeping with one of the most basic stylized facts of long-run growth in advanced capitalist economies. See, for example, Maddison (1991, pp. 48–52).

10. Although this model is usually presented without time subscripts (see, for example, Thirlwall (1980)), the lag structure in equations [3.1]–[3.4] is imposed in order to simplify exposition of the dynamic interaction of these equations.

11. Verdoorn's Law states that there exists a positive relationship between the growth of manufacturing output and productivity growth. See Thirlwall (1983) for further discussion of this law.

12. Thirlwall (1980, pp. 270–2) shows how this particular problem can be overcome. By introducing an import function and balance of payments equilibrium condition, he derives an expression for the rate of growth in region j which is consistent with long run balance of payments equilibrium in this region.

13. This assumption, which is analogous to assuming constant wage relativities over time (that is, $\dfrac{w_{jt}}{w_{wt}} = c$ for all t, where c is some constant) is a key feature of Kaldor's exposition of cumulative causation. It is discussed in more detail in Section III(i), where its relaxation is considered.

14. This assumption rules out any influence of $\dot{Y}_j$ on $\dot{Y}_w$ and hence may be more or less objectionable depending on the size of region j in the world economy. Our second simplifying assumption, then, does involve some loss of generality.

15. Setterfield (1995b) provides a more extensive investigation of the variety of non-equilibrium interpretations of the model that are possible. These include cases of instability when $\lambda_j\alpha_j\beta_j > 1$, and also the special case of a unit root ($\lambda_j\alpha_j\beta_j = 1$) in equation [3.7].

16. Some insight into the truth of this statement can be gained even at this stage by inspection of equation [3.8], in which γ_j plays a key role in determining $\dfrac{\dot{Y}_j^*}{\dot{Y}_w}$.

17. Given that $0 < \lambda_j\alpha_j\beta_j < 1$, it is straightforward to verify that as $t \to \infty$, so:

$$(\lambda_j\alpha_j\beta_j)^t \to 0$$

whilst:

$$\sum_{i=0}^{t-1}(\lambda_j\alpha_j\beta_j)^i \to \frac{1}{1 - \lambda_j\alpha_j\beta_j}$$

from which it quite clearly follows that equation [3.8] is the limit result of [3.10].

18. This can be demonstrated as follows. Define total world income as $Y_{Tt} = Y_{jt} + Y_{wt}$. Deleting time subscripts for simplicity, it follows that:

$$\dot{Y}_T = \dot{Y}_j \cdot \frac{Y_j}{Y_T} + \dot{Y}_w \cdot \frac{Y_w}{Y_T}$$

$$\Rightarrow \quad \dot{Y}_T = \dot{Y}_j \cdot \left(1 - \frac{Y_w}{Y_T}\right) + \dot{Y}_w \cdot \frac{Y_w}{Y_T}$$

$$\Rightarrow \quad \dot{Y}_j - \dot{Y}_T = \frac{Y_w}{Y_T} \cdot (\dot{Y}_j - \dot{Y}_w) > 0$$

since $\dot{Y}_j > \dot{Y}_w$ by hypothesis. This, in turn, implies that:

$$\frac{d\left(\frac{Y_j}{Y_T}\right)}{dt} \cdot \frac{Y_T}{Y_j} = \dot{Y}_j - \dot{Y}_T > 0$$

$$\Rightarrow \quad \frac{d\left(\frac{Y_j}{Y_T}\right)}{dt} > 0$$

since $Y_T, Y_j > 0$ by assumption – that is, region j's share of world income is increasing over time.

19. Note that if $\dot{P}_{jt} \leq \dot{P}_{wt}$ in any period t, then:

$$\dot{y}_{jt} = \dot{Y}_{jt} - \dot{P}_{jt} \gg \dot{Y}_w - \dot{P}_{wt} = \dot{y}_{wt}$$

given that $\dot{Y}_{jt} > \dot{Y}_w$. Defining $y_{Tt} = y_{jt} + y_{wt}$, reasoning analogous to that applied in the previous endnote dictates that under the hypothesized conditions, we will observe:

$$\frac{d\left(\frac{y_j}{y_w}\right)}{dt} > 0$$

that is, region j's share of world per capita income will be increasing over time.

20. Note that e is defined throughout the present analysis as the number of units of region j's currency per unit of region w's currency. Hence $\dot{e}_t < 0$ implies an appreciation in the value of region j's currency.

4 The Supply Side and Macroeconomic Performance I: Technological Evolution

1. This is easily verified, since under the hypothesized conditions:

$$v_{jn} = \varepsilon_{jn} - \varepsilon_{jn-1} = \varepsilon_{jn}$$

and

$$v_{jn+1} = \varepsilon_{jn+1} - \varepsilon_{jn} = -\varepsilon_{jn}$$

$$\Rightarrow \quad -v_{jn+1} = \varepsilon_{jn}$$

2. The size of the root $\lambda_j \alpha_j \beta_j$ – which, as suggested in Chapter 3, can take on different magnitudes according to different disequilibrium interpretations of equation [3.10] and hence equation [4.5] – also plays an important role in motivating this result. Inspection of [4.6] reveals that under the hypothesized conditions ($\varepsilon_{jn} > 0$, $\varepsilon_{ji} = 0$ for all $i \neq n$), we can, in fact, have:

$$\theta_j < 0 \text{ if } \lambda_j \alpha_j \beta_j \in (0, 1)$$

$$\theta_j > 0 \text{ if } \lambda_j \alpha_j \beta_j > 1$$

$$\theta_j = 0 \text{ if } \lambda_j \alpha_j \beta_j = 1$$

3. Frankel also argues that similar interconnections will likely develop between an economy's institutions. This possibility is explored in Chapter 5.

4. Similar problems may arise due to fluctuations in asset values resulting from changes in the state of long-run expectations in an environment of fundamental uncertainty.

5. In this case, of course, we would expect the relative efficiency and competitiveness of the region to be adversely affected. These issues are taken up in Section III.

6. Recall that interrelatedness refers to interconnections arising between components of the production process. These interconnections can be expected to multiply as the economy develops and the division of labour increases – that is, as production becomes more specialized and technically advanced. See Frankel (1955).

7. This possibility is developed by Richardson (1965a) in the context of a discussion of British experience in the 1930s. We will draw on Richardson's empirical observations in more detail in Chapter 7.

8. In the following analysis, we will consider the sensitivity of α_j and γ_j to past values of $\dot{Y}_{jt}$ rather than $\dfrac{\dot{Y}_{jt}}{\dot{Y}_w}$. This is done purely for simplicity of exposition. Hence note that $\dfrac{\dot{Y}_{jt}}{\dot{Y}_w}$ varies in direct proportion to $\dot{Y}_{jt}$, since $\dot{Y}_w$ is assumed constant. The sensitivity of α_j and γ_j to past values of $\dot{Y}_{jt}$ therefore implies their sensitivity to $\dfrac{\dot{Y}_{jt}}{\dot{Y}_w}$ in a straightforward manner, and statements about the growth path of region j translate into statements about the relative growth path of region j in a similarly straightforward fashion.

9. Note that even if $D\alpha = 0$, an increase in α_w motivated by changes in the 'rest of the world' (such as industrialization in late industrializing nations) will depress $\dfrac{\dot{Y}_{jt}}{\dot{Y}_w}$, since from [3.10]:

$$\frac{\partial \left(\dfrac{\dot{Y}_{jt}}{\dot{Y}_w} \right)}{\partial \alpha_w} = -\lambda_j \beta_j \cdot \sum_{i=0}^{t-1} (\lambda_j \alpha_j \beta_j)^i < 0$$

given that α_j, β_j, $\lambda_j > 0$. Hence even a *relative* diminution of α_j can bring about a relative growth climacteric similar to that discussed in the text.

10. Recall from Chapter 3 our assumption that $\dfrac{Y_j}{P_j} > \dfrac{Y_w}{P_w}$ initially, where P_i, $i = j$, w denotes total population. Therefore, 'catch up' is only a *possibility* when $\dot{Y}_w > \dot{Y}_j$, because although region j is growing relatively slowly, it is doing so from a higher initial base level of per capita income.

11. Maddison's notion of changes in economic leadership is actually defined in terms of levels of productivity rather than per capita income. However, these variables are obviously closely related.

12. According to this rationale, we would have to contemplate the *absolute* decline of an industry or region in order to conceive of a reduction in the level of interrelatedness and the alleviation of the problem of lock-in.

5 The Supply Side and Macroeconomic Performance II: Institutional Evolution

1. For recent surveys of the different branches of this literature, see the *Review of Political Economy*, Vol. 1, No. 3, 1989, and Hodgson (1993).

2. Whether or not institutions are functional to the goal orientation of individual actors and if so, to what degree, are issues that will be discussed subsequently.

3. Although this does not, of course, preclude the possibility of an explanation of institutions based on the aggregate effects of individual action.

4. Efficiency here refers to allocative efficiency, that is, a situation where '... the marginal rates of substitution between any two commodities or factors ... [are] the same in all their different uses' (Hayek, 1945, p. 519).
    It should be noted that Hayek has more recently expressed a greater interest in the role of institutions in a capitalist society. See Rutherford (1989) for a review.

5. Although this, of course, takes as given the definition of the commodities available on the market – that is, what goods and services are provided through the market, and why any particular commodity exists in the precise form that it does.

6. In this respect, Olson's argument bears superficial resemblance to the thesis which will be advanced in Section VI, which emphasizes the adverse effects on long-run growth of lock-in to an inefficient institutional regime. However, this superficial resemblance obscures fundamental methodological differences, not least because of our treatment of institutions as an endemic feature of all forms of economic organization, rather than mere veneers or 'imperfections'.

7. One exception to this would be if a single, deterministic, 'true' model of economic activity exists and is known to all individuals. Then any one agent might form expectations of how others will react to a given signal simply by equating their response with his/her own response to that same signal, based on the 'true' model. However, Richardson is considering decision making under conditions of fundamental uncertainty, which does not admit this possibility.

8. The importance and influence of Richardson's precise hypothesis, that institutions are an endemic and fundamental feature of capitalism because of fundamental uncertainty, is indicated by its now widespread acceptance amongst approaches such as Post-Keynesianism (see, for example, Lavoie, 1992) and heterodox institutionalism (see, for example, Hodgson, 1988).

9. Following Rutherford (1989), the term 'old' institutional economics is used here '. . . [not] to imply that the tradition concerned is no longer vital, only that it represents the longer history of continuous and central concern with institutional questions'. (Rutherford, 1989, p. 300).

10. This way of thinking about institutions certainly seems to contrast with their conception in some branches of the NIE. For example, North (1990) *defines* institutions as '. . . humanly devised *constraints* that shape human interaction' (p. 3, emphasis added).

11. This is particularly troublesome since, for many institutionalists, the notion that institutions are not immutable but subject to change over time is central to the OIE. See, for example, Miller (1978, pp. 14–17).

12. See also Hodgson (1993, pp. 4–6) for the argument that methodological individualism is the central common feature of the NIE, despite other theoretical and policy differences which can be found within this approach.

13. This is usually coupled with the further claim that these institutions will be efficient. This aspect of the NIE will be discussed in more detail subsequently.

14. See, for example, Brunner (1987).

15. This appears to suggest that institutions are conceived as preferences in the NIE – that they are ends in and of themselves. However, institutions can also be 'positively valued' as means to more narrowly defined selfish (usually pecuniary) ends. This treatment of 'institutions as decision rules' is consistent with the methodological individualism of the NIE as described earlier (Griffith and Goldfarb, 1991). Indeed, it would appear to be the more typical interpretation of what institutions are, especially in game theoretic strands of the NIE.

16. This involves the same game being played repeatedly in consecutive periods. The repetition mechanism in games of strategy can be thought of as a metaphor for time in what is otherwise a static framework of analysis.

17. Chiefly the notion that competition will give rise to a process of 'economic natural selection' amongst institutional forms.

18. North (1990) departs somewhat from this methodology by allowing for the influence of ideology on individual behaviour and hence the formation of institutions. Indeed, North's treatment of ideology changes not only his perception of the individual decision making process, but also his perception of the relationship between the individual and his/her environment (which includes pre-existing institutions). Hence Denzau and North (1994) conceive ideologies as examples of *shared* mental models within a society. It therefore transpires that '. . . an individual's experiential learning . . . is based on a culturally provided set of categories and priors so that each person does not need to begin as a *tabula rasa*' (pp. 4–5) – which sounds very much like the notion of the socialized individual found in the OIE. In general, however, NIE theorists treat individuals as maximizing, asocial atoms, whose behaviour is independent of any form of social structure.

19. Bardhan (1989) distinguishes between efficiency enhancing and distributional institutional changes, where the latter are related to control over economic outcomes, that is, the exercise of power. Distributional claims of this nature may motivate the 'vested interests' identified by Rutherford.

20. See also Hodgson (1993, pp. 8–9) on this point. According to Hodgson (1993, p. 9), Field's criticism effectively '. . . undermines any "new institutionalist" claim that the explanation of the emergence of institutions can start from some kind of institution-free ensemble of individuals in which there is supposedly no rule or institution to be explained'.

21. Whilst existing institutions will define the *actual* choice sets faced by individuals and groups (for example, the law places bounds on consumption sets) it is important to note that even if they only define *perceived* choice sets, institutions may still influence the nature of economic activity. Hence social norms which bind some individuals to traditional lifestyles and communities may affect labour mobility, despite the fact that they place no literal constraint on an individual's choice of occupation and place of residence.

22. Note that the model itself does not *predict* this form of institutional evolution, but is *compatible* with it due to the distinction made within the model between short and long-run aspects of institutional evolution.

23. Institutions are conventionally regarded as 'socially efficient' in the sense of being Pareto optimal – that is, no alternative set of institutions exists that could make one individual better off whilst leaving no others worse off. In general, however, there is nothing compelling about this particular definition of efficiency. Indeed, other definitions may be more appropriate when discussing institutional efficiency. We will introduce these alternative definitions in due course, as need for them arises.

     Note, also, that some NIE authors have begun to back away from making claims about the efficiency of institutions. See, for example, North's (1990, p. 7) account of the development of his own thought on this issue.

24. In what follows, we will concentrate on explaining the emergence and persistence of inefficient institutions for reasons associated with path dependency. This is not to suggest that other factors, such as power, are not instrumental in explaining these same phenomena; the exclusivity of what follows is justified solely by our greater emphasis on the importance of sequential causality and path dependency in explaining long-run outcomes.

25. Note, then, that what is being contemplated here differs from an explanation of institutional inertia couched purely in terms of vested interests. The latter may arise because some party *knows* that a certain institutional change is in their distributional interest, whereas the mechanism outlined relies simply on one party *suspecting* that distributional consequences will arise from what may be described by some other party to the institution as mutually beneficial change.

26. This is to say nothing of the competitive decline the economy may experience if the inefficient institution subsequently affects its relative economic performance. This issue is taken up in more detail later.

27. This emphasis on a sequential, competitive struggle taking place *over time* makes the natural selection mechanism compatible with the methodology of hysteresis, discussed in Chapter 2. This contrasts with the repetition mechan-

ism in game theoretic variants of the NIE (see footnote 18), in which institutional outcomes are determined at a *point in time* as a result of a dynamic programming exercise by individual agents. The repetition mechanism is therefore fundamentally incompatible with the methodology of hysteresis, and is therefore not considered further. See also Setterfield (1993b).

28. Suppose, for example, that Type I firms account for 78 per cent of the market. Then $\pi_I = 78 < 79 = \pi_{II}$. The marginal firm in this market (that is, the new entrant) therefore has an incentive to be of Type II.

29. Notice that any conception of these institutions as 'efficient' now involves conceiving institutional efficiency in terms of 'macroeconomic' and/or 'dynamic' efficiency, defined respectively as the full employment of resources at a point in time and the realization of 'high' rates of accumulation and growth over time.

30. These 'new demands' were related to concerns including control of the work process, hiring and firing practices, and the overall level of employment. They were accompanied by enhanced distributional claims by a labour movement buoyed by conditions of full employment.

31. Note that in this example, the economy is engaged not only in the creation of inefficient institutions, but also the destruction of previously efficient institutions. The latter theme is discussed by Schumpeter (1942), and also by Hirsch (1976), who argues that capitalism inexorably erodes values inherited from the pre-capitalist past (for example, values associated with religion). This is despite the fact that these pre-capitalist values may be instrumental in forming the 'social prerequisites of markets' – shared values on such issues as the appropriate sphere of market activity – and may therefore, as authors such as Adam Smith and J.S. Mill believed, be functional to the successful operation of capitalism.

32. Another potentially fruitful approach would be to concentrate on monetary institutions. According to Post-Keynesian economists, the use of money and associated money contracts are institutional responses to decision making under uncertainty, and have real effects on the economy. This treatment of money as a non-neutral institution suggests that the evolution of monetary institutions is ripe for incorporation into the extended model of cumulative causation we are currently developing. As it is, the model appears bereft of monetary relations, although it might be argued that it appeals implicitly to a crude form of the horizontalist theory of credit money (see Moore, 1988), in which the demand for credit at a given interest rate is always accommodated by a perfectly elastic supply of credit.

33. This point is also emphasized by Lazonick (1990).

34. The reader is referred back to the arguments of Section V of Chapter 4 with respect to this claim.

35. Notice that the interpretation of capitalism that arises from this extended model – that of a transforming system which encounters different epochs in its development characterized by different technological and institutional 'regimes' – is similar to that which arises from traditions such as the French Regulation School (see, for example, Boyer, 1990), and the American Social Structure of Accumulation school (see, for example, Bowles *et al.*, 1990).

36. Dialectics is used in this context to denote a theory of historical motion based on conflict between contradictory forces (see Elster, 1985, pp. 37–48).

Part III   The Evolution of a Macroeconomy: Growth and Structural Change in the British Economy since 1780: Introduction

1.   See Lorenz (1991, pp. 3–5) for a summary of the arguments which suggest that, by virtue of its competitors' industrialization, some part of Britain's relative economic decline after 1870 was inevitable.

6   A Brief History of the British Economy since 1780

1.   Throughout Part III, we will use the term 'rest of the world' in reference to France, Germany, Italy, Japan and the USA, the economies that were destined to emerge as Britain's major industrial competitors during the nineteenth and twentieth centuries. Initially, we will also include the Netherlands in this group, due to its significance as the 'lead' economy prior to 1820 (Maddison, 1982, 1991).

2.   The decade 1876–85 is the earliest period for which reliable export share data are available. See Harley and McCloskey, 1981.

3.   That Britain's economic performance 1870–1913 was not greatly inferior to that achieved during the preceding period may be explained, in part, by the fact that the British economy was never particularly fast growing in absolute terms, even during the period of its unchallenged dominance of the world economy (Maddison, 1982).

4.   Floud (1981, p. 8) calculates real GDP growth rates 1873–1914 in Britain, the USA and Germany as 1.8 per cent per annum, 4.5 per cent per annum and 2.8 per cent per annum respectively.

5.   Inspection of Tables 6.1, 6.2, 6.4, 6.7, 6.8 and 6.10 reveals that Britain experienced not just relative, but also *absolute* declines in its rates of export and output growth after 1870 as compared with the early mid-Victorian era. Tables 6.3 and 6.9 do not support the notion of a comparable slowdown in the rate of growth of labour productivity. However, Matthews *et al.* (1982, pp. 207–10) do find evidence of a slowdown in Britain's rate of growth of total factor productivity, from 1.4 per cent per annum 1856–73 to 0.5 per cent per annum 1873–1913.

Although Britain's historical growth slowdown dates from 1873, evidence suggests that this slowdown is most pronounced after 1899 (Feinstein *et al.*, 1982; Matthews *et al.*, 1982, pp. 606–7). This implies that the notion of an Edwardian climacteric 1899–1914 is more useful than that of a 'Great Depression' 1873–96 for the understanding of British economic history in the late nineteenth and early twentieth centuries.

6.   The years 1913–50 proved to be extremely turbulent for the German economy, its average economic performance suffering accordingly. Indeed, Germany's poor average performance after the Great War clearly biases downwards the rest of the world's performance in Tables 6.7–6.10, flattering Britain by comparison.

7.   The possibility that since the 1960s, the US has entered a growth climacteric and is following a development path similar to that previously experienced by Britain is not investigated here. However, this possibility is beginning to draw the attention of a number of authors. See, for example, Elbaum (1990) and Elbaum and Lazonick (1986).

8. The six original members of the EEC from 1957–73 were West Germany, France, Italy, Belgium, the Netherlands and Luxembourg.
9. By the end of the nineteenth century, textiles still accounted for about 40 per cent of the value of British exports (Harley and McCloskey, 1981) whilst as late as 1910, textiles, iron and steel, machinery and shipbuilding comprised 70 per cent of British manufactured exports (Elbaum, 1990).
10. 63 per cent of value added in the British textile industry was labour cost, and wages were substantially higher than in the textile industries of competing nations, except the US (Elbaum, 1990). Clark (1987, p. 14) documents the substantial labour cost advantages that European textile industries enjoyed relative to the British textile industry as early as the 1830s.
11. In spite of their specialization, British ship yards did not mass produce a standardized vessel, and relied upon skilled labour to facilitate product variation within a given class of vessel. See Lorenz (1991, pp. 26–8).
12. The contribution of overseas markets to the demand for British textile machinery is illustrated by the fact that Britain dominated international trade in ring frames, despite the fact that this technology accounted for so little of Britain's own cotton spinning capacity. See Chapter 7 on the slow adoption of ring frame technology in Britain.
13. See also Elbaum (1990) and Elbaum and Lazonick (1986) for the argument that institutional factors have been the most important elements in Britain's accelerated relative economic decline during the twentieth century.

7 Technological Interrelatedness and Lock-In in the British Economy, 1870–1930

1. Although Aldcroft does not explicitly define the composition of 'industrial output,' it is clear from the context in which he uses the term that this category comprises the output of the manufacturing and mineral extraction sectors.
2. It is important to note that Richardson originally defined the term 'over commitment' in connection with the sectoral composition of Britain's output. However, he acknowledges the importance of technological change within individual industries, and in fact describes over commitment to traditional lines of production as a problem relating to the adoption of new *technologies* associated with new industries. It does not, therefore, involve a great aberration of Richardson's original meaning to extend the use of the term 'over commitment' to describe the concentration of Britain's capital stock in certain traditional technologies and associated techniques of production.
3. Richardson (1965b, pp. 240–1) stresses that the over commitment thesis is not contingent on the assumption of irrational behaviour on the part of firms. Note, however, that the over commitment/lock-in thesis can be reinterpreted as entrepreneurial failure from a Schumpeterian perspective. The key question from this perspective is why British firms failed to innovate around constraints inherited from the past. See, for example, Lazonick (1992, p. viii).
4. Notice that interrelatedness *within* firms cannot explain why new entrants in a region fail to adopt the latest technology, and hence why an entire industry should remain locked in to an obsolete technology. *Inter* (as opposed to *intra*)

firm interrelatedness is therefore important in the explanation of the latter phenomenon, since this affects both new entrants and current incumbents alike.

Note also that the existence of inter firm interrelatedness begs the question as to why consolidation does not occur in an industry. The issues of market entry and consolidation are addressed in the course of the historical case studies that follow – the latter in some detail in Section II(iii).

5. Britain's share of world trade in cotton goods fell from 82 per cent in 1882–4 to 58 per cent in 1910–13.

6. These and other details of the spinning and weaving processes can be found in Sandberg (1974).

7. Weaving involves passing a shuttle containing yarn (known as weft) between orthogonal strands of yarn (known as warp).

8. The mule placed less strain on yarn during spinning, and was consequently capable of spinning a wider range of cotton qualities than the ring frame.

9. According to Coase (1937), the nature of the firm is dictated by profit maximizing considerations, with organization supplanting the market (as in the case of the integration of technically separable production processes) whenever this appears profitable.

10. The ease of sea communication between the coalfields of South Wales and North East England and the markets of Europe and South America gave Britain a substantial cost advantage in haulage at a time when transporting coal over land was expensive. See Taylor (1968, p. 41).

11. By way of comparison, it may be noted that by 1900, 20 per cent of the output of the US coal industry was machine cut (Taylor, 1968, p. 56).

12. The term 'new industries' is used to denote those industries, such as the chemical and motor vehicle industries, which emerged in the late nineteenth century.

13. The relative positions of these nations did, however, vary from product to product.

14. By 1890, the price of Leblanc alkali was just one third of its level in the early 1870s (Richardson, 1968, p. 284).

15. This allowed Leblanc producers to differentiate their product from that of their Solvay competitors, who produced mainly pure soda.

16. Although the possibility is not explored in detail here, lock-in to traditional industries may also have an effect on the ability of a region to realize dynamic increasing returns, as reflected in the size of α_j in the model developed in Part II. This is possible if new industries form 'development blocks' which it is necessary for a region to move into if it is to sustain the same productivity growth rate on the basis of a given rate of growth of output. Hence Cantwell (1991) provides evidence that technological progress in late Victorian Britain was self reinforcing. In so doing, he concludes that after 1890, Britain was locked in to a development block comprising a set of staple industries in which the possibilities for technological advancement were nearly exhausted. This, he concludes, was likely detrimental to Britain's rate of productivity growth.

17. Svennilson applies the term 'contracting industry' to those industries whose share of total world trade in manufactures exhibited a declining trend over the period 1913–50.

18. The total decline in Britain's share of manufactured exports between 1899 and 1937 was 10.1 percentage points.
19. Many of the traditional industries which were steam powered in Britain could be powered (often more efficiently) by electricity, making their power demands compatible with those of new industries such as aluminium, and providing a sufficiently large market to stimulate the large scale investment necessary for the creation of efficient electricity generating facilities. See Kennedy (1987, p. 138) on the importance of this last point.
20. The loss of common land due to the enclosure movement, and the subsequent loss of livelihood experienced by rural workers was a key factor promoting labour mobility during Britain's initial industrialization.
21. This conclusion draws particularly on his extensive study of the decline of the British cotton industry. See Sandberg (1974).
22. See also Lazonick (1990, pp. 157–62) for the argument that Sandberg significantly underestimates the extent to which productivity growth declined in British industry from the late nineteenth century onwards.

8 Institutional Hysteresis and the Performance of the British Economy after 1914

1. Emphasis is placed on the twentieth century because, as noted earlier, it has been the concern of a number of authors to suggest that institutional factors were the single most important source of Britain's competitive failure during this period. See, for example, Elbaum (1990) and Elbaum and Lazonick (1986).
2. Once again, it is important to bear in mind that our focus on the industrial relations system is not meant to suggest that this is the only institution that may have contributed to Britain's relative economic decline. A more general theory of inefficient institutional evolution might also take into account Britain's commitment to the conventions of free trade and domestic *laissez-faire* (Bowles and Eatwell, 1983), the role of financial institutions (Best and Humphries, 1986; Kennedy, 1987) and the nature of corporate structure and industrial organization in the British economy (Elbaum and Lazonick, 1986).
3. The Taff Vale Decision ruled that trade unions were liable for damages brought about by their sponsorship of industrial action. It effectively undermined the financial feasibility of strikes.
4. Following Hibbs (1978), we can define three dimensions which make up the profile of a strike: size (the number of strikers per strike); duration (the number of person days lost per striker); and incidence (the number of strikes per thousand workers). It is widely agreed that strike volume – the product of these three dimensions – is the most appropriate aggregate indicator of strike activity (see Hibbs, 1978).

   Note, however, that the volume of strike activity is an imperfect indicator of the state of industrial relations. As Naples (1981, 1986) notes, strikes are only one form of industrial action – phenomena such as absenteeism and even high quit rates may also be symptoms of labour unrest. Furthermore, a low level of strike volume may indicate trade union weakness rather than capital–labour cooperation. It is important to bear these shortcomings in mind when assessing the contents of Table 8.1.

5.   War and the preparations for it also drastically reduced the rate of unemployment, a major source of social strife in inter-war Britain. Unemployment fell from a peak of 23 per cent in 1932 to 9 per cent by 1937, although it then increased again between 1938–9 to 12 per cent despite re-armament (Pollard, 1962, p. 243). It would have likely continued to increase had it not been for the outbreak of World War II, following which unemployment fell to the extent that it had been 'virtually abolished' by 1941 (Pollard, 1962, p. 347).

6.   The number of unofficial strikes during this period was also indicative of a problem that was to re-emerge in subsequent periods – the battle for control of the labour movement between national leadership and shop stewards.

7.   In 1945, the Labour Party won what remains the largest ever majority in the House of Commons in British parliamentary history.

8.   Productivity agreements were designed to link conditions of employment – in particular, wages – to productivity growth.

9.   These Acts also affected other aspects of union activity, such as the legality of the closed shop.

10. Recall that even during the post-war years, the British economy did not develop social democratic industrial relations structures, such as those which typified the Scandinavian economies, or 'plant level corporatist' institutions such as those defining capital–labour relations in Japanese firms. In fact, as will be emphasized, Britain made no radical break from the structure of the industrial relations system it had inherited from the late nineteenth/early twentieth centuries.

11. On the importance of technological change and its relationship to efficiency in the cotton industry, see Chapter 7.

12. This opposition was made known when the FMCSA sought legal backing for its price fixing arrangements in an effort to discipline spinning firms who persisted in defecting from the terms of these arrangements.

13. Again, the lack of any trend towards consolidation in this key British industry seems to have played an important role in its subsequent institutional and technological development. For a discussion of the relative lack of merger activity in late nineteenth and early twentieth century Britain, the reader is referred back to Section II(iii) of Chapter 7.

14. In 1890, Britain accounted for 80 per cent of the world market in shipbuilding. This share diminished to 60 per cent by 1900, to 35 per cent during the inter-war years, and to 15 per cent by the 1950s, after which the continued decline of the British shipbuilding industry threatened its very survival (Lorenz and Wilkinson, 1986, p. 109).

15. It is not clear, however, that the advantages of this rapidly expanding market accrued evenly to all shipbuilding nations. Lorenz (1991, p. 84) argues that Britain's major competitors – especially Japan and Sweden – benefited disproportionately from their faster growing and protected domestic markets.

16. Some illustration of this is provided by the fact that in 1913, Ford produced over two hundred times as many cars as Wolseley, the largest British producer, whilst employing only three times as much labour (Lewchuk, 1986, p. 139; Saul, 1962, p. 25).

17. The British motor vehicle industry was largely non-union up to the 1950s (Lazonick, 1990, p. 183).

18. Again, the reader is referred to Chapter 6 for comparative historical statistics on Britain's post-war dynamic macroeconomic performance.

19. The view that the emergence of post-war welfarism in Britain derived from the conditions of the preceding era can be found in the Beveridge Report, which stresses the emergence of sentiments such as 'national unity' during World War II. An alternative hypothesis, forwarded by Goodin and Dryzek (1987), is that the degree of uncertainty created by the war amongst all sections of the British population generated widespread demands for 'socialized risk sharing', and so to the growth of state welfarism.

20. See Cornwall (1990) for a more detailed exploration of the links between institutions and the post 1945 macroeconomic performance of Britain and other capitalist economies.

21. Much has been made of the apparent 'renaissance' of British productivity growth since 1979. See, however, Crafts (1993, pp. 49–52) for the view that this chiefly constitutes a once and for all increase in the *level* of productivity during the 1980s.

22. Several of these authors offer an international perspective on the rise and demise of these 'regimes' in industrial relations. They have begun to receive particular attention in the context of the US economy, with accompanying indications as to how changes in industrial relations regimes have affected the dynamic efficiency of this economy (see, for example, Weisskopf *et al.*, 1983; Naples, 1981, 1986).

23. The reader is again reminded of the significant difference between *organizations* such as trade unions, and *institutions* which govern the relationship between organizations, such as the industrial relations system.

24. In some of the 'new' industries, of course, such as the motor vehicle industry discussed in Section II(iii), the problem of institutional inefficiency arose from the *creation* of (by now) inefficient institutions as well as their subsequent persistence. Given the precise nature of industrial relations in the motor vehicle industry, however, the fact that we can produce industry level evidence on the creation of inefficient institutions merely reinforces our greater point concerning the lack of systemic change in the basic nature of British industrial relations during the twentieth century, and their continued dominance by quintessentially nineteenth century practices.

25. Recall that labour relies on its control of production to generate income and employment security, which is not otherwise automatically forthcoming, in the context of craft production.

26. For the view that Fordist mass production has since been superseded by the Japanese flexible manufacturing system, and that the latter now constitutes the technique of production within which the most dynamically successful economies are accumulating, see Lazonick (1990).

Conclusion

1. See, for example, Elbaum and Lazonick (1986).

2. A similar point could be made about the British experience, based on the role of commercial policy and imperialism in securing sources of raw materials and export markets for British industry.

References

Akerlof, G. (1970) 'The market for "lemons": quality uncertainty and the market mechanism', *Quarterly Journal of Economics*, 84, 488–500.

Akerlof, G. (1976) 'The economics of caste and race and other woeful tales', *Quarterly Journal of Economics*, 90, 599–617.

Alchian, A. (1950) 'Uncertainty, evolution and economic theory', *Journal of Political Economy*, 58, 211–21.

Aldcroft, D.H. (1964) 'The entrepreneur and the British economy, 1870–1914', *Economic History Review*, 17, 113–34.

Aldcroft, D.H. (ed.) (1968) *The Development of British Industry and Foreign Competition, 1875–1914*, London, Allen and Unwin.

Aldcroft, D.H. (1968) 'Introduction: British industry and foreign competition, 1875–1914', in D.H. Aldcroft (1968) *op. cit.*

Amsden, A. (1989) *Asia's Next Giant*, Oxford, Oxford University Press.

Arrow, K. (1959) 'Towards a theory of price adjustments', in M. Abramovitz, A. Alchian, K.J. Arrow, P.A. Baran, P.W. Cartwright, H.B. Chenery, G.W. Hilton, H.S. Houthakker, C.E. Lindblom, M.W. Reder, T. Scitovsky, E.S. Shaw and L. Tarshis, *The Allocation of Economic Resources*, Stanford, Stanford University Press.

Arrow, K. (1962) 'The economic implications of learning by doing', *Review of Economic Studies*, 29, 155–73.

Arthur, W.B. (1988a) 'Self reinforcing mechanisms in economics', in P.W. Anderson, K. Arrow and D. Pines (eds) *The Economy as an Evolving Complex System*, Reading, Mass., Addison–Wesley.

Arthur, W.B. (1988b) 'Competing technologies: an overview', in G. Dosi, C. Freeman, R. Nelson, G. Silverberg and L. Soete (eds) *Technical Change and Economic Theory*, New York, Pinter.

Ayres, C. (1962) *The Theory of Economic Progress*, New York, Schocken Books.

Bardhan, P. (1989) 'The new institutional economics and development theory: a brief critical assessment', *World Development*, 17, 1389–95.

Barkin, S. (1975) 'The third post-war decade (1965–75): progress, activism and tension', in S. Barkin (ed.) *Worker Militancy and its Consequences, 1965–75*, New York, Praeger.

Basu, K., E. Jones and E. Schlicht (1987) 'The growth and decay of custom: the role of the new institutional economics in economic history', *Explorations in Economic History*, 24, 1–21.

Baumol, W.J., S.A.B. Blackman and E.N. Wolff (1989) *Productivity and American Leadership: The Long View*, Cambridge, Mass., MIT Press.

Best, M.H. and J. Humphries (1986) 'The City and industrial decline', in B. Elbaum and W. Lazonick (eds) *op. cit.*

Bowles, S. and J. Eatwell (1983) 'Between two worlds: interest groups, class structure and capitalist growth', in D.C. Mueller (ed.) *The Political Economy of Growth*, New Haven, Yale University Press.

Bowles, S., D.M. Gordon and T.E. Weisskopf (1990) *After the Wasteland*, Armonk, New York, M.E. Sharpe.

Boyer, R. (1990) *The Regulation School: A Critical Introduction*, New York, Columbia University Press.

Boyer, R. and P. Petit (1991) 'Kaldor's growth theories: past, present and prospects for the future', in E.J. Nell and W. Semmeler (eds) *Nicholas Kaldor and the Mainstream Economics*, New York, St. Martin's Press.

Bromley, D. (1989) *Economic Interests and Institutions*, Oxford, Basil Blackwell.

Brown, W. (1972) 'A consideration of "custom and practice"', *British Journal of Industrial Relations*, 10, 42–61.

Brunner, K. (1987) 'The perception of man and the conception of society: two approaches to the understanding of society', *Economic Inquiry*, 25, 367–88.

Cairncross, A. (1981) 'The post-war years, 1945–77', in R.C. Floud and D.N. McCloskey (eds) *op. cit.*

Cantwell, J. (1991) 'Historical trends in international patterns of technological innovation', in J. Foreman-Peck (ed.) *New Perspectives on the Late Victorian Economy*, Cambridge, Cambridge University Press.

Church, R.A. (1975) *The Great Victorian Boom, 1850–1873*, London, Macmillan.

Clark, G. (1987) 'Why isn't the whole world developed? Lessons from the cotton mills', *Journal of Economic History*, 47, 141–73.

Coase, R. (1937) 'The nature of the firm', *Economica*, 4, 386–405.

Coates, K. and T. Topham (1986) *Trade Unions and Politics*, Oxford, Basil Blackwell.

Coddington, A. (1972) 'Positive economics', *Canadian Journal of Economics*, 5, 1–15.

Coddington, A. (1975) 'The rationale of general equilibrium theory', *Economic Inquiry*, 13, 539–58.

Commons, J.R. (1961) *Institutional Economics*, Madison, University of Wisconsin Press.

Cornwall, J. (1972) *Growth and Stability in a Mature Economy*, London, Martin Robertson.

Cornwall, J. (1977) *Modern Capitalism*, Oxford, Martin Robertson.

Cornwall, J. (1990) *The Theory of Economic Breakdown*, Oxford, Basil Blackwell.

Cornwall, J. (1991) 'Prospects for unemployment in the 1990s with hysteresis', in J. Cornwall (ed.) *The Capitalist Economies: Prospects for the 1990s*, Aldershot, Edward Elgar.

Cornwall, J. and W. Cornwall (1987) 'The political economy of stagnation', *Journal of Economic Issues*, 25, 535–50.

Cornwall, J. and W. Cornwall (1992) 'Export led growth: a new interpretation', in W. Milberg (ed.) *The Megacorp and Macrodynamics*, Armonk, New York, M.E. Sharpe.

Crafts, N.F.R. (1993) *Can De-Industrialisation Seriously Damage Your Wealth?* London, Institute for Economic Affairs.

Cross, R. (1987) 'Hysteresis and instability in the natural rate of unemployment', *Scandinavian Journal of Economics*, 89, 71–89.

Cross, R. (1991) 'The NAIRU: Not an interesting rate of unemployment?', University of Strathclyde Working Paper.

Cross, R. (1993) 'On the foundations of hysteresis in economic systems', *Economics and Philosophy*, 9, 53–74.

Cross, R. and A. Allen (1988) 'On the history of hysteresis', in R. Cross (ed.) *Unemployment, Hysteresis and The Natural Rate Hypothesis*, Oxford, Basil Blackwell.

Crouch, C. (1978) 'The intensification of industrial conflict in the United King-dom', in C. Crouch and A. Pizzorno (eds) *The Resurgence of Class Conflict in Western Europe since 1968 Volume 1*, New York, Holmes and Meier.

David, P.A. (1985) 'Clio and the economics of QWERTY', *American Economic Review*, 75, 332–7.

Davidson, P. (1988) 'A technical definition of uncertainty and the long-run non-neutrality of money', *Cambridge Journal of Economics*, 12, 329–37.

Davidson, P. (1991) 'Is probability theory relevant for uncertainty?', *Journal of Economic Perspectives*, 5, 129–43.

Deane, P. and W.A. Cole (1962) *British Economic Growth 1688–1959*, Cambridge, Cambridge University Press.

Denzau, A.T. and D.C. North (1994) 'Shared mental models: ideologies and institutions', *Kyklos*, 47, 3–31.

Dixit, A. (1989) 'Hysteresis, import penetration and exchange rate pass through', *Quarterly Journal of Economics*, 104, 205–28.

Dixon, R. and A.P. Thirlwall (1975) 'A model of regional growth rate differences along Kaldorian lines', *Oxford Economic Papers*, 27, 201–14.

Dixon, R. and A.P. Thirlwall (1978) 'Growth rate stability in the Kaldorian regional model', *Scottish Journal of Political Economy*, 25, 97–9.

Dopfer, K. (1991) 'Toward a theory of economic institutions: synergy and path dependence', *Journal of Economic Issues*, 25, 535–50.

Dornbusch, R. (1987) 'Exchange rate economics: 1986', *Economic Journal*, 97, 1–18.

Dowie, J.A. (1968) 'Growth in the interwar period: some more arithmetic', *Economic History Review*, 21, 93–112.

Dunlop, J. (1958) *Industrial Relations Systems*, New York, Holt.

Eatwell, J. (1984) *Whatever Happened To Britain?* New York, Oxford University Press.

Elbaum, B. (1990) 'Cumulative or comparative advantage? British competitiveness in the early twentieth century', *World Development*, 18, 1255–72.

Elbaum, B. and W. Lazonick (eds) (1986) *The Decline of the British Economy*, Oxford, The Clarendon Press.

Elbaum, B. and W. Lazonick (1986) 'An institutional perspective on British decline', in B. Elbaum and W. Lazonick (eds) *op. cit.*

Elster, J. (1976) 'A note on hysteresis in the social sciences', *Synthese*, 33, 371–91.

Elster, J. (1985) *Making Sense of Marx*, Cambridge, Cambridge University Press.

Elster, J. (1989a) 'Social norms and economic theory', *Journal of Economic Perspectives*, 3, 99–117.

Elster, J. (1989b) *The Cement of Society*, Cambridge, Cambridge University Press.

Farnie, D.A. (1979) *The English Cotton Industry and the World Market 1815–1896*, Oxford, Oxford University Press.

Feinstein, C.H. (1972) *National Income, Expenditure and Output of the United Kingdom 1855–1965*, Cambridge, Cambridge University Press.

Feinstein, C.H., R.C.O. Matthews and J.C. Odling Smee (1982) 'The timing of the climacteric and its sectoral incidence in the UK, 1873–1913', in C.P. Kindleberger and G. di Tella (eds) *Economics in the Long View Volume 2: Applications and Cases Part I*, New York, New York University Press.

Field, A.J. (1984) 'Microeconomics, norms and rationality', *Economic Development and Cultural Change*, 32, 683–711.

Floud, R.C. (1981) 'Britain 1860–1914: a survey', in R.C. Floud and D.N. McCloskey (eds) *op. cit.*

Floud, R.C. and D.N. McCloskey (eds) (1981) *The Economic History of Britain Since 1700 Volume 2: 1860 to the 1970s*, Cambridge, Cambridge University Press.

Frankel, M. (1955) 'Obsolescence and technological change in a maturing economy', *American Economic Review*, 45, 296–319.

Franz, W. (1990) 'Hysteresis in economic relationships: an overview', *Empirical Economics*, 15, 109–25.

Friedman, M. (1953) 'The methodology of positive economics', in *Essays in Positive Economics*, Chicago, Chicago University Press.

Friedman, M. (1968) 'The role of monetary policy', *American Economic Review*, 43, 1–17.

Georgescu-Roegen, N. (1971) *The Entropy Law and the Economic Process*, Cambridge, Mass., Harvard University Press.

Giavazzi, F. and C. Wyplosz (1985) 'The zero root problem: a note on the dynamic determination of the stationary equilibrium in linear models', *Review of Economic Studies*, 52, 353–57.

Goodin, R.E. and J. Dryzek (1987) 'Risk sharing and social justice: the motivational foundations of the post-war welfare state', in R.E. Goodin and J. LeGrand, *Not Only the Poor*, London, Allen and Unwin.

Gordon, D., R. Edwards and M. Reich (1982) *Segmented Workers, Divided Work*, Cambridge, Cambridge University Press.

Gordon, R.J. (1989) 'Hysteresis in history: was there ever a Phillips curve?', *American Economic Review*, 79, 220–5.

Gordon, W. (1980) *Institutional Economics*, Austin, Texas, University of Texas Press.

Griffith, W.B. and R.S. Goldfarb (1991) 'Amending the economist's "rational egoist" model to include moral values and norms, part 2: alternative solutions', in K.J. Koford and J.B. Miller (eds) *Social Norms and Economic Institutions*, Ann Arbor, University of Michigan Press.

Grossman, G.M. and E. Helpman (1991) *Innovation and Growth in the Global Economy*, Cambridge, Mass., MIT Press.

Hahn, F. (1970) 'Some adjustment problems', *Econometrica*, 38, 1–17. Reprinted in F. Hahn (1984) *op. cit.*

Hahn, F. (1974) 'On the notion of equilibrium in economics', inaugural lecture, Cambridge University, Cambridge University Press. Reprinted in F. Hahn (1984) *op. cit.*

Hahn, F. (1982) 'Reflections on the invisible hand', *Lloyds Bank Review*, 1–21. Reprinted in F. Hahn (1984) *op. cit.*

Hahn, F. (1984) *Equilibrium and Macroeconomics*, Oxford, Basil Blackwell.

Handbook of International Economic Statistics (1986) Faculty of Economics, Cambridge University.

Harley, C.K. and D.N. McCloskey (1981) 'Foreign trade: competition and the expanding international economy', in R.C. Floud and D.N. McCloskey (eds) *op. cit.*

Hayek, F.A. (1945) 'The use of knowledge in society', *American Economic Review*, 35, 519–30.

Henin, P.Y. (1986) *Macrodynamics: Fluctuations and Growth*, London, Routledge and Kegan Paul.

Hibbs, D. (1978) 'On the political economy of long run trends in strike activity', *British Journal of Political Economy*, 8, 153–76.

Hirsch, F. (1976) *Social Limits to Growth*, Cambridge, Mass., Harvard University Press.

Hodgson, G.M. (1986) 'Behind methodological individualism', *Cambridge Journal of Economics*, 10, 211–24.

Hodgson, G.M. (1988) *Economics and Institutions: A Manifesto for a Modern Institutional Economics*, Cambridge, Polity Press.

Hodgson, G.M. (1989) 'Institutional rigidities and economic growth', *Cambridge Journal of Economics*, 13, 79–101.

Hodgson, G.M. (1991) 'Economic evolution: intervention contra Pangloss', *Journal of Economic Issues*, 25, 519–33.

Hodgson, G.M. (1993) 'Institutional economics: surveying the "old" and the "new"', *Metroeconomica*, 44, 1–28.

Hont, I. (1983) 'The "rich country-poor country" debate in Scottish classical political economy', in I. Hont and M. Ignatieff (eds) *Wealth and Virtue: The Shaping of Political Economy in the Scottish Enlightenment*, Cambridge, Cambridge University Press.

Ingrao, B. and G. Israel (1990) *The Invisible Hand*, Cambridge, Mass., MIT Press.

Jenkinson, T. (1987) 'The natural rate of unemployment: does it exist?', *Oxford Review of Economic Policy*, 3, 20–6.

Kaldor, N. (1934) 'A classificatory note on the determinateness of equilibrium', *Review of Economic Studies*, 2, 122–36.

Kaldor, N. (1970) 'The case for regional policies', *Scottish Journal of Political Economy*, 18, 337–48. Reprinted in *Further Essays on Economic Theory* (1978) New York, Holmes and Meier.

Kaldor, N. (1972) 'The irrelevance of equilibrium economics', *Economic Journal*, 82, 1237–55.

Kaldor, N. (1981) 'The role of increasing returns, technical progress and cumulative causation in the theory of international trade and economic growth', *Économie Appliquée*, 34, 593–617. Reprinted in *Further Essays on Economic Theory and Policy*, New York, Holmes and Meier, 1989.

Kaldor, N. (1985) *Economics Without Equilibrium*, Cardiff, University College Cardiff Press.

Katzner, D. (1993) 'Some notes on the role of history and the definition of hysteresis and related concepts in economic analysis', *Journal of Post Keynesian Economics*, 15, 323–45.

Kennedy, W.P. (1987) *Industrial Structure, Capital Markets and the Origins of British Economic Decline*, Cambridge, Cambridge University Press.

Keynes, J.M. (1936) *The General Theory of Employment Interest and Money*, London, Macmillan.

Kirman, A. (1989) 'The intrinsic limits of modern economic theory: the emperor has no clothes', *Economic Journal*, 99, 126–39.

Kirman, A. (1992) 'Whom or what does the representative agent represent?', *Journal of Economic Perspectives*, 6, 117–36.

Kitson, M. and S. Solomou (1989) 'The macroeconomics of protectionism: the case of Britain in the 1930s', *Cambridge Journal of Economics*, 13, 155–69.

Kregel, J.A. (1976) 'Economic methodology in the face of uncertainty: the modelling methods of Keynes and the Post-Keynesians', *Economic Journal*, 86, 209–25.

Krugman, P.R. (1989) *Exchange Rate Instability*, Cambridge, MIT Press.

Lamfalussy, A. (1961) *Investment and Growth in Mature Economies*, New York, Macmillan.

Lamfalussy, A. (1963) *The UK and the Six*, Homewood, Irwin.

Langlois, R.N. (1986) 'The new institutional economics: an introductory essay', in R.N. Langlois (ed.) *Economics as a Process*, Cambridge, Cambridge University Press.

Lavoie, M. (1992) *Foundations of Post-Keynesian Economic Analysis*, Aldershot, Edward Elgar.

Lawson, A. (1985) 'Uncertainty and economic analysis', *Economic Journal*, 95, 909–27.

Layard, R., S. Nickell and R. Jackman (1991) *Unemployment: Macroeconomic Performance and the Labour Market*, Oxford, Oxford University Press.

Layton, D. (1973) 'Low pay and collective bargaining', in F. Field (ed.) *Low Pay: Acton Society Trust Essays*, London, Arrow Books.

Lazonick, W. (1979) 'Industrial relations and technical change: the case of the self acting mule', *Cambridge Journal of Economics*, 3, 231–62.

Lazonick, W. (1981) 'Factor costs and the diffusion of ring spinning in Britain prior to World War I', *Quarterly Journal of Economics*, 96, 89–109. Reprinted in W. Lazonick (1992) *op. cit.*

Lazonick, W. (1983) 'Industrial organization and technological change: the decline of the British cotton industry', *Business History Review*, 57, 195–236. Reprinted in W. Lazonick (1992) *op. cit.*

Lazonick, W. (1986) 'The cotton industry', in B. Elbaum and W. Lazonick (eds) *op. cit.*

Lazonick, W. (1990) *Competitive Advantage on the Shopfloor*, Cambridge, Mass., Harvard University Press.

Lazonick, W. (1992) *Organization and Technology in Capitalist Development*, Aldershot, Edward Elgar.

Lee, C.H. (1986) *The British Economy since 1700: A Macroeconomic Perspective*, Cambridge, Cambridge University Press.

Lewchuk, W. (1986) 'The motor vehicle industry', in B. Elbaum and W. Lazonick (eds) *op. cit.*

Lorenz, E. and F. Wilkinson (1986) in B. Elbaum and W. Lazonick (eds) *op. cit.*

Lorenz, E. (1991) *Economic Decline in Britain*, Oxford, Oxford University Press.

Lucas, R.E. (1975) 'An equilibrium model of the business cycle', *Journal of Political Economy*, 83, 1113–44.

Lucas, R.E. (1976) 'Econometric policy evaluation: a critique', in K. Brunner and A.H. Meltzer (eds) *The Phillips Curve and the Labour Market*, Amsterdam, North-Holland.

Maddison, A. (1982) *Phases of Capitalist Development*, Oxford, Oxford University Press.

Maddison, A. (1991) *Dynamic Forces in Capitalist Development*, Oxford, Oxford University Press.

Matthews, R.C.O., C.H. Feinstein and J.C. Odling-Smee (1982) *British Economic Growth 1856–1973*, Stanford, Stanford University Press.

McCloskey, D.N. (1983) 'The rhetoric of economics', *Journal of Economic Literature*, 21, 481–517.

McCombie, J.S.L. and A.P. Thirlwall (1994) *Economic Theory and the Balance of Payments Constraint*, London, Macmillan.

McGoldrick, J. (1982) 'Crisis and the division of labour: Clydeside shipbuilding in the Inter-war period', in A. Dickson (ed.) *Capital and Class in Scotland*, Edinburgh, John Donald and Co.

Miller, E.S. (1978) 'Institutional Economics: philosophy, methodology and theory', *Social Science Journal*, 15, 13–25.

Mitchell, B.R. (1988) *British Historical Statistics*, Cambridge, Cambridge University Press.

Moore, B.J. (1988) *Horizontalists and Verticalists: The Macroeconomics of Credit Money*, Cambridge, Cambridge University Press.

Myrdal, G. (1957) *Economic Theory and Underdeveloped Regions*, London, Duckworth.

Naples, M.I. (1981) 'Industrial conflict and its implications for productivity growth', *American Economic Review*, 71, 36–41.

Naples, M.I. (1986) 'The unravelling of the union-capital truce and the US industrial productivity crisis', *Review of Radical Political Economics*, 18, 110–131.

North, D.C. (1990) *Institutions, Institutional Change and Economic Performance*, Cambridge, Cambridge University Press.

OECD (1990) *OECD Historical Statistics*, Paris.

Olson, M. (1982) *The Rise and Decline of Nations: Economic Growth, Stagflation and Social Rigidities*, New Haven, Yale University Press.

Pasinetti, L.L. (1981) *Structural Change and Economic Growth*, Cambridge, Cambridge University Press.

Payne, P.L. (1974) *British Entrepreneurship in the Nineteenth Century*, London, Macmillan.

Pelling, H. (1972) *A History of British Trade Unionism*, London, Macmillan.

Pollard, S. (1957) 'British and world shipbuilding, 1890–1914: a study in comparative costs', *Journal of Economic History*, 17, 426–44.

Pollard, S. (1962) *The Development of the British Economy 1914–50*, London, Edward Arnold.

Pollard, S. (1989) *Britain's Prime and Britain's Decline*, London, Edward Arnold.

Pollard, S. and P.L. Robertson (1979) *The British Shipbuilding Industry, 1870–1914*, Cambridge, Mass., Harvard University Press.

Pratten, C. and A. Silberston (1967) 'International comparisons of productivity in the automobile industry, 1950–1965', *Oxford Bulletin of Economics and Statistics*, 29, 373–94.

Reid, A. (1991) 'Employer's strategies and craft production: the British shipbuilding industry 1870–1950', in S. Tolliday and J. Zeitlin (eds) *The Power to Manage?* London, Routledge.

Richardson, G.B. (1959) 'Equilibrium, expectations and information', *Economic Journal*, 49, 223–37.

Richardson, H.W. (1962) 'The basis of economic recovery in the 1930s: a review and a new interpretation', *Economic History Review*, 15, 344–63.

Richardson, H.W. (1965a) 'Over-commitment in Britain before 1930', *Oxford Economic Papers*, 17, 237–62.

Richardson, H.W. (1965b) 'Retardation in Britain's industrial growth, 1870–1913', *Scottish Journal of Political Economy*, 12, 125–49.

Richardson, H.W. (1967) *Economic Recovery in Britain 1932–9*, London, Weidenfeld and Nicolson.

Richardson, H.W. (1968) 'Chemicals', in D.H. Aldcroft (ed.) *op. cit.*

Ricoy, C.J. (1987) 'Cumulative causation', in J. Eatwell, M. Milgate and P. Newman (eds) *The New Palgrave: A Dictionary of Economics*, London, Macmillan.

Robinson, J. (1974a) 'History versus equilibrium', *Thames Papers in Political Economy*, London, Thames Polytechnic. Reprinted in *Collected Economic Papers Vol. V*, (1980) Cambridge, Mass., MIT Press.

Robinson, J. (1974b) 'The abdication of neoclassical economics', in A. Mitra (ed.) *Economic Theory and Planning: Essays in Honour of A.K. DasGupta*, Calcutta, Oxford University Press. Reprinted in *Collected Economic Papers Vol. V* (1980) Cambridge, Mass., MIT Press.

Robinson, J. (1980) 'A lecture delivered at Oxford by a Cambridge economist', in *Collected Economic Papers Vol. IV*, Cambridge, Mass., MIT Press.

Romer, P. (1994) 'The origins of endogenous growth', *Journal of Economic Perspectives*, 8, 3–22.

Rowthorn, R.E. and J.R. Wells (1987) *De-industrialization and Foreign Trade*, Cambridge, Cambridge University Press.

Rutherford, M. (1989) 'What is wrong with the new institutional economics (and what is still wrong with the old)?', *Review of Political Economy*, 1, 299–318.

Sandberg, L. (1974) *Lancashire in Decline*, Columbus, Ohio State University Press.

Sandberg, L. (1981) 'The entrepreneur and technological change', in R.C. Floud and D.N. McCloskey (eds) *op. cit.*

Saul, S.B. (1962) 'The motor industry in Britain to 1914', *Business History*, 5, 22–44.

Saul, S.B. (1968) 'The engineering industry', in D.H. Aldcroft (ed.) *op. cit.*

Saul, S.B. (1969) *The Myth of the Great Depression*, London, Macmillan.

Schmookler, J. (1966) *Invention and Economic Growth*, Cambridge, Mass., Harvard University Press

Schotter, A. (1981) *The Economic Theory of Social Institutions*, Cambridge, Cambridge University Press.

Schumpeter, J. (1942) *Capitalism, Socialism and Democracy*, New York, Harper.

Scitovsky, T. (1956) 'Economies of scale and European integration', *American Economic Review*, 46, 71–91.

Setterfield, M.A. (1992) *A Long Run Theory of Effective Demand: Modelling Macroeconomic Systems with Hysteresis*, PhD thesis, Dalhousie University, Canada.

Setterfield, M.A. (1993a) 'Towards a long run theory of effective demand: modelling macroeconomic systems with hysteresis', *Journal of Post Keynesian Economics*, 15, 347–64.

Setterfield, M.A. (1993b) 'A model of institutional hysteresis', *Journal of Economic Issues*, 27, 755–74.

Setterfield, M.A. (1994a) 'Adjustment asymmetries and hysteresis in simple dynamic models', Trinity College, mimeo.

Setterfield, M.A. (1994b) 'Recent developments in growth theory: a Post Keynesian view', in P. Davidson and J. Kregel (eds) *Employment, Growth and Finance: Economic Reality and Economic Growth*, Aldershot, Edward Elgar.

References

Setterfield, M.A. (1995a) 'Historical time and economic theory', *Review of Political Economy*, 7, 1–27.

Setterfield, M.A. (1995b) 'History versus equilibrium and the theory of economic growth: a critique and extension of Kaldor's model of cumulative causation', *Cambridge Journal of Economics*, forthcoming.

Shackle, G.L.S. (1958) *Time in Economics*, Amsterdam, North Holland.

Shalev, M. (1978) 'Lies, damned lies and strike statistics', in C. Crouch and A. Pizzorno (eds) *The Resurgence of Class Conflict in Western Europe since 1968 Vol. 1*, New York, Holmes and Meier.

Shubik, M. (1981) 'Game theory models and methods in political economy', in K.J. Arrow and M.D. Intriligator (eds) *Handbook of Mathematical Economics*, Amsterdam, North Holland.

Skott, P. (1983) 'An essay on Keynes and general equilibrium theory', *Thames Papers in Political Economy*, London, Thames Polytechnic.

Skott, P. (1985) 'Vicious circles and cumulative causation', *Thames Papers in Political Economy*, London, Thames Polytechnic.

Soskice, D. (1978) 'Strike waves and wage explosions 1969–70: an economic interpretation', in C. Crouch and A. Pizzorno (eds) *The Resurgence of Class Conflict in Western Europe since 1968 Vol. 2*, New York, Holmes and Meier.

Stiglitz, J.E. (1987) 'The causes and consequences of the dependence of quality on price', *Journal of Economic Literature*, 25, 1–48.

Sundrum, R.M. (1990) *Economic Growth in Theory and Practice*, London, Macmillan.

Svennilson, I. (1983) *Growth and Stagnation in the European Economy*, New York, Garland.

Targetti, F. and B. Kinda Hass (1982) 'Kalecki's review of Keynes' General Theory', *Australian Economic Papers*, 21, 244–60.

Taylor, A.J. (1961) 'Labour productivity and technological innovation in the British coal industry, 1850–1914', *Economic History Review*, 14, 48–70.

Taylor, A.J. (1968) 'The coal industry', in D.H. Aldcroft (ed.) *op. cit.*

Thirlwall, A.P. (1980) *Balance of Payments Theory and the UK Experience*, London, Macmillan.

Thirlwall, A.P. (1983) 'A plain man's guide to Kaldor's growth laws', *Journal of Post Keynesian Economics*, 5, 345–58.

Tyson, R.E. (1968) 'The cotton industry', in D.H. Aldcroft (ed.) *op. cit.*

Tyszynski, H. (1951) 'World trade in manufactured commodities, 1899–1950', *The Manchester School of Economic and Social Studies*, 19, 272–304.

Varian, H.R. (1984) *Microeconomic Analysis*, New York, Norton.

Veblen, T.B. (1919) *The Place of Science in Modern Civilisation and Other Essays*, New York, Huebsch.

Veblen, T. (1975) *The Theory of Business Enterprise*, Clifton, Augustus M. Kelley.

Walker, J. (1981) 'Markets, industrial processes and class struggle: the evolution of the labour process in the UK engineering industry', *Review of Radical Political Economy*, 12, 46–69.

Weisskopf, T.E., S. Bowles and D.M. Gordon (1983) 'Hearts and minds: a social model of US productivity growth', *Brookings Papers on Economic Activity*, 2, 381–441.

Wilber, C.K. and R.S. Harrison (1978) 'The methodological basis of institutional economics: pattern model, storytelling, and holism', *Journal of Economic Issues*, 12, 61–89.

Williamson, O.E. (1985) *The Economic Institutions of Capitalism*, New York, The Free Press.

Witt, U. (1991) 'Reflections on the present state of evolutionary economic theory', in G.M. Hodgson and E. Screpanti (1991) *Rethinking Economics*, Aldershot, Edward Elgar.

Wulwick, N.J. (1993) 'What remains of the growth controversy', *Review of Political Economy*, 5, 321–43.

Wyplosz, C. (1987) 'Comments', in R. Layard and L. Calmfors (eds) *The Fight against Unemployment*, Cambridge, Mass., MIT Press.

Young, A. (1928) 'Increasing returns and economic progress', *Economic Journal*, 38, 527–42.

Zeitlin, J. (1987) 'From labour history to the history of industrial relations', *Economic History Review*, 40, 159–84.

Index